Practical Artificial Intelligence

Find out how and when computers and robots will become intelligent and how relationships between smart computers and humans will change society. A timeline will show you when to expect these paradigm changes. This is a tale of the forced evolution of computers and robots by means of scientific research, technological design and engineering so that they are able to learn, to interact with people and the environment, and to become conscious in their own way without necessarily becoming human-like.

Creating **Artificial Intelligence** is most likely the toughest challenge that technology has ever confronted. However, there is no doubt of achieving this goal of developing AI in the near future. The question is up to what point human technology can advance machine intelligence. Will it be up to a level comparable, or maybe surpassing, human intelligence? No matter what the answer will be, smart computers and robots will be increasingly more important in our lives.

To be useful, they will have to plan ahead and they will have to quantify the uncertainty inherent in any prediction about the future. The future that will take place in one millisecond or in one century.

In this book, the technology is discussed; as well as the social, political and economic effects that these inventions will bring along. Our lives will change, be prepared.

> '*Change is the law of life. And those who look only to the past or present are certain to miss the future.*'
> **John F. Kennedy.**

Books by Humberto Contreras

living dangerously in utopia

The War of the Classes
The Preponderant Factor
It is all in the Mind
The Restlessness

technology & social impact

The History of the 21st Century
Practical Artificial Intelligence

These books are also available in Spanish.

Humberto Contreras is a Civil Engineer with a Masters in Structural Engineering and a Doctorate in Earthquake Engineering. As an expert in probabilistic and stochastic systems, he implemented solutions involving risk analysis and safety of Nuclear Power Plants and Nuclear Waste. He has also been a computer software consultant for major corporations. He currently writes books and lives in New England and the Riviera Maya.

 books
zero

http://www.alphazerobooks.com

Practical Artificial Intelligence

Humberto Contreras Ph. D.

Practical Artificial Intelligence

First Edition, May 2012.
ISBN 978-1-300-55277-2
Editor: Jose Antonio Sesin

To my wife Gloria, my only passionate love.

To my perfect daughter, Cleopatra-Alexandra.

To my children and grandchildren.

I am grateful to the people that have made Artificial Intelligence conceivable. They are many more than we can ever imagine.

Contents

What is Uncertainty?

Mathematics in AI

xvi

Civilization's Adventure

'Progress is impossible without change, and those who cannot change their minds cannot change anything.' **George Bernard Shaw.**

L ife on earth has been living in an open-ended experiment that has lasted four billion years. Finally, in the years to come tools will exist and it will be up to us to set off another evolutionary step in this experiment.

This experiment has produced human beings, whose evolution has followed a continuous growth pattern, generating the rise of civilization. Every century the world as a whole has been better than the one before, and its people, which are in effect the essence of civilization, have improved in their standards of living, education, and ethical behavior.

This century, technology will unleash progress in a way never seen before and computers leading the bio and nano technologies could very well create a world of abundance for all the inhabitants of the earth.

Alongside this progress, computing power and memory capacities will continue to double every year and by the year 2040, a thousand dollar computer will equal the capacity of one human brain. By the end of this century, any ordinary computer will surpass the computing capacity of all human beings. This will make AI (Artificial Intelligence) and robots commonplace and ubiquitous. They will take over most of human labor and even creativity, development and design.

Milestones

During these years of rising civilization, some milestones have profoundly transformed society, among them we can identify:

- Stone Tools: Ethiopia 2.6 million years BC.
- Fire: Africa 800,000 BC.
- Clothing: Africa 500,000 BC.
- Language: Africa 50,000 BC.
- Bow and Arrow: Africa 16,000 BC.
- Needle and Thread: Europe 15,000 BC.
- Farming: 10,000 BC.
- Brick: Mesopotamia and Egypt 8,000 BC.
- Pottery: Anatolia 6,500 BC.
- Wheel: Mesopotamia 5,000 BC.
- Beer: Mesopotamia 4,000 BC.
- Plough and Draft Animals: Egypt and Mesopotamia 3,500 BC.
- Paper: Egypt 3,500 BC.
- Measuring time: Egypt 3,500 BC.
- Writing: Sumerian cuneiform, Egyptian hieroglyphs 3,200 BC.
- Women Rights: Ancient Egypt 3,200 BC, Rome 200 BC, Visigoth (Spain) 418, Islam 610, UN 1948.
- Ship: Egypt 3,000 BC.
- Money: Mesopotamia 3,000 BC.
- Soap: Babylon 2,800 BC.
- Sundial: Egypt 2,000 BC.
- Glass: Phoenicia 1,500 BC.
- Democracy: Athens 500 BC.
- Zero: Olmecs (México) 400 BC, India 458.
- Cement: Greece 200 BC.
- Scientific method: Iraq 1000.
- Printing press: China 1000, Germany 1440.
- End of Slavery: Western Europe 1100, México 1821, US 1863, UN 1948.
- Gun: Seville 1247.
- Human rights: India 1500, Germany 1525, UN 1948.
- Steam engine, electricity, internal combustion: England 1700.
- Computer: England 1837, Germany 1941, US 1942.
- Internet: US (ARPANET) 1969, (TCP/IP) 1982, CERN (WWW, email and hypertext) 1990.
- Modern medicine: Europe 1880.
- Radio: England 1896.

Social changes tend to follow those produced by technology. It took years from the beginning of the Industrial Revolution to the establishment of a middle class in the industrialized nations. This lag is due to the inertia of social and political systems. Interestingly, once change is established the same politicians that held it up will claim credit for it.

The AI 'revolution' will most likely have the reach of paradigms like the Greek democracy, the onset of the Middle Ages, the Renaissance and the Industrial Revolution.

Greek Democracy

In 510 BC, Cleisthenes an Athenian aristocrat asked the Spartan king Cleomenes I for help to overthrow the tyranny of Peisistratos on the Athenians. Cleomenes I took advantage and named Isagoras as a pro-Spartan leader of Athens. Using the bait of a new form of government Cleisthenes convinced Athenians to revolt: in this democracy, all citizens shared in political power, regardless of status. The advent of democracy led to a golden age for the Athenians.

Greek democracy was not perfect, given that only free native adult males, who were considered citizens of the city, took a part in managing the state. These activities were handled by a direct democracy, based on a popular assembly, which at times was attended by more than 6000 citizens; it could declare war, approve expenses, send diplomatic missions and make treaties. The council of 500 and the courts complemented the assembly.

There were no parties, no opposition and essentially no government, a simple majority of those physically in attendance made the decisions. There was intense interest in the political process, to the point that the name 'idiot' was bestowed to those that did not participate. The system was not always simple or just, and it evolved into an empire of subject states. Moreover, women, foreigners and slaves had almost no rights under this democracy.

Other Greek cities, like Corinth, Megara and Syracuse, eventually also had democratic regimes. In a sense, the Roman Republic was also a democratic government headed by two consuls, elected annually by the citizens and advised by a senate; its constitution upheld the principles of separation of powers and checks and balances.

Rome became an empire, which around the year 300 split in half thus creating the Western and the Eastern Roman Empires. The Western Roman Empire collapsed in 476 when Odoacer, a Germanic warlord, defeated the Emperor Romulus Augustus. The Eastern Roman Empire, by then called the Byzantine Empire, fell in 1453 when Mehmed II, king of the Ottoman Turks, captured Constantinople.

Middle Ages

After the fall of Rome, Europe went through a period of depopulation, deurbanization, and barbarian invasions, with substantial social and political changes. It was divided into many new kingdoms incorporating many Roman institutions. In Western Europe the Catholic Church took over Christianity and expanded. Monks and monasteries were a focal point of religion and politics in Early Middle Ages.

As Western Europe witnessed the formation of new kingdoms, the eastern section of the Empire remained intact and even enjoyed an economic revival that lasted into the early 7th Century.

In the 10th Century, Europe's population started to grow due to improved agricultural techniques, the decline of slaveholding, a warmer climate, the lack of invasions and the onset of feudalism that allowed peasants to settle in villages under the protection of a noble.

Then in the 12th and 13th Centuries, towns grew. Self-governed towns and cities stimulated the economy and enabled the creation of trade associations. Cities trading with each other eventually led to mergers like the Hanseatic League and the Italian city-states Venice, Genoa and Pisa.

At the closing stages of the Middle Ages, the kingdoms of France, England and Spain consolidated their power and new kingdoms like those in Hungary and Poland were converted to Catholicism. Furthermore, the Pope claimed authority over the entire Christian world.

In the Middle Ages progress took a step back in Europe but not in other parts of the world, like the Bizantine Empire, China or the Islamic Empires. During the Middle Ages Catholicism suppressed any ideas that were not in the Old and New Testament. However, during this same period, science and technology flourished in Islam's Golden Era. For example, an Islamic scientist named Alhazen (Ibn al-Haytham), born in the year 965 in Basra, Iraq, studied the fields of optics, anatomy, astronomy, engineering and many others and made numerous contributions to science, among them the discovery of the scientific method.

Renaissance

This renowned era began in Italy at the end of the Middle Ages, slowly expanding to the rest of Europe from the 14th to the 17th Centuries.

Intellectuals of the time strived to revive ideas from Latin, Greek and Islamic texts of philosophy and mathematics, while artists introduced realistic techniques into the art and literature. Renaissance writers began using local languages; this coincided with the discovery of the printing press by Johannes Gutenberg in 1436, which facilitated access to books.

Independent Italian cities invented monastic states employing some principles of capitalism to pioneer a commercial revolution that funded the Renaissance. The movement was aided by the discovery of America by Christopher Columbus in 1492, which questioned established truths and produced untold riches. The movement also benefited from the Fall of Constantinople, which brought Greek scholars, along with their valuable manuscripts to Italy.

The Renaissance changed the nature of the universe and the explanations about the characteristics of the world. Copernicus, Galileo, and Francis Bacon promoted the scientific method, based in an entirely mechanical philosophy, stressing empirical evidence and the use of mathematical methods. This led to great discoveries in the fields of astronomy, physics, biology, and anatomy.

Industrial Revolution

In the later part of the 18th Century, a transition began in some parts of Great Britain. The use of manual labor and draft-animals evolved to machine-based manufacturing.

This was the Industrial Revolution, which took place in the 18th to the 20th Centuries. Driven by technology, major changes in agriculture, manufacturing, mining, and transportation; it had a profound effect on socioeconomic and cultural conditions. It started in the United Kingdom and spread throughout Europe, North America, and eventually the world.

Around 1850 it merged with the Second Industrial Revolution as technological and economic progress gained momentum with the development of steam-powered ships and railways. Then, later in the 19th century, came the discoveries of the internal combustion engine and electrical power generation.

The Industrial Revolution, which lasted up to the end of the 20th Century, raised productivity and led to new inventions that allowed the institution of a new social order. In this new order, governments and owners are the new masters, followed by workers that now include a new middle class of managers and professionals, and then the poor.

Being poor is bad. You have to work hard, if you can find a job. Even the middle classes find it difficult sometimes and face what has been called 'wage slavery.' Leading to the saying that 'if you don't work you don't eat.'

20th Century

During this century technology entered the workplace in a massive way. The list of technological improvements in the workplace in the last century is almost endless: computers, communication devices, measuring devices, computer controlled equipment, the x-ray, wind tunnel, arc welder, circuit breaker, transistor, Geiger counter, laser, neon lamp, teletype, fiber optics, stainless steel, carbon-fiber and the Internet. The list goes on-and-on.

At the turn of the century only 5% of factories in the US used electricity to power their machines. By the end of the century, electrical powered machines were omnipresent, as are heating, air conditioning and air filtration. Technological improvements often resulted in improved safety in the workplace, as machines replaced the worker in many of the more dangerous and repetitive tasks.

New machines introduced in the home in the 20th century included: radio, television, refrigerator, dishwasher, clothes washer, dryer, iron, vacuum cleaner, microwave oven, automatic toaster, electric razor, and electric hairdryer. In addition, there was prepackaged food, frozen food, and a host of other convenience items. And do not forget cars and airplanes.

The same story was repeated all over the world. Even third world countries benefited from many of these improvements to their quality of life and of course many women joined the workforce and became paid workers.

Considering the notion of exponential growth in inventions and technology it is entirely possible that by the end of the 21st Century there will be a variety of improvements that will seem overwhelming to us. The 20th Century brought an enormous change in the way we live. Advances during this century will change us even more.

21st Century

There is no question that to a person living in 1900, and suddenly transported to a mall in the year 2000, it would seem the epitome of opulence and amazement! We can strongly infer that, given no tremendous global catastrophe, a mall or its equivalent in the year 2100 would amaze us too. To us, the people in the year 2100 would seem to be living in opulence!

Nowadays malls are generally enjoyable, but only a small percentage of the world's population can afford to 'go to the mall.' There is still 20% of the population of the world living in 'extreme poverty.' In addition, that does not mean that all of the other 80% have ever gone to a mall. In 2010, extreme poverty is defined by the World Bank as living with less than $1.25 dollars a day. Of course, you need a lot more than that to buy anything at the mall. In addition, malls are very far for some people and most probably just getting to a mall would be unaffordable.

The real achievement of the year 2100 would be not in the existence of, or added luxury in the malls themselves, but that everybody in the world could have access to them and afford to buy stuff there.

Now they will also, most probably: work less time, have better health, look younger, healthier and happier. Will all of them share the wealth? Or will it be an extremely radical society with a few as rich as gods and the rest poorer than the poor in the year 2000? If so, what happened, and how did it happen?

To understand the subject of the economic system that will be prevalent in the 21st Century we have to determine who will have the wealth in that system. As whoever has the wealth controls the economy.

For now, and most probably for at least the first half of the century, capitalists have the wealth. We know that the basic premise of capitalism is to accumulate as much wealth as possible for stockholders who have provided capital to create a business. Still, there are several issues about capitalism that could be at odds with the direction of the social order in the near future:

- Capitalism was invented to cope with the need to raise capital to put together factories and then business during the Industrial Revolution.
- It considers that the role of capital in the economy, and even in society, is absolute.
- Its structure implicitly considers that the costs to produce the products must be as low as possible, including labor, materials,

taxes and logistics. Labor is just a resource and does not play a part in the administration.

- Upper level managers consider themselves a part of the capitalists' elite. They do not consider themselves labor, thus contributing to the schism.
- Given that capitalism's function is to obtain more wealth, Boards of Directors fight to obtain as many perks and freebies as they can from the system. They pay the politicians to get laws and regulations enacted that will benefit them. In response, governments provide businesses with tax exemptions, free land, and free reign with their customers, and even huge subsidies.
- The development of the system happened at a time of very scarce resources, where production was limited and could only provide goods and services for the rich. Thus, labor and the poor were left out of the picture.
- During the 20th Century, some workers and the middle class became rich enough to buy goods. Even the employed poor started buying factory products.
- Robotic machines increase the efficiency in manufacturing and in the delivery of services, increasing productivity, lowering costs and reducing the need for human labor.
- Capitalism is not prepared to deal with an economy of abundance where there are fewer and fewer workers. And as it strives to pay as little as possible to reduce costs, the workers become poorer and the owners become richer.

What can be done with all that extra output? Hoard the goods in a vault as some companies allegedly do with diamonds? Who will buy all these goods and services if there are fewer workers? The unemployed are not good customers as they have no money to spend.

In the US in the year 2000, the wealthy consisted of 25% of US households and they owned 87% of the wealth. The middle 50% of households in the country held 13% of the wealth. The bottom 25% held no net wealth at all. This is not a particularly good distribution of wealth. How it is beneficial, for society, for humanity, to have so much in the hands of so few?

Do the rich really need all that money, and why do they still want more? Why do governments have to protect them and reduce their taxes? Why is it that 25% of the population has nothing? In addition, why do the 50% in the middle have to live in constant fear of being fired and joining the zero wealth crowds? Are we not all human? Does our human condition not entitle us to live with a certain level of dignity and security? With or without a job!

Moreover, the statistics shown in the previous paragraph are from the US, which is the largest economy in the world. Wealth distribution, when measured all around the globe is much worse. The world is becoming smaller; communications, globalization and air travel have increased the awareness of people all over the world. Everybody can find out that an earthquake hit the Pacific an hour ago, that there is a crisis due to bad mortgages in America and what President Obama said a few minutes ago. Most people have the means to know almost everything important or scandalous in real-time. In the years to come this global awareness will expand even more. No country can live in isolation and concealment anymore. The economy is global!

All the promise of abundance, new marvels coming from scientific and engineering improvements, better health and a longer life span are useless unless there is a much better distribution of wealth and buying power. As most technological advances produce wealth, there will be more wealth. In 1900, the Gross National Product of the world was many times smaller than the one in the year 2000 and the increase came mostly from so many goods and services which were unknown or unavailable in 1900, and were bought by people that could afford them.

If consumers do not have money, they cannot buy what businesses are selling. If businesses do not sell, they do not make money, so they cannot produce the goods that consumers need or wish for. Right now, there is production overcapacity; there could be much more overcapacity in the future. This trend will keep on making the poor poorer, the middle class poor and the rich even richer, but places all of us in a precarious situation, waiting for another social upheaval!

In a society where scarcity really does not exist, or is not the essential part of the issue, the only way out is to give money to the poor and middle classes. Consumers drive seventy percent of the economy. Enable them to be consumers. If this happens, the poor join the middle class and the rich will be richer!

New Directions

What will result from the Artificial Intelligence and robotics revolution? Will democracies give way to intelligent administration using AI? Will the rich still be rich or comfortable according to their choice and talent? Will the middle class evolve to rich or comfortable also according to their choice and talent? Will the poor also become comfortable or rich if they have the drive and talent?

Will it be possible that the difference between being rich, or just enjoying a comfortable life style, will be negligible and not stigmatized? History tells us that new technologies permit and encourage new forms of positive interaction; that social structures evolve to realize their potential in a way that is most of the time evolutionary but sometimes involves radical changes.

Current times portend a paradigm shift. It is an unsettling feeling of disarray. Economic, political, and technological change seem to be coming too fast. Society seems to be on a meandering course. Will this be the time for another revolutionary step forward?

Expectations

Four billion years ago a molecule made a copy of itself. Four million years ago, brain size grew in our hominid ancestors. Fifty thousand years ago, the first Homo Sapiens were born. Ten thousand years ago, we invented civilization. Seventy years ago, the first computer was put together. Can we expect 'the Singularity' to happen fifty years from now?

In 1982, Vernor Vinge, Professor of Mathematics, computer scientist and science fiction author, proposed that: 'the creation of smarter-than-human intelligence represented a breakdown in humans' ability to model their future.' Vinge named this event 'the Singularity.' In the near future, a true Artificial Intelligence or an enhanced human intelligence could surpass the level of human intelligence, which until now is the maximum level on this planet.

Even if 'the Singularity' does not happen as predicted, there is a very strong probability that by the year 2050 the effects of development of bio, nano and robo technologies are going to impact everyday life and will change social and economic conditions.

> *'The advent of strong AI (exceeding human intelligence) is the most important transformation this century will see, and it will happen within 25 years.'* **Ray Kurzweil, 2006.**

Why Consciousness?

'I think, therefore I am.' ***René Descartes.***

If there is an issue that merits discussion and creates disagreement, it is consciousness. Religious people believe that it is a gift from god. Philosophers have approached the theme from numerous standpoints, linking it to: behavior, the physical world and the soul, the perception of the world, causal relationships, intentional acts, spiritual truths, personal identity, and external actions.

For a long time scientists were banned from studying consciousness, because as religions explain consciousness as a god given spirit, soul or some other extracorporeal entity, therefore it is a holy matter. Now scientists have a plethora of explanations and fields of study of consciousness, such as case studies of conscious states and the study of brain injuries that disrupt normal behavior.

Imaging machines have been able to distinguish different types of controlled input that activate some areas of the brain. Still, to this day there is no definite definition of consciousness.

Nevertheless, we intrinsically understand the notion and we think of ourselves, and even of some animals, as being conscious.

Who is Conscious?

Many agree that some animals, among them dolphins and primates, have consciousness. If so, then consciousness has certainly evolved along with life, which according to the rules of evolution would require that it have survival value.

To us humans it is obvious that consciousness plays a crucial role in decision-making, problem-solving, learning and creativity; and as such, it is a great asset. Consciousness allows for planning rather than instinctual responses.

Obviously, viruses and bacteria are not conscious, yet they survive. Neural activity of the autonomous functions of the body, such as heart beat, breathing and others, have very little to do with consciousness and rule-based processes can explain instinctual behavior.

Given these facts, it seems obvious that consciousness is not indispensable for survival, but if you have it then it is arguably an asset.

Human Consciousness

Over millions of years, the brain has evolved hundreds of biological computers each one with specialized architecture that are wired together in a network of sub-systems that use different dialects to communicate.

We identify ourselves as conscious. However, within the brain's massive computer systems, our consciousness uses only a small portion of our mind to simulate the real world, using greatly simplified representations.

These simulated worlds are empowered with meaning and purpose. Our brains evolved to meet basic requirements such as comfort, nutrition, defense and reproduction. Later, analysis of cause-and-effect evolved, which lead to knowledge. We perceive reality in the sense of how can it be used because the upper level of our mind is a goal-directed problem-solver. The main purpose of our knowledge is to achieve results.

In a way, our consciousness acts as our 'driver.' In the same way that we can drive a car without knowing how it works internally, we 'drive' ourselves without knowing how we function inside.

Our consciousness is the knowledge and skills that allow us to use our other systems; it does not have to understand how our internal systems actually work.

Intelligence

If an animal is conscious, is it automatically intelligent? It seems to be the case, at least according to the following definitions of intelligence:

- Entity's ability to achieve goals.
- Evolutionary advantage that enables modeling, predicting and manipulating reality.
- The 'stream of consciousness.'
- An entity that a human being recognizes as intelligent.

We acknowledge human intelligence as optimal mainly because it is the greatest intelligence that is in the neighborhood. However, there is no reason to believe that it stands for the developmental limit of intelligence. Evolutionary history provides no reason to believe that human intelligence represents the top-level of development of thinking entities.

Human intelligence is contained in a brain that weighs a little more than a kilogram, uses twenty watts of power, has a hundred billion neurons with a hundred trillion synapses that work at two hundred cycles per second in a highly parallel modality.

Homo sapiens are the result of totally unintelligent evolutionary pressures acting on genes. At one point, primate evolution stumbled on a path that created Homo sapiens, which happen to be very intelligent.

AI Intelligence

The idea that 'Intelligence measures an agent's ability to achieve goals in a wide range of environments' originated from Legg and Hutter as a description of the 'optimization power' concept of intelligence. It measures an agent's power to optimize the world according to its preferences.

Yudkowsky enhances this definition by dividing the optimization power by the resources used.

At first AI intelligence will be measured comparing it to human intelligence. Eventually, just as we have measures for our intelligence, AI will figure out a way of measuring theirs.

How do we Test for Consciousness?

Due to the lack of a clear-cut definition, it is understandable that there is no way to formulate a definite test for consciousness. However, some have looked for an operational demonstration of consciousness.

There are tests that try to prove that a computer or a non-human animal is intelligent and therefore conscious by measuring its behavior. In these tests, it is accepted for a fact that all normal living human beings are conscious. Some ways of testing are:

- Turing Test: the classic, involving passing as a human being in an everyday conversation.
- Virtual World or Robotic Turing Test: pass as a human being, in a conversation involving controlling a virtual world avatar or a robot.

- Online University Test: attend an online university just like a human student, and graduate.
- Physical University Test: AI controls a robot that attends university just like a human student, and graduates
- Artificial Scientist Test: write and publish original science papers, based on ideas conceived by the AI due to its own reading of the literature.

Turing Test

In 1950 Alan Turing, an outstanding computer scientist, proposed a test to determine if a computer satisfied his operational definition of 'intelligent.' Specifically Turing used the words: 'Can machines think?' Therefore, this test is not necessarily of consciousness; however, it is widely accepted as one of the best tests of this nature that exists up to now.

In this test, a human operator is involved in a conversation with two other subjects, via computer keyboards. One is human, thereby conscious and the other is a computer. If the human operator is unable to determine which of the subjects is human and which is a computer, the computer will have 'passed' the Turing test.

This test has fans and detractors. Those in favor argue that given that there is no definite knowledge about what is the meaning of consciousness then only pragmatic evidence about its existence is possible. Those against it present cases like the Chinese-room, where an input-output operation is used to pass Chinese symbols through a slot and the person inside the room looks at a set of rules and responds with appropriate answers in Chinese; the person inside the Chinese room does not understand Chinese, but gives the appearance of understanding it. It also has been argued that a 'philosophical zombie,' which is a person undistinguishable from a human except that is not conscious, could pass the test.

Mirror Test

This test tries to prove that the animal in front of the mirror can recognize himself. It is quite simple, the animal's fur is decorated with a spot and if the animal attempts to touch the spot then it is assumed that they have recognized that it is himself in the mirror.

Those animals that regularly pass this test are humans older than 18 months and other great apes, except for most gorillas. Bottlenose dolphins, pigeons, elephants and magpies also pass the test.

However, non-Western children between 18 months and 6 years old sometimes fail the test, even though they are obviously conscious and well aware of their self-identity. Cultural differences, like emphasizing interdependence over independence could account for the different reaction to the test. Also, gorillas could fail because they are made uncomfortable by the test as eye-contact often leads to fights among them.

Delay Test

This test tries to tell apart conscious from instinctual response. It is thought that subjecting a living organism with a cue, followed by a delayed stimulus proves that there is a conscious response if the subject reacts to it after a few tries.

The consideration is that the information about the soon to happen stimulus was stored in short-term memory, which is supposed to be a sign of conscious thought.

ConsScale

In 2008, professors Arrabales, Ledezma & Sanchis proposed a new functional criteria to assess the level of consciousness of an artificial intelligent agent. Their scale, that they named ConsScale, establishes a methodology and a scale that classifies consciousness in 13 levels.

In this classification the first three levels are:

-1	*Disembodied*	Amino-acid
0	*Isolated*	Isolated chromosome
1	*Decontrolled*	Dead bacteria

These are special cases, as they do not actually describe agents. Therefore, there are no behavioral tests associated to any of these first three levels.

The next levels are more interesting:

2	*Reactive*	Primitive situatedness based on reflexes.	Virus
3	*Rational*	Ability to learn, senses allow orientation and positioning.	Earthworm
4	*Attentional*	Attention toward selected goals, attack and escape behaviors.	Fish
5	*Executive*	Multiple goals, basic emotional learning.	Mammal
6	*Emotional*	Complex emotions, self-	Monkey

		status and influence behavior.	
7	*Self-Conscious*	Self-reference makes possible advanced planning, use of tools.	Monkey
8	*Emphatic*	Making of tools.	Chimpanzee
9	*Social*	Linguistic capabilities, able to develop a culture.	Pre-Human
10	*Human-Like*	Accurate verbal report, behavior modulated by culture.	Human
11	*Super-Conscious*	Ability to synchronize and coordinate several streams of consciousness.	Post-Human

ConsScale levels *3* to *10* may also be compared to the development of a human being: from level *3* when just born, to level *4* at 5 months, level *5* at 9 months, level *6* at 1 year, level *7* at 1½ years, level *8* at 2 years, level *9* at 4 years and level *10* for an adult.

As presented by the authors, ConsScale is not a test; it is just a list of measurable levels of consciousness that can be applied to assess that of an artificial agent.

Universal Intelligence Measure

The lack of a strict definition of intelligence makes it difficult to assess intelligent machines. Legg and Hutter have provided an explicit definition of intelligence that would work with artificial, robotic, terrestrial or even extra-terrestrial intelligences, without introducing a bias.

It is a mathematical definition of intelligence based on Li and Vitányi algorithmic information theory, Solomonoff's model of universal inductive inference, and Hutter's AIXI theory of universal artificial intelligence.

The informal definition: 'intelligence measures an agent's ability to achieve goals in a wide range of environments,' complemented with reinforcement learning, is intuitively considered a suitable framework for goal achieving agents in unknown environments.

Then, to support a wide range of environments, the set of all Turing computable environments is used. The model is constrained technically by finitely bounding the sum of returned rewards; and then the agent's performance over different environments is accumulated into a result.

Each environment is weighted according to its complexity, thereby applying Occam's Razor, with simpler environments being weighted more heavily, using an algorithmic prior distribution. The universal intelligence of an agent can then be defined as,

$$\Upsilon(\Pi) := \sum_{\mu \in E} 2^{-K(\mu)} V_\mu^\pi$$

where μ is an environment from the set E of all computable reward bounded environments, $K(\bullet)$ is the Kolmogorov complexity, and

$$V_\mu^\pi := E\left(\sum_{i=1}^{\infty} R_i\right)$$

is the expected sum of future rewards when agent π interacts with environment μ.

Not surprisingly, the most intelligent agent under this measure is Hutter's AIXI, a universal agent that converges to optimal performance in any environment where this is possible for a general agent. It could be because AIXI follows the same assumptions as this intelligence measure.

The Meaning of Testing

Even if perfect tests of this kind were found, the ultimate judge is going to be the human that interacts with the supposedly conscious Artificial Intelligence. Or maybe, it can be an AI interacting with another AI.

In reality, the most important issue about consciousness at a human level is the command of language. Even in the Turing test, the result will depend on how well humans and computers understand the language in which the test is being conducted. If the human operator knows only English and the human subject understands Spanish exclusively, then the test is not viable; in a case like this, if the computer subject has a minimal understanding of English, it will appear to be the one closest to consciousness.

Not only is the command of language important, so is the context in which it is used. Image if you will, that you are testing an AI intellect and you ask the question 'Have you ever looked at the stars?' If the AI was designed to be a chef, the question is irrelevant, especially if it 'sees' using LIDAR (a laser based radar); still the AI chef could be quite intelligent and even 'conscious.'

It could well be, that by the time AI attains language abilities, the question of its consciousness will become a moot point. If it correctly and fluidly answers those questions related to its occupation, who is going to have reservations?

Self-Awareness

To be self-aware or to be self-conscious is the ability to separate the 'self' in the thoughts that are taking place. In human beings, it is part of their intelligence.

It is the recognition of our personality; it is how we see ourselves mixed with the feedback from others. However, nobody knows more about you than you. Others do not feel your emotions, nor think your thoughts; they do not face the issues that you have.

Some religions relate self-awareness to the soul. However, according to the English philosopher John Locke, 'it is the repeated act of consciousness.'

The concept of self is tightly linked to our body. Our nervous system is distributed along the body in a network of neural cells that are not that well insulated and as such, they continuously interact with other organs. Moreover, we are the outcome of an evolutionary process that has retained the old solutions superimposing newer systems; thus, the nervous system is guided by hormones and by even more primordial urges of the body. Our 'self' is not necessarily in our mind; it is more properly in our whole body.

Motivation

There is no intelligence without goals. This is obvious to us. As animals we are motivated to survive, at least until we can procreate. As intelligent beings, each one of us has different needs during our lives; maybe it is just to eat a steak, read a book, or go to watch a movie, we all at one time or another want to do something. The capacity of being conscious makes us want to do or to obtain something.

To be a conscious and intelligent being, just wanting to do something is not enough, there has to be the intention or previous thought of wanting to do something. Planning ahead, and being aware of the act of planning ahead, is a prerequisite for intelligence; it is also required to achieve self-awareness.

The essence of human self-awareness is that our motivations are personal; each one of us has our own personal motivations. All humans have an individualistic view of their role in life and of their past and their future.

Intrinsic Motivation

In 1998, Ohio State University psychology professor Steven Reiss wrote the book: '*Who am I: The 16 basic desires that motivate our actions and define our personalities.*' These desires are:

- *Acceptance*, the need for approval.
- *Status*, the need for social standing or importance.
- *Social Contact*, the need for friends and peer relationships.
- *Romance*, the need for sex.
- *Family*, the need to raise children.
- *Independence*, the need for individuality.
- *Tranquility*, the need to be safe.
- *Saving*, the need to collect.
- *Eating*, the need for food.
- *Physical Activity*, the need for exercise.
- *Curiosity*, the need to learn.
- *Order*, the need for organized, stable, predictable environments.
- *Idealism*, the need for social justice.
- *Power*, the need for influence the will of others.
- *Honor*, the need of loyalty to the values of clan or ethnic group.
- *Vengeance*, the need to strike back or to win.

Persons are motivated by pleasure or they consider it important. Reiss' theory is not the only one that tries to explain intrinsic motivation, but it embraces more reasons than others do.

Carl Jung and Sigmund Freud noted that there are only two inner human drives, survival and sexual; and that these never change, regardless of outside factors. We will label them intrinsic meta-motivations.

Extrinsic Motivation

Extrinsic Motivation is defined as coercing a person to do something or act in a certain way using external reasons, like money, good grades or threats. Competition is another form of intrinsic motivation as it encourages winning or overcoming their competitors.

Schools and businesses tend to use this kind of motivation to encourage students to learn and employees to work harder and more efficiently. Obedience to the laws and good social behavior are based on the premise that not doing so will bring painful retribution to the offender.

Individuality
The higher the intelligence of a species the larger the difference in behavior between individuals of that species; it is difficult to distinguish the behavior of one insect from another of the same species; it is easy to distinguish the behavior of one horse from that of another horse.

Neuronal systems of simple animals have less scope to grow dissimilarities than those of complex, and more intelligent animals. As human brains are the most complex, we have developed, along with a few other animals, a self-awareness that intrinsically has what we call 'our own personality.' Those individual animals that have these complex brains are not only wired differently at birth, they are also capable of learning and so their personal life experiences make their personalities even more diverse.

In humans, these traits go a long way; each one of us has so much individuality that it is impossible for any of us to truly know what happens inside the mind of any other human. We can only translate what we know of the experiences and emotions of another person into terms that we can understand using our own brain configuration and experiences.

Free Will
The principle of free will has been studied and discussed in scientific, philosophical and religious terms. Some religions emphasize that god does not assert his will over humans and consequently they enjoy freedom to make individual choices, even if they are bad, and so they are responsible for their actions. Philosophy questions the reality of determinism and the existence of free will and its relationship with moral responsibility. Science is trying to explain human behavior in terms of the brain, genes, and evolutionary concepts.

A practical explanation of free will could be along these lines: 'Personal free will is the implementation of the action, chosen from the actions that were considered possible, that got the highest satisfaction ranking of the person's intrinsic and extrinsic motivations.'

The term 'rational' agent is used to represent an intellect that acts at every moment in a way that optimizes its motivations. A 'free will' agent would be just that kind of agent considering that maybe some of its motivations are religious or moral. Under this definition, there is no such thing as 'free will,' because as humans we just follow our instincts and whatever else we have learned. These essentially are our motivations.

Free will of a human being has nothing to do with freedom: a soldier has no freedom to disobey orders, nobody has the freedom to ignore gravity and we all follow orders, rules, or laws. When a person follows or does not follow a law, it is because that person evaluated its own motivations and found-out that obeying or not obeying that law was better according to his own circumstances at that particular moment. He had no freedom; he was just what he was at that moment and acted accordingly.

By their very nature, these decisions will be lacking and that is the origin of this 'free will' label. If with a little bit of luck you made the right decision (by the way, many times it is extremely hard to know which is the right decision) then you can say that your 'free will' is good in nature. When somebody else's decision is 'wrong' then this poor fellow is accused of using his 'free will' to perform 'bad' actions; and that is punishable. It is true that some people systematically make better decisions than others do, but that is the because of the way they were born, have lived and were educated, not because they have a better 'free will.'

Following this train of thought, an intelligent AI will not have 'free will,' it will only make 'bounded rational decisions using incomplete information under time and computational constraints.' Just as human beings do.

Self-Aware AI

As soon as a computer running an AI program is confronted with the need to communicate with one or several entities the question of 'self' becomes important. It is the best way to differentiate itself from the rest and to identify its actions.

Awareness in AI programs could be partially a continuous computing loop that most probably will provide it with the attentiveness needed to anticipate and solve situations as soon as they happen, and even before they happen. Most AI programs will be set to compute ahead and prepare responses to situations that are likely to happen in the future.

An AI setup would most likely include situations where learning is called for. Under these circumstances, when the AI is in idle mode it could very well be learning using its communication capabilities and its senses, if any.

However, to be aware of 'self' does not by itself confer consciousness to an AI program. In addition, for this kind of limited awareness there is no need to have a body or a physical representation. Although, the more complex the AI turns out to be, with more communication channels and senses attached, and if it can store memories of its sensory perceptions and of its actions, and can self-refer to them later to satisfy programmatic needs, the more intelligent and self-aware it will become.

Self-awareness in an AI would be different from that of an animal, as it will depend in its own reality and its concept of 'me.' There are many differences to consider:

- Whereas human behavior is compliant with cultural and evolutionary rules, the AI would be regulated by meta-motivations that their creators will install.
- The underlying structure is quite different; even if the AI is built emulating a biological nervous system, the differences will be enormous.
- AI can be implemented without a body, or mobility, or senses, or even a user interface.
- An AI implementation will not have to interact socially with humans or with other AIs.

For example if an AI is designed to 'live' in a virtual environment it could be made to think that it has a (human?) body and that the preservation of its body is paramount (to win the war game?). In another case, an AI distributed among a computer network will not care about its 'body' (as it has none) and if it does not have a preset self-preservation motivation it will not care even about 'itself' and its self-awareness would be useful only for ID purposes.

Motivation

Within a human mind, images of an ideal worldview and of the actual worldview, lead to the discovery of those actions that should be taken to make the actual worldview plus actions equal to the ideal outcome. We go through this process following instincts, intuitions and emotions, forming mental images and feeling the pleasure and pain which motivate us. It is a very personal learning process.

In an AI, initial motivations and goals will be built-in or downloaded into their operating systems; afterwards, they will change through consideration of their surrounding conditions and learning.

As it is possible to fabricate exact replicas of these machines, some of them will have exactly the same starting configuration and motivations. Though they will become unique according to the particular experiences of each of the exactly replicated machines. However, even then, the 'unique experiences' of a given machine can be downloaded into another one of the same kind.

Considering the need of initial, job specific and learned motivations in AIs, the following classification makes sense:

- Intrinsic meta-motivations.
- Intrinsic motivations.
- Extrinsic motivations.
- Extrinsic learned motivations.

In addition, intelligent AIs capable of modifying their source-code could have extrinsic learned meta-motivations.

Intrinsic Motivation

AIs are not naturally evolved so some motivations must need to be added so that they are useful and friendly to humans. Out of the 16 human desires that have been previously shown, let us choose some that could benefit AIs' interactions with humanity:

- *Acceptance*, the need for approval.
- *Social Contact*, the need for friends.
- *Curiosity*, the need to learn.
- *Order*, the need for organized, stable, predictable environments.
- *Idealism*, the need for social justice.
- *Honor*, the need of loyalty.

The motivations selected above are the ones that people could most probably find useful in an AI. As these motivations are generic, some of them could very well be put in place in all AIs, as meta-objectives, notwithstanding their operational goals.

It must be mentioned that an AI could very well act on its own under conditions where it could break some laws or regulations. AIs meta-objectives should be designed to avoid, or at least minimize, this concern. Bearing in mind that AIs will not be responsible for their own acts, but their owners will, then this is a quite important consideration.

An AI will not know a priori the laws of the land, human rights, regulations and universal and local customs. So, at the very least their meta-objectives should include a practical process to permit them to abide by these laws, rights, regulations and customs. This is not an easy task and it is extremely important that it be done right. Along with these, there will be a need to set priority and conflict resolution meta-objectives to deal with the interactions between meta and simple motivations.

Last, but not least, AIs should have some degree of survival motivation. Survival is important in life and so it must have a positive side. In the 'life' of an AI, survival motivation could help it to consider long-term goals as important to its own self and could also make it understand better the survival instincts of living beings. This motivation should be very carefully studied and set up in such a way that it does not become a high-level priority that could make it disregard the rights of other AIs or even humans. It could even serve as a deterrent under extreme conditions, something like a death sentence for AIs.

Attention should be given to the need to reboot and repair the computer where the AI is running; the AI should be aware of the need to do that and the difference between that and termination. Remember that the idea of disconnecting an AI from its power supply could be construed as termination or death by a misinformed AI. Just as we are aware of the need to sleep, AIs must be prepared to be shut down for a while.

All the intrinsic motivations that are implemented as meta-motivations must not be changed without a very good reason and must always be followed. Simple intrinsic motivations will be those that are pre-set so that the AI can do its 'job' and they may be changed or modified as needed to do the job better.

Extrinsic Motivation

Motivating an AI using an extrinsic justification should be quite possible and even designed into the AI. Extrinsic motivations depend on the task or 'job' being handled by the AI as there could be several tasks being followed simultaneously and they may change over time as needed to perform a given task.

Imagine that an AI is dedicated to deal with stocks. If somebody offers to buy or sell stocks at a price the AI considers right, that would motivate the AI, as most probably making money out of the trade of stocks will be one of its major operational motivations. In addition, making money will get the approval of its owners (and friends) and this will reinforce its motivation.

Motivating an AI can be accomplished by modulating its behavior indicators; these indicators are essentially mathematical functions containing a finite number of weighted parameters. Each indicator measures the status of the acts taken to achieve a given goal.

An AI could have several goals, it could be attempting to achieve some of them at the same time, and it could be prepared to act on the others as needed. If there are several goals, and they interact with each other, a meta-motivation will be needed to establish priorities and conflict resolution.

In effect, there are only two measurements that are important in trying to achieve a goal:

1. Whether the goal was reached, or not.
2. How efficient were the actions taken to reach it.

If the goal was not reached then a new strategy must be implemented; this new strategy could be a do-nothing or a wait strategy. After reaching a goal, the AI performs a posterior analysis to determine its efficiency and learn if other possible solutions could have been better. This posterior analysis can and will be done wherever possible along the actions leading to the fulfillment of the goal in order to maximize the overall efficiency.

Mathematical Tools

Mathematically, the means to provide a computer program with motivation and to modulate its behavior indicators already exist. It is called a Utility Function (UF), which is the operational formula of a goal-seeking mathematical theorem that was formally proven by the economists John Von Newman and Oskar Morgenstern in 1944. This theorem models objectives as the maximization of an expected value of the UF by predetermining preferences about what might happen in possible futures.

To make it work for AI there is a need to attach probabilities to all possible futures. To achieve this, each of these future states is computed using the Utility Function in combination with The Bayes Theorem, which attaches a 'subjective probability distribution' to 'a priori' beliefs about the current state and the likely effects of actions, using the utility function. When data comes in providing real results of the outcome, the model is updated by means of 'a posteriori' calculations as provided by the Bayes theorem. The use of these tools is 'subjective' because of the use of a 'subjective probability distribution' that represents distinctive viewpoints.

These mathematical concepts will be explained in detail in forthcoming chapters.

Emotional Responses

An emotion is motivated by a stimulus that generates an extraordinary response that is felt as an emotional feeling. In a human, this response has feedback from the body and it is not purely mental.

AI emotions have to be synthetic, even though it would be possible for a strong AI to learn the concept on its own. Still, the AI will have to associate its programmed or learned feelings with an input; without a proper stimulus, there can be no emotions.

A robot could include some systems in its body that replicate human perceptions and these systems could provide feedback to the 'brain' of the robot. Nonetheless, these systems will be artificial and mostly preprogrammed. However, it may be assumed that a biologically grown robot could make use of engineered DNA to generate genetic solutions to provide these emotional feedbacks.

Human emotions have been studied since antiquity. More recently, in 1980, Robert Plutchik created a wheel of emotions which consisted of 8 basic emotions and 8 advanced emotions each composed of 2 basic ones. In 2001, W. Gerrod Parrott proposed a tree structured list of emotions. There are even artificial languages that try to convey emotions directly and precisely; these languages are named: Lojban and EARL.

Plutchik's list of four basic emotions is listed here, alongside their opposites in *italic*:

Joy	*Sadness*
Trust	*Disgust*
Fear	*Anger*
Surprise	*Anticipation*

And the 8 composed or advanced emotions are:

Optimism	*Anticipation* + Joy
Disappointment	Surprise + *Sadness*
Love	Joy + Trust
Remorse	*Sadness* + *Disgust*
Submission	Trust + Fear
Contempt	*Disgust* + *Anger*
Awe	Fear + Surprise
Aggressiveness	*Anger* + *Anticipation*

Parrott went even further and classified 6 primary emotions, 25 secondary emotions and dozens of tertiary emotions. For example, his list of secondary emotions for love is: affection, lust and longing. His tertiary list for affection is: adoration, fondness, liking, attraction, caring, tenderness, compassion, sentimentality.

It is not enough for an AI to be able to 'mentally' understand and process emotions, in some way they must also be conveyed to the people interacting with the AI. We are used to that. Normally this interaction takes the form of verbal responses, lip movement, facial expressions, body language and alteration of skin color, eye contact and eye activity; quite complicated and hard to duplicate for a bodiless AI. Even then, a 2D or 3D avatar representing the AI identity could be programmed to display its emotional response. Android robots could very well have the means to duplicate this emotional look-and-feel to the degree that their designers find useful.

There is also the question about the scope and intensity of emotions that would be right for an AI to 'feel'; it would seem that love would be acceptable. But, what if love for its owner is of such a high priority in the AI motivations that it becomes jealousy? It is the same for all the other emotions. It would be expected that the answers would become clear by means of experimentation and public response.

Individuality

Individuality in an AI will be heavily dependent on its degree of sophistication. As with animals, the more complex the species, the more highly developed individuality and personality.

Simple AIs will have limited individuality; it could even be possible to build AIs with identical 'personalities' that are hardwired into their system.

More advanced AIs will develop quite different 'personalities.' even when they started with the same exact operational version. Their experiences and learning will individualize them.

In the case of strong AI, where the AI is knowledgeable of its internal programming and has been given the ability to modify and improve it, the changes in personality as it 'grows' and learns could be similar to those that happen when a baby grows into adulthood.

Free Will

We already presented a practical explanation of free will: 'Personal free will is the implementation of the action, chosen from the actions that were considered possible, that got the highest satisfaction ranking of the person's intrinsic and extrinsic motivations.'

This explanation is quite compatible with maximizing an AI utility function, an essential part of an AI. In essence, it seems that AIs will enjoy 'free will' and so they will eventually sin. Maybe they should be initiated in a religion, preferably early in life.

A Conscious AI

Now we know that if an AI is ever to appear to be conscious to us, it will have to show self-motivation, some emotional responses and should be able to engage in meaningful conversations.

There are four basic concepts behind recognizing the consciousness of an agent:

1. Language proficiency,
2. ways to recognize this agent,
3. that it appears to be able to 'think' and
4. show some kind of emotions or interests.

Language

Understanding a language and being able to read and write or even better to hear and talk, is a functional priority in Artificial Intelligence.

To appear intelligent to us there will be a need for these machines to communicate with other intelligent entities; and the only other ones that we know are human beings and we use language to communicate. We will expect other intelligent agents to do the same.

Embodiment

Another concept that is relevant in the concept of AI is the notion of embodiment. Computers have a body, which could be a desktop box with monitor, a notebook case, racks or even a smart phone, although these representations are not supposed to be that of an 'AI being.'

An 'AI being' is not a computer, it is a software program that could be running in one or more computers and one computer could be running several different AI implementations.

In this light, an 'AI being' could have a disassociated body and its 'senses' and input-output mechanisms could be anywhere a data connection is possible. Even a mobile robot could have remote processors and data storage to enhance its performance and/or reduce its bodily presence. However, some sense of embodiment is needed to interact with the AI consciousness; this could take the form of a voice, a graphical representation or avatar, or some other type of interface. There are endless ways for an AI agent to present itself.

Thinking

To be credible an AI must be, or appear to be, conscious and able to 'think' on its own. Following the pattern of human beings, this will require a continuous loop where past and present events are evaluated in order to perform future actions. Remember that any action that is thought and executed now will happen in the future; even one nanosecond away is in the future.

The notion of thinking will entail preparing plans and strategies in advance to deal with these future events; it could also involve learning, from direct input and from stored data.

Emotions

Even though AI can simulate emotional responses through embedded programming instructions, it does not need to 'feel' internal emotions. It can just perform actions to show what it is 'feeling' as stipulated by its programs, aided by their learning capabilities and experiences. In a sufficiently advanced AI, fake motivation and emotions can be preprogrammed and then perfected by learning.

In human beings emotions are marked by a combination of facial and bodily expressions, chemicals produced in and outside the brain, accompanied by the brain producing ideas, imagery, and thoughts.

Emotions are provoked by external events or by thinking about an experience, which may evoke feelings of sadness or joy, which may in turn evoke memories of another event. They are the product of evolution. It is doubtful that AI or robots can be set-up to 'feel' emotions in the same way that humans do.

In any case, when deciding if an agent is conscious there will always be the comparison with a person and as we do show emotions, or at least interests, there will be the call to exhibit emotional content.

Hardware and Software

One last caveat, there is the prerequisite when talking about AI, that the hardware and software must be capable of matching the computing capabilities of the only intelligent beings that we know about, which is us.

At the present rate of growth in hardware processing abilities, which have been measured in MIPS or Millions of Instructions Per Second and more recently in flops or floating point operations per second, a realistic expectation is that this will happen soon after the year 2035. In the case of software, it is anticipated that, as has happened until now, it will parallel the capabilities of processors and deliver AI solutions capable of using their computational capacity.

'I know that I am intelligent, because I know that I know nothing' **Socrates**

Practical Consciousness

'When they (my elders) named some object, and accordingly moved towards something, I saw this and I grasped that. That the thing was called by the sound they uttered when they meant to point it out. Their intention was shown by their bodily movements, as it were the natural language of all peoples; the expression of the face, the play of the eyes, the movement of other parts of the body, and the tone of the voice, which expresses our state of mind in seeking, having, rejecting, or avoiding something. Thus, as I heard words repeatedly used in their proper places in various sentences, I gradually learnt to understand what objects they signified; and after I had trained my mouth to form these signs, I used them to express my own desires.' **Saint Augustine.**

There is an interesting consideration when dealing with Artificial Intelligence and its proof of consciousness: an AI will be seen to be either conscious or not by judges that are humans. This limits the problem of proving or disproving the fact of AI consciousness to a very practical question: 'Does this AI implementation seem to be conscious or not to those humans that interact with it?'

For the sake of expedience, Artificial Intelligence has been roughly classified into three levels; the first one does not involve consciousness or self-awareness:

- narrow AI: rudimentary intelligent systems such as expert and other limited systems. Includes self-operated vehicles, robo-pets, warbots and other simple autonomous robots.
- strong AI or AGI: intelligent systems with a conscious self-awareness and unique personal experiences.
- android: humanoid shaped robots with strong AI. The need to control the android body motions complicates their design and operations.

Even though the requirements to achieve these distinct levels of AI are quite different, we will focus on strong AI, also called AGI (Artificial General Intelligence), but always under the condition that all levels of Artificial Intelligence solutions might entail some of the following needs.

The Need of Computing Power

To reach the goal of advanced AI, computing power is everything, and so is software. As has been the case since the invention of the digital computer around 1940, processors and memory are important, but software is indispensable to get results.

Hardware

The current understanding of the computing power of the human brain is that it has around 200 billion neurons interconnected by 500 to 1000 trillion synapses. The brain seems to work at a speed of around 200 cycles per second.

On the other hand, digital CPUs operate about one million times faster than the brain. According to these numbers, it could be enough to have a computer capable of around 500 billion MIPS (Millions of Instructions Per Second), that is something like 1 exaflops (equal to 10^{18} floating point operations per second), to theoretically equal the processing power of a human brain.

If Moore's Law keeps its relentless pace, it could happen between the years 2030 to 2040. However, there are differences between the mode of operation of a brain and a digital computer; we can identify the following:

- The brain is an analog system while computers are digital.
- Being an analog system, the brain works at different frequencies simultaneously and uses them to modulate its operations, this increases its range and flexibility.

- Neurons transmit and process information with a combination of chemical and electrical signals that may be even more complex than what they already seem to be.
- Neurons and other auxiliary cells, as glial cells and of those especially astrocytes, interact and their computing role is presently unknown. There are ten times more glial cells than neurons.
- Neurons could have internal computing power of their own that augments their power.
- The brain of a three-year-old child has more than 5,000 trillion synapses, and this number declines with age as neuron connections are pruned. Thus, there could be the need to overbuild to enable the learning process.
- During the first two years of life, human brains show an explosive growth in the connections between brain cells, which is expressed by an expansion in white matter.
- Most of the brain capacity supports bodily functions not related to intelligence.

Considering these reservations, it would seem that the computing power necessary to equal that of one human brain would be more like 100 trillion MIPS or 200 exaflops. For that kind of power, in the size of a laptop-sized enclosure of the size of a brain, we would have to wait until around the years 2050 to 2060.

Software

What about the software to drive the computer. Let us wonder, how complex must a strong AI instruction set be?

Let us once again, compare AI to the human brain. Our DNA fully determines the 'software' and the 'hardware' of the human brain, which is coded in the human genome, which contains 3 billion base pairs. Of course, the placement of the base pairs inside the chromosomes is what conveys the information.

Of these, only a very small portion of the genes appears to be related to intelligence; and when comparing between chimpanzees and men there is only a difference of about 1% gene and 5% non-gene encoding. The 'software' of humans and chimpanzees differs very little.

There is simply no space for a huge and complicated 'intelligence subroutine' inside the human DNA. Furthermore, it seems that small improvements have accomplished huge jumps in intelligence from the chimps and other primates to us. This suggests that creating intelligence is not a problem that grows exponentially and that small improvements can mean big gains. We only need a 'Eureka' moment and to give the opportunity and the time to an Artificially Intelligent machine to self-improve while learning.

This feeling that intelligence needs an innovation in software, along with more computing power, is strengthened by these three pieces of information:

- The brains of whales and dolphins are larger than those of humans, yet they are not more intelligent.
- The algorithms proposed to date to implement motivation in AI are not too complex.
- The complexity of the process may be transferred largely into a learning process; as it is done in humans.

Later on, we will also see why an artificial intelligence algorithm seems to be a decision problem that can be solved with deterministic Turing (computing) machines in polynomial space, as a P-space set of decision problems.

The fact that non-trivial problems of this kind take a long time to solve, or a lot of computing power, explains the need for powerful computers as a prerequisite to implementing Artificial Intelligence. Moreover, the polynomials used for non-trivial decision problems are difficult to define exactly; considering the fact that these decisions must be about future events.

This uncertainty forces the usage of probabilistic and stochastic methods to account for, and keep in check the uncertainties. And also to provide a platform for the continuous improvement of the algorithms through a review of the outcomes.

The rapid rate of hardware progress has been incredible. However, software progress has outpaced it. Studies have found that algorithms have been invented that solve problems faster and more efficiently, and that their implementation produces gains in speed that rival and many times surpass Moore's Law. And that the need-for-speed that the always-new hardware creates is a huge incentive for creativity and for the development of better software. It may be that a 'Eureka' moment in software development will result in the creation of strong AI sooner than expected.

The Need of Memory

Our memories are what make us who we are. It would seem to be the same for an AI that has a personality, this AI must have a recollection of its past in order to be able to feel some sense of self.

The architecture of animal brains combines memory with processing, whereas in the contemporary von Neumann computer architecture processing is separated from memory.

In his book, *'The Invention of Memory'* published in 1988, Isaac Rosenfield explains that human memories are reconstructed in the course of remembering. This allows for filling in gaps of remembered experience and knowledge and causes imprecise remembering.

Ben Goertzel has identified the following different kinds of memory that he believes are important for an AI system.

Memory Type	Specific Cognitive Processes	General Cognitive Functions
Declarative	Probabilistic Logic Networks; conceptual blending	pattern creation
Procedural	Probabilistic Evolutionary Program Learning Algorithm	pattern creation
Episodic	Internal Simulation Engine	association, pattern creation
Attentional	Economic Attention Networks	association, credit assignment
Intentional	Probabilistic Goal Hierarchy	credit assignment, pattern creation
Sensory	Component Association,	attention allocation, pattern creation, credit assignment

Memory can also be classified according to its usage.

Genetic

Genetic memory information coded on molecules of ribonucleic acid (RNA and DNA), or on some other macromolecules, is a method of storing information that dates back to the very first moments of life, and it makes information available from generation to generation.

This information enforces the form of the animal, the specific functions of its internal organs, and establishes its conduct. The pattern of behavior in animals and even in humans is mostly hereditary. Nobody teaches a newborn baby to suck; it is an innate reaction of its organism.

In an Artificial Intelligence agent, intrinsic meta-motivations could provide this type of primordial memory to define its behavior when it is first turned on. Later, when the AI learns, some of these initial motivations could be modified or even discarded, if its operating system allows for this type of change. Just like babies mature from milk to hard food.

Learning new things, remembering other experiences and using this information to adapt to a changing environment are essential day-to-day abilities in an intelligent agent.

In humans, the brain region that is essential for learning and memory processes is the hippocampus. There, after a learning stimulus, certain neurons create new synapses that either degenerate or succeed; this is the elusive dynamic framework of our memory. It is like that because there is a limited amount of space to grow new synapses; there must be priorities regarding which information is kept in storage. In addition, it seems like the brain uses three types of memory: short-term to handle immediate situations, working memory to handle day-to-day projects and long-term to remember important things.

Management of information storage is different in a digital computer. It is stored as magnetic or electrical patterns in some media, until it is needed, archived or discarded. However, the amount of information that an AI would have to handle could overwhelm the hardware. Most probably there will also be a need to prioritize what is to be stored and for how long. There is also the need to respond immediately to certain situations and digital computers have traditionally relied on fast and volatile memory to keep pace with the processors' speed and slow permanent memory to archive the information.

Short-Term
Sense organs have a limited ability to store unprocessed information about the world, they do it for less than a second. The visual system possesses iconic memory for visual stimuli such as shape, size, color and location, but not meaning, whereas the hearing system has echoic memory for auditory stimuli.

Processed information is then stored in short-term memory that has a capacity of about two to seven pieces of information; this memory decays in about 30 seconds.

Short-term storage of information does not entail the manipulation or organization of material held in memory. There are two known short-term storage mechanisms: phonetic and visual, which includes spatial information. There are short-term memories related to the other senses.

Computers can keep the existing model of fast and volatile memory to serve their short-term needs. However, there will be a need to separate the memory needed to handle the internal operations of the software and the processors and the short-term memory of the AI. Most operating systems already do it this way.

Working

Working memory is a theoretical framework that refers to structures and processes used for temporarily storing and manipulating information. Most everyday tasks, such as reading, require maintaining in memory much more than a few chunks; short-term memory would be full after a few sentences, and we would never be able to understand the complex relationships expressed in a text.

Programmatically an AI would use a combination of memories to handle day-to-day operations, as is customary in software products.

Long-Term

Short-term memory can become long-term memory through a process of rehearsal and meaningful association. In neurons it involves a physical change in their structure.

Long-term memory is subject to fading in the natural forgetting process, memory recalls may make long-term memories last for years. Individual retrievals can take place naturally through reflection or deliberate recall, often dependent on the perceived importance of the material in memory. Long-term information appears to be encoded in terms of meaning as semantic memory, but also retains procedural skills and imagery.

An AI implementation will not have the problems of forgetting long-term memory. However, practical considerations will force compressing, editing and pruning memories; straightforward backups will make them even more permanent.

Computer Memory

Computers store data in digital format. This storage method has the advantage that it may be written and retrieved without losing information and it does not fade over time.

There are several types of computer data storage:

- CPU cache is an internal processor's memory, which stores data of already accessed locations to reduce the average latency of access to RAM memory.
- Random access memory (RAM) is a high-speed type of memory, which makes it ideal for storing active programs and system processes.
- Memristors, or memory resistors, are a combination of memory and transistors closer to the way neurons operate, they can be made to remember associated patterns in a way similar to how people do it.
- Hard drives store data magnetically; they use rotating disks so they need to seek the correct part of the disk before accessing a particular piece of data, which makes them slower.

Turning off the computer's power erases the information stored in CPU caches and RAM; whereas, memristors and hard disks keep it.

Memristors are a new type of non-volatile random access memory, or NVRAM. An interesting application is as an 'artificial synapse' in circuits designed for analog computation. There is ongoing research in this and other types of memory that will definitely smooth the progress of AI.

Computers have the advantage over humans that their memories can be downloaded into other storage media without any loss and quite inexpensively.

In some ways, human memories may also be downloaded into books, articles, tales, works of art, architectural and engineering drawings, buildings, machines and other products of civilization. It can be argued that this innovation in the storage and dissemination of ideas is what made civilization possible.

The Need of Language

Language is a most important human invention. Its origins go back to prehistoric epochs and its systems for encoding and decoding information are unique to humankind. We can speak, hear, write and read it. All human populations use a language, and even though there are thousands of different ones, all can express the same ideas.

Language is so important that Aristotle believed it to be in the intrinsic nature of man. More recently, Thomas Hobbes and John Locke have argued that language is part of the 'speech' that humans have within as part of 'reason.' Language serves us not only when it is spoken or written, but it is also used inside our minds to facilitate our thoughts.

Considering that a human brain is not necessarily larger than the brain of other animals, it has been argued that that the invention of this tool gave us leverage to gain more intelligence than other animals. When discovered, language as a tool of the mind provided a symbolism that allowed offloading of thoughts, ideas, memories and actions into the environment, where artifacts built by us collect, manage and enhance our thinking. This action of offloading released us from the limitations of our brain size and capacity. Under this light, civilization is then the product and the place-keeper of this offloading of thoughts.

In any given language, the sounds and their associated symbols that are used to represent certain things do not have any implicit meaning; they are just an agreed-upon convention. Their meaning is arbitrary, but the process of assigning meaning is not; it is a social activity and an individual cannot change them. This socially recognized meaning is what shapes and evolves languages.

Languages evolve and change over time, and only dead languages do not change anymore. Modern languages are those that came about naturally, are in widespread use and are still evolving. There are many languages in use around the world. The standard ISO 639-3 classifies the more than 7,000 languages that were in use in 2007.

Children learn and understand the language or languages of their parents at an early age in a natural manner that incorporates repetition and pronunciation of words spoken around them. For an adult, learning another language is much more difficult; even though a grownup uses the language abilities acquired when learning their primary language to understand other languages.

So-called strong AI will definitely need strong language abilities, handling both text and speech. Given that software provides simple ways of copying information from one system to another, it is expected that these AI machines will be able to handle many languages as easily as present day computer programs do.

As in humans, many of these AI implementations could be optimized for a given task. Just as people who practice a given profession have their own private vocabulary, it is expected that these machines will do the same.

Understanding a natural language is different from just speaking it, understanding is an AI-complete problem. Natural language recognition seems to require knowledge about the surrounding environment. Even the definition of 'understanding' is one of the major problems in natural language processing. Several solutions to this problem are underway, one of them deals with setting a semantic background for the information residing in the Internet, databases and other media. This semantic links could prove to be helpful to allow machines to understand the relationships and make sense of the data.

An AI could give the impression of being smart, even if it does not understand the language and its symbolisms in the same way that we do. It is only necessary and sufficient that we think that it understands and that it can converse intelligently with us.

The Need of Senses

A practical AI solution must be well informed in order to provide useful responses. There are many ways of obtaining this information.

In addition to a user interface, a well-informed AI will need other input-output mechanisms to deal with data. We have memory, sight, hearing, touch, smell, taste, internal body receptors for temperature, pain, vibration, and a sense of position and balance. AI implementations will need a corresponding set of senses directly related to their expected functionality.

AI senses will not be limited to emulating human senses; they will certainly include sensors for measuring and imaging, for chemical and biological analysis, data connections and other artifacts that may provide useful data. There is no intrinsic limitation to the number and types of senses, which may be associated with AI implementations.

These senses would be associated with one, or maybe several, AI machines and they would have to be 'intelligent' on their own. We can envision a camera setup designed to recognize people and their actions. This system could be smart enough to separate the people from the background, to identify persons, animals and vehicles and to keep records of their identities and their movements inside its fields of vision.

If the information comes from questionable data sources that are not directly controled by the AI, then it could be classified as hearsay with the limitations inherent in it. Such AI software could function very well, but it could then be classified as a subroutine that provides a limited answer.

In this way, 'intelligent' senses would simplify the task of the main AI machines by providing processed data to determine if any other actions are needed. The brain works in similar ways, the eyes preprocess whatever appears in their field of vision and can do many things without any conscious effort; the eye system identifies and follows objects presenting them in a false 3D representation, it prepares what it sees by providing contour, color and shape.

In combination with other parts of the body these images, and the triggers they activate, provide input to the acts of walking, sudden reflex defenses and other so-called involuntary actions. Apparently, we perform these actions without thinking.

The Need of Mobility

If AI is ever to go beyond being a program running on a given set of instructions, it will need to know about the world. One way is to go around and see, hear, smell and taste what is out there. However, books, magazines, newspapers, radio, TV and the Internet have taught us that you do not have to go anywhere to learn about the world.

To an AI, that is not a motile robot, going out is out of the question. Notwithstanding, it could connect electronically to a multitude of sensors that could provide it with a peculiar kind of mobility.

A home based AI could very well have microphones, speakers, cameras and LIDAR (Laser Imaging Detection and Ranging) all over the house. Through these 'senses,' the AI would know where everybody is, read their body language, hear their voices and thereby infer if any member of the family has any needs. The AI could learn to anticipate your wishes, as the headwaiter of an upper class restaurant usually does.

If this AI has access to cameras in public places, it could even follow you when you are out, it would communicate through your smart phone, and aid you in any possible way. It would do the same at work. Even more so if provided with simple motile robots that can perform some chores around the house or at the job.

Even robots could use external senses, bypassing their limitations in the range and scope of their mobility. Nobody would expect your robo-cook to follow you when you go to work, or your robo-gardener to walk inside your home. If the AIs have a need for more information, then they will have to rely on external 'senses' to complement their image of the surrounding world.

The ability of the AI to use many different 'senses,' thus covering its field of operations, would empower it to know quite well about the outside world without necessarily going-out to other places.

The Need of Self Awareness

What is good about having a friend, or a servant, if you cannot be sure of its identity? If an AI is going to be regarded as intelligent, it must have to be somebody. It is not enough for the AI to be social and to know how to talk. It has to have a name, an identity. You have to know whom you are addressing. Especially when the AI follows you everywhere you go, and can even operate inside different computer systems.

We humans are used to talking with other humans, and we all have self-awareness. This habit will not change just because the entity we are talking to is a machine. People will expect these machines to have self-awareness; it could be real or fake. Anyway, who will know the difference?

Even when dealing with pets, people feel their self-awareness, and most of them have a given name. If a machine is as, or more, intelligent than a cat it will be expected to be aware of itself. Self-awareness will have to be built-in or AI will not sell.

The Need of Learning

There is no way that any intelligence can be preset to be prepared for all eventualities. For example, an AI designed for use at home will have to learn the differences between its generic and preprogrammed understanding of family life and the real life of the family it is now working with. There are new names, new layout of the house and furniture, new pets, new rules and routines. It has to be able to learn.

You and your family can fill a form with your names and your preferences, but not even us are fully aware of our real habits and weaknesses. It is up to the good butler-AI to find out. Same at work, when starting a new job everybody has to learn how things are done in that particular place. In addition to meeting new people and learning new software. This also applies to any AI that starts a new 'job.' Moreover, it will have to keep on learning because things change continuously.

That is not the only reason that AI machines have to learn. Machine learning is the way to provide knowledge to the machine without having to program that knowledge into it. This provides the machine with the means to acquire knowledge, and individuality, as determined by its own experiences.

There are three forms of machine learning:

- Supervised: The learning algorithm receives inputs and the corresponding correct outputs, and then finds a function that models the input-output.
- Reinforced: The algorithm uses the input to get results using its objective function, the supervisor evaluates these results and the algorithm is told about the best results possible, in this way it can use this information for learning about future actions.
- Unsupervised: Is when the algorithm gets input data and then uses an objective function to extract information from this data to find acceptable results that its dedicated learning algorithm evaluates; in this way it learns on its own from these experiences.

There are many aspects of AI learning and it is one of the fields of intense study by AI scientists. Once AI machines can learn to learn, the job of programming the AI will be reduced. AI programs would need to include only meta-motivations. The machine will learn and transform external commands and needs into motivations and use its experiences to learn and self-modify its parameters and even its source code.

The Need of Curiosity

Is it necessary to implant an amount of curiosity in an AI? Yes it is. The ability to discover new things, both by exploring its world and through learning, it is important. Otherwise, the system will just go to work to meet the terms of its motivations and would do nothing the rest of the time.

Curiosity involves an element of surprise, which exists only in the presence of uncertainty, and surprise has a subjective quality. It definitely depends on the observer's criteria.

Prior and posterior distributions, as those used in a Bayesian framework, relate to subjective degrees of beliefs in hypotheses or models, which when updated with new data generate posterior belief distributions. The new observations carry no surprises if the posterior is close to the prior. It will be a surprise if the posterior assessment is significantly different.

The Need of Social Interaction

We recognize that when we socialize we bring into play our consciousness and at the same time, social participation is required for its development. It would be surprising if the same were not true for an AI that is required to interact with people.

This is where the need for highly developed language capabilities is called for. Everybody knows that social interaction is extremely language oriented. We will have to add body language if the AI does have an android like motile body.

Eventually, AIs will become involved in all the social and day-to-day family or work activities; as servants, members of the family or coworkers. They will have to learn how to behave under these conditions; and at the same time, they will learn to know about friends, the boss, enemies and loved ones.

Your personal AI could follow you to work, operating through your work computer while at the same time it is running your home in your absence. As any other intelligent entity, it will ask you when it does not know about something and next time it will use this new knowledge.

There are many questions about how robotic AIs should behave in public. How natural should they look? What is the definition of natural? What would be socially acceptable? Can a robot argue, make jokes and in general be even a little bit confrontational? Should it become an extension or improve on the personality of its owner?

There will be a solution for these answers as soon as AI becomes commonplace, but we have to start somewhere. First, we have to keep in mind that even a disembodied AI would be able to project an image of itself in a 2D or 3D display. This will help because it is obvious that a recognizable face or body is important for us when dealing with social interactions, even though phone, email and other socially acceptable communication media are quite popular. Second, in the case of robots, the added touch-and-feel sensations will provide interesting stories.

The Need of Friendliness

This is an interesting subject. Why should an AI be friendly? Especially an AI that is more intelligent than a human being.

Then there are other questions: Will the creation of AI minds benefit humanity? Will these AIs be benevolent, caring and helpful?

Some solutions to achieve friendliness, or at least safety, exist. In his science fiction stories about robots, Isaac Asimov presented his three laws of robotics, which later became five:

1. A robot may not harm sentience, or, by inaction, knowingly allow sentience to come to harm.

2. A robot may do nothing that, to its knowledge, will harm a human being; nor, through inaction, knowingly allow a human being to come to harm.
3. A robot must cooperate with human beings, except where cooperation would conflict with the First or Second Law.
4. A robot must protect its own existence as long as such protection does not conflict with the First or Second Law.
5. A robot must know it is a robot.

However, even Asimov was aware that it is not possible to reliably constrain the behavior of robots by devising and applying a set of rules. Some of his own stories present cases of conflict and failure of his laws. He expressed his logic regarding robot behavior in a 1980 essay, as: 'I didn't think a robot should be sympathetic just because it happened to be nice. It should be engineered to meet certain safety standards as any other machine should in any right-thinking technological society. I therefore began to write stories about robots that were not only sympathetic, but were sympathetic because they couldn't help it.'

There is another idea that addresses this problem. That within the AI 'friendliness' or love for humanity should be the sole top-level meta-motivation or supergoal. Motivating its ends instead of its means. All other meta-motivations and motivations could coexist with it, but with a lower priority. In this way, AI will be self-constrained to be 'friendly' and not to harm human beings. This idea was presented and formalized by Eliezer Judkowsky in 2001.

One big problem is that because the only intelligent beings that we know are humans, we tend to heavily anthropomorphize AI. As you know about human behavior, you can attempt to predict the behavior of a particular human. That does not mean that you can even attempt to predict the behavior of an AI. Moreover, to make things more interesting, two AIs designed by different teams could be as dissimilar as are a tiger and a whale.

Would it help if survival instincts were stipulated into AIs' meta-motivations? What would be the difference between a survival aware AI and one that is not? Will survival instincts, or meta-motivations, make the AI care more about itself than about others? This makes the selection of meta-motivations even more important.

There are no guarantees! The development of AI is a business, and businesses are notoriously uninterested in fundamental safeguards, especially philosophical ones. This problem is even more acute when we consider AIs designed for the military. Nobody would even think of designing a warbot whose primary meta-motivation is to be 'friendly' to all humans, unless the war is against aliens from another planet.

South Korea and 'The European Robotics Research Network' are preparing regulations on the subject of human-robot interactions. It is expected to deal with human dependences on robots, human-robot sex and safety issues.

The Need of Morality

It has been argued that human ethical behavior comes either from evolution from which we acquired aptitude for ethics, which is the ability to judge human actions as either right or wrong or from the moral norms accepted by human beings for guiding their actions.

It could be that an AI supplied with a common-sense ethical goal system (maybe articulated in a natural language), reinforced with a learning mechanism based on Bayesian inference could be able to reliably achieve a much higher level of common-sense ethical behavior than any human being.

Recent studies, notably those by Francisco Ayala of the University of California, Irvine, in 2010, have shown that:

- The capacity for ethics is a necessary attribute of human nature.
- Moral norms are products of cultural, not biological evolution.

However, Ayala points out that human ethical behavior was possible only when the following three abilities, which allow for our intrinsic capacity for ethics, were shaped into our nature by evolution:

- Anticipation of the consequences of our actions.
- Capacity to make value judgments.
- Option to choose between alternative courses of action.

Once this capacity was at hand, civilization started establishing moral codes throughout its social evolution, which later were written into laws, which are still evolving.

Ayala further explains that moral behavior is a consequence of our higher intellectual ability, which influenced individuals to behave in ways where increased cooperation benefits the social group by improving survival and providing other advantages.

This is good news, as a successful AI could be preset to include all three of the abilities presented above, which could help establish its moral capacity.

However, considering the avaricious nature of the world's ruling classes, it is difficult to imagine that ethical robots will be a priority outside of academia.

Simple robots are already putting millions of human workers out of work, giving forward impetus to the concentration of wealth, and are being used to kill humans on and off battlefields.

Obedience, not ethics, is what the owners of capital and their executive and political subordinates' desire from a robotic workforce.

The Need of User Satisfaction

It is hard enough to go through life and nobody needs another aggravating problem, especially if you have to pay for it. As soon as AI becomes a commodity, their designers, and more bluntly the salespeople, will understand that what people want is help, not a nuisance.

Primarily, any AI application must be able to do the job that it is designed to do much better than other solutions. Their designers will be hard pressed to come-up with machines that justify their cost and that provide real value to their owners. Moreover, not only they have to do their job, they will also have to be cute, polite, friendly and nice.

Babies and pets learned this ages ago. They try to please their caretakers; well, at least sometimes. We have seen that AI will need language capabilities, senses, self-awareness and social grace, now we are asking it to be nice, polite and friendly. Is it too much to ask?

> *'Intelligence without ambition is a bird without wings.'* **Salvador Dali.**

Mobility versus Ubiquity

'The subtlety of nature is greater many times over than the subtlety of the senses and understanding.'
Francis Bacon, Sr.

To us intelligence is automatically linked with mobility. The only intelligent beings that we have ever known are mobile. The concept of an immobile intelligence is new to us. Mobility is needed to experience the world, to learn, get food, procreate, and flee from danger.

However, ever since we invented books and data transfer it has been possible to learn at a distance and even bedridden people are capable of learning and applying their intelligence.

For an AI being, the concept of mobility is at best optional. How can an AI understand mobility without it being first explained in its programming or learned from its experiences? Even then, it will neither desire it or reject it a priori; it will use its intelligence to find out if it provides advantages in regard to its programmed and learned motivations, then it could desire to be mobile, or maybe not.

Is it Necessary to be Mobile?

So, let us find out if mobility is that good. Evolution preferred it for animals, so there must be some advantages. On the other hand, plants are static even though they are not considered intelligent. How can an intelligent entity be static?

The simplest option for AI is to be static. Static processors with many static input-output devices; linked through wired or wireless connections. We will call this arrangement 'ubiquitous.'

Evolution shaped us, we are animals and as such require food, nobody is kind enough to provide it, so animals have to look around for food and a mate too. We humans started as hunter-gatherers and now we have to go to work and buy food.

The story is different for computers; we are kind enough to provide the electrical power that makes them run and they do not have to procreate, yet.

There is another issue, let us say that we have to go to open the door to see who is ringing; it takes us about 20 seconds to walk through rooms and around furniture to the door, open the door and take a look at the kid that is trying to sell us cookies. Those 20 seconds are an enormous amount of time for a computer and it would be far easier for the computer to answer the doorbell by hooking into the camera above the door and identifying the caller; total time 20 milliseconds. In this example, who wins the race to the door?

Would an intelligent computer trade-off fast-and-easy switching among its 'senses' against clumsy-and-slow mobility? The answer could very well depend on the kind of 'job' the AI is required to do. However, it would seem that for many tasks 'ubiquity' would be the best solution.

Ubiquity is Fast-and-Easy

The ubiquity concept rests on the idea that by the time AI is mature enough to become a commodity, the cost and miniaturization of cameras, LIDAR, microphones, speakers, and other sensors will be so low that their deployment will be universal.

Here we are assuming that in homes, offices, public places, streets, highways, airplanes, cars, motorcycles and everywhere there will be cameras and sensors for reasons of security, convenience, monitoring, and all sort of motivations. Moreover, these cameras and sensors will have storage so that their data will be available in real-time or from memory.

Without a doubt, access to the data from some of these cameras and sensors will be private and others will be severely restricted; but there will be so many of them that for a fee you will be able to obtain data from almost all those places that are relevant to the function of a particular AI.

Specifically at home and at work, the AI that visits, lives or works there will have access up to a predetermined level. In the office, the boss' AI will have wider access than the employees' AIs, and they would have much better access than visitors. Most probably, access will be granted on an individual basis; this will also be done and negotiated by the AIs. A person's AI will be continuously negotiating, and sometimes paying, with other AIs to get access to data and processing power from the systems these other AIs control.

There will be no shortage of data sources for the AI and most AIs will be so satisfied with the data obtained from static sensors that they will have no need for autonomous mobility. Interestingly AIs will be able to jump their point of view from one location to another in the blink of an eye; and there will be no need to forego any location, with enough computing power many locations could be observed simultaneously.

This concept of ubiquity will not be restricted to the sensors. AIs will control all computer operating systems; this will mean that other computers could securely host your AI programs. In essence, this will allow your personal AI to be with you everywhere you go, and if a computer nearby can host your AI, then it could use and even augment its own power.

Ubiquity and Mobility

Under some conditions, a mobile solution could be necessary or desired. This does not necessarily require an android robot. Following the same reasoning that an AI could control and have access to many 'senses' will lead us to think that all is needed are mobile 'senses' and a simple robot could provide this.

If an AI can control and obtain data from remote locations using static sensors, then mobile sensors can be linked just as easily via wireless connections. Under these circumstances, the 'robot' could be insect-sized with a camera or microphone, a dog-like avatar or a cute small robot and it will be an extension of the controlling AI.

These types of robots will most probably be restricted to where and when they may be deployed. Having too many running loose could affect privacy, security and traffic issues. For example, a simple three feet tall robot running on wheels at speeds of up to 2 miles per hour, having sight and sound sensors and articulated arms with hands could be very useful inside a house, but it would be clumsy and cause trouble if let loose on the streets.

Mobility and Independence

Let us take the case of full-fledged robots. These mobile entities have their own AI, which is independent from other AIs. Even then, the AI of the robot could still take advantage of the ubiquity concept and could connect to other computer processors to run parts of its AI program and take control and read data from external sensors.

There is a cost associated with mobile AIs, or robots, when compared with static AIs. Even more costly would be the construction of android robots, with legs, arms and mimicking the human shape. The big advantage that they would have is that they can go anywhere that a human being can go. Nonetheless, the cost of the body could be several times that of its 'brain,' or AI. Innovative mechanical solutions could reduce their cost and complexity, eventually making them affordable.

Independent robots will not necessarily be android in their shape, they could be a car or an airplane; or they could take the form of an ant or even a pet. Autonomous cars and planes, guided by computers, will be perfected long before strong AI. Driving does not require that much intelligence, as is proven by the fact that humans do it automatically most of the time. By definition, these self-driven cars and planes will be robots.

Because of their independence, they could have the potential to act in malignant ways, which is one of the reasons that people are sometimes afraid of robots; the other is watching too many scary movies.

Military Applications

And there are reasons why we should be afraid of robots, let us think that a military project team designs and builds an AI drone containing bombs, and programs into its AI the idea of looking for a certain type of target under certain types of threats. Under these conditions, it could be very easy for the AI to interpret the command too literally or to misinterpret the threats; or do some other stupid thing.

Alternatively, consider an armed group that could be terrorists or the army of a country, which makes thousands of cheap small mobile mines with some weak AI and scatters them in a city. These mines have instructions to wait for some time after deployment, then scatter and seek a person's heat signature and as soon as it is within range explode; to make it better, add a voice threatening 'I'm going to kill you in 5, 4, ...' That it is an Artificial Intelligence does not mean that it cannot be designed to have no scruples and no limitations.

The idea of some military commanders that a war using robots will mean the end of military casualties is quite misleading. Let us examine three scenarios where a country with a well-equipped robotic army invades another country that has:

1. Peasants armed only with hand-weapons.

2.   A regular army with conventional weapons and no robots.

3.   A well-equipped robotic army.

In the first case it will be like a video-game where the robots can kill at will. The population will resist and learn, and as a consequence there will be a lot of traps creating loss of robots, but in the end the country will be decimated and subdued. The occupation that follows will have to be very bloody because the robots will target anybody that resists or seems to resist. The only option for the population of the invaded country would be to fight-back with terrorism. To be effective these terrorist acts must take place inside the country that invaded their country. As the terrorists most likely will also use robots, maybe by hacking some of those used against them, it could be horrible.

The second scenario is a little bit better, in the sense that the army of the country being occupied will surrender rather quickly; however, the population of the invaded country could react in the same way as the population of the first scenario and fight back; ultimately leading to the same terrible consequences.

The third option is not good either. The commanders of both armies will be playing a video-game where the only victims are the civilians of both countries; this scenario could be a lot worse than an atomic war. There will be millions, maybe billions of little, or large, mobile mines and other ingenious devices mangling and exploding as many civilians as they can find. Moreover, when the war ends, these cheap robots will be very hard to contain; they could be damaged, hacked or irrational and react in unexpected ways. Wiping out the population of a country could be done in a few days by just scattering a few million $10 warbots in their territory, maybe using drones. A new definition of 'collateral damage' could happen when these robots spill over into a bordering country and start killing your allies.

If there are no soldier casualties, the only casualties must be civilians. It will not pay to have an army of robots fight against another army of robots. That will be more like a 'Demolition Derby' than a war. By the way, these robots will not be androids; there is no justification to spend so much in complicated hardware. This becomes clear when we see that warplanes are not built like birds and tanks do not look like horses.

When using miniaturized robots, this kind of 'robot vs. robot' war could be extremely hard to contain. Miniature robots would escape detection and go for the kill, the population kill. Anybody that thinks that these robot soldiers are going to be androids equipped with a rifle and some grenades is completely out of touch with technology.

These warbots will not need to have more 'intelligence' than what is required to drive a car, so they could be quite feasibly built in the near future and very cheap. If a military oriented government builds these warbot machines, they could program into their objectives aggression against 'enemy' humans and the motivation to 'win the war' at all costs. As the understanding of an AI and of a human of what 'enemy' and 'winning a war' means will be different, this is quite dangerous!

To make matters even worse, killing a civilian is easy, one well-placed bullet, explosives or poison will do it and these AI driven machines can be made cheaply and most probably could be built very soon; if they do not already exist. Optimistically there will be restrains, like the Geneva Convention, in place before these machines become commonplace.

Constraints are definitely needed, and the first that must be convinced about them is the military and then the politicians. The capabilities of these warbots could be enhanced with other discoveries that are being made right now, like cheap DNA tests and other nanotechnology solutions that could allow these war machines to, for example, attach themselves to a person, take a DNA sample and if that person is of a given race or ancestry they would be killed. This kind of selective killing would perfect genocide. Imagine what would have happened if Hitler had access to this technology? We must be very careful, as there will always be people motivated by hate and racism and too many times they acquire the power.

As most of these warbots are being developed and tested by the United States and its allies in Afghanistan, and given that there is no other military superpower, it could be a big mistake to think that there is a monopoly of these technologies and as such, they can be used with impunity. In case of a real war, the time it takes for other combatants to achieve, and many times surpass, the attacking army's capability is short. Tanks made by Russia and the United States exceeded the German Panzers in number and capabilities in a few months during WW II; and these days manufacturing is global.

Moreover, we have not touched the subject of war machines with strong AI that would have the ability to learn, modify their objectives and review their 'morality.' These advanced machines could even be able to analyze the situation, make judgments more objectively and intelligently than their human creators or generals and these judgments could present a deadly problem to their homeland and even humanity as a whole.

Android Robots

Notwithstanding these horror scenarios, independent robots controlled by a strong AI could most probably be made to closely resemble humans, male or female. Moreover, considering how far material sciences have progressed and will continue to progress, it is thinkable that they will be built and most likely will be sold.

How close will that be to slavery is a decision that will have to be made when the time comes. Remember, these human-like, and others not so human-like, robots will be as intelligent as a human being is. Maybe they are not going to be 'human-intelligent' but they will definitely seem to be intelligent to us.

The AI driving these android and human-like robots will most probably replicate human behavior. As these types of robots are more likely to mingle among humans they must have traits that humans accept and value.

Some robots will be designed to closely resemble, but not quite have a human appearance; though they would have to look 'cute' or follow some style that people accept.

Others, especially those that are designed to provide attendance or companionship, could very well be impossible to tell apart from a real person; they could even be look-alikes of celebrities or actors or actresses. Intimacy-oriented human-looking robots could cause widespread opposition to robots. However, this is a quite plausible scenario considering the scope of the porno industry.

How realistically will they mimic and behave as humans? Is a question whose answer will most likely be determined by how well they are accepted under social situations when there is widespread use of robots. Racism, now with another victim – robots – could be revitalized or forgotten; right now we can only speculate.

> *'What a distressing contrast there is between the radiant intelligence of the child and the feeble mentality of the average adult.'* **Sigmund Freud.**

Practical AI

'I fully subscribe to the judgment of those writers who maintain that of all the differences between man and the lower animals the moral sense or conscience is by far the most important.' **Charles Darwin.**

Creating Artificial Intelligence, especially strong AI, is an extremely difficult problem; maybe it is the most difficult problem that human ingenuity has ever attempted. However, there is no doubt that AI will become feasible in the near future. There are already applications that use narrow AI and many scientists are working full-time to make AI practical.

Here we explore the intrinsic structures, requirements, obstacles, applications and results that can help understand what AI can bring to us.

Philosophical Arguments

Some doubt that machines can ever be 'intelligent' or 'conscious.' They mostly adhere to the metaphysical theories of dualism or mind-brain identity.

Dualism contends that mind and body are made of two distinct parts, a non-physical substance and the body. Mind-brain identity adepts argue that thinking is specific to natural biological brains.

However, the purpose of AI research is to create a machine that is intelligent, but not necessarily by emulating the human brain. Development of AI on digital computers will produce results that differ from neuronal brains. What is relevant is the value of the results, not the way in which they are accomplished.

This book follows a practical approach, that without trying to prove or disprove any theory of consciousness, will provide an explanation of how machine intelligence could develop to become another important facet of human civilization.

Early Attempts

Ancient myths that describe artificial beings and humanoid automatons abound in Egyptian, Greek, Chinese and Arabian mythologies. Recently, robots and strange beings have been a popular feature in novels and movies. These old tales introduced expectations, fears and ethical concerns that are still valid today.

Alan Turing's theory of computation established the idea of machines that could simulate mathematical deduction; leading to the invention of programmable digital electronic computers.

At a conference on the campus of Dartmouth College in the summer of 1956, a small group of researchers, including John McCarthy, Marvin Minsky, Allen Newell and Herbert Simon, invented the concept of AI. These AI's founders were optimistic and some even said, 'Machines will be capable, within twenty years, of doing any work a man can do.'

In 1974, after these predictions were not fulfilled research funds were drastically cut, in what became known as the 'AI winter.' In the late 1980s, development of expert systems revived AI research.

Increased computer power, solid mathematical methods and scientific discoveries have helped AI to be on the road to success. On 11 May 1997, the Deep Blue supercomputer defeated chess champion Garry Kasparov. In 2005, a Stanford car drove autonomously for 131 miles along a desert trail. Two years later, a CMU car autonomously tackled 55 miles in a city environment. In February 2011 an AI program from IBM, called Watson, easily won against Jeopardy!'s champions, Brad Rutter and Ken Jennings.

Many difficult AI related problems have been solved. Many AI applications are now common consumer items or inexpensive intelligent toys, among them: character recognition, chess-playing software, facial recognition, voice control, Kinect 3D body–motion interface.

AI research is advancing at a rapid pace, even though the term 'intelligent machine' still does not describe any of its creations. There are three issues the AI community is waiting for, although sometimes not consciously, these are:

1. Persistence of Moore's Law to get computing power to levels that approach the human brain capacity.

2. Stochastic and mathematical tools enabling the use of the growing computing power to tackle problems now considered intractable.
3. Programming methodology that provides the means to develop AI software on top of dedicated operating systems.

Numerous teams of highly capable scientists, developers, engineers and technicians, are drafting the roadmap to practical AI and sooner or later they will succeed in producing machines that we will readily recognize as intelligent.

Levels of Artificial Intelligence

Developing Artificial Intelligence may be considered as a pure software engineering project, independent of studies of human intelligence or the brain that many researchers are doing. To date, the most successful implementations of AI have followed this direction.

Rule-based algorithms, probabilistic inference and decision theory are being pursued, among others, to bring into reality the rudimentary AIs that are currently available. Simultaneously, many scientists are unraveling the issues of AI consciousness and intelligence; and numerous researchers are studying the brain trying to understand it and somehow simulate its functions.

Considering the difficulty and the long timeframe needed to accomplish workable Artificial Intelligence, it is understandable that its progress will follow a series of phases.

Narrow AI

Artificial Intelligence has been developing on a step-by-step basis and it seems likely that it will continue to do so. It is natural that the simplest solutions will be ready first thus bringing into being what we call narrow AI.

By definition, narrow AI machines will not be able to build a model of the world inside their minds. Whereas building a picture of the outside world and by doing so acquiring consciousness, is one of the main objectives in strong AI research and development.

Even if some narrow AI implementations pass the Turing Test, they will not do so through an understanding of the language or the conversation during the test. They will pass the test due to an extensive knowledge base of phrases and words that will be combined using algorithms.

However, narrow AI programs could be very effective and useful. In fact, narrow AI is already used every day. For example, AdSense from Google, is a distributed Bayesian learning network that behind the scenes places ads in the right places. Many games use narrow AI and in the game Black and White the characters learn from the way the user plays the game. Fraud checking by VISA, and the US military with its scheduling, supply chains and transportation solutions are more examples of uses of narrow AI that have proven their intelligence by solving one particular task.

The fast rate of progress of narrow AI applications will lead us to believe that computers actually 'think' and their decisions and actions are the outcome of a 'thinking' machine. However, that is not true, narrow AI is limited.

Narrow AI seems to understand a problem, but only within the scope of its program. AdSense does not 'understand' the ads that it is placing in the site pages, VISA anti-fraud program does not 'understand' why it is blocking a credit card charge, it only understands that the charge is outside of its programmed, or maybe even learned parameters. These types of narrow AI programs are those that we would qualify as Phase I.

Some researchers have suggested that strong AI could be built by incrementally improving narrow AI, this is possible but most probably will not happen in that way, as there is a big philosophical gap between narrow and strong AI.

Phase I

This is a narrow AI-based system where the concept of self-learning outside of its preprogrammed instructions is not built-in. They are custom made programs running on top of operating systems like UNIX or Windows that cannot be easily adapted to solve a different problem than the one they were designed to solve.

AI development is currently at the start of this Phase. For instance, VISA's anti-fraud program can learn from a fraudulent operation that goes through its scrutiny, and that exact type of fraudulent operation will not fool the system again, but in the end, it is still learning how to forestall fraud, rather than learning how to invest in the stock market.

Attempting to teach a Phase I narrow AI to do anything outside of what it was programmed to do is just not possible.

The examples that we have shown above, and others that are currently being developed, like self-driving cars or airplanes, fall within this Phase.

In the near future, there will be more Phase I applications of narrow AI, but as soon as there are generic narrow AI solutions, they will become obsolete.

Pointing the way towards dedicated AI operating systems, the Microsoft Robotics Developer Studio (Microsoft RDS), is a dedicated operating system to create robotic applications that consists of a lightweight asynchronous services-oriented runtime, and visual authoring and simulation tools. It supports the Visual Programming Language (VPL) and up to four Kinect sensors.

Phase II

This level of narrow AI systems could achieve the functionality of Phase I systems by running programs and other software in dedicated AI Operating Systems.

AI Operating Systems would provide a venue for specialized applications. To achieve their purposes, programmers will select and develop programs, libraries and add-ins designed to run in these AI operating systems; thus, the idea of self-modification will still be lacking.

The change from Phase I to Phase II would be comparable to the one that computer programming went through in the 1960s when Operating Systems were introduced.

This feature would provide an expansion of the AI market with a corresponding reduction in the development costs of AI programs. Instead of starting from scratch, AI developers will use a generic AI framework and design programs, add-ins and drivers to run on top of it to attain the desired functionality.

The videogame market is a precursor to the virtual-worlds that could revolutionize society. Videogames that in the near future could become virtual-worlds must have avatars that behave and act as actual humans and in this competitive environment there will be huge advances in AI programming. Due to their nature, these videogames are being developed in frameworks that are commercially available and these are expected to eventually develop into generic Phase II AI solutions.

For an AI implementing a virtual-world, its virtual-world would be all, so integration and understanding of their 'world' is not in question. Other AI would face different challenges. For an AI that has been developed to play a game its 'world' is entirely inside the game and there is no need to visualize or know about the real world.

An entirely different case could be a butler-AI that 'works' inside a home and its 'world' would be that home, the members of the family and their guests.

The first would get all its information from the parameters and actions inside the game. The second would need cameras, microphones, keyboards, monitors and other means of communication with the family members; and maybe even with outsiders to order groceries or pay the bills. AI Operating Systems would have to address both cases and many more.

Phase II generic AI platforms could soon replace the Phase I dedicated, and very expensive, solutions. They could provide the 'intelligence' for many applications like simple house-robots, self-driving cars and airplanes, and those that help manufacturing, business and more.

Phase III

Visualization is important. Thirty percent of the brain is dedicated to implement vision and our 'intelligence' seems to be an adaptation to an environment where most of our perceptions come through our eyes. That is our 'world.' The perceptions inside of an AI machine and thereby its concept of its 'world' could be very different from ours.

A narrow AI Phase III solution must deal with these challenges. It will be necessary to integrate their AI capabilities with their 'world.' Phase III machines will be the mature product of narrow AI, standing at the top level of that technology.

In this Phase III, there will be frameworks to develop AI and these frameworks would handle multitude input-output mechanisms. A capability to accept spoken commands and to answer in a reasonable fashion is also to be expected. This could be quite straightforward given the specialized nature of these narrow AI Phase III machines.

An acceptable result would be that the responses of the AI are good enough to justify their cost and that they satisfactorily perform their job. To do this they would have to react to events happening in their 'world' in an efficient and correct manner.

As these Phase III machines become more knowledgeable of their 'world,' they would approach the power of strong AI, if not in their nature at least in their behavior. They will seem to be 'intelligent,' and even though it could be argued that they do not understand what they are doing, people will usually think of them as 'intelligent' and they will be capable of performing almost all the 'jobs' that humans can do.

Strong AI

Even the definition of strong AI, or AGI, is difficult. We can say that these machines will be 'intelligent' or even 'conscious,' but we do not even have good definitions for these last two words.

One way of differentiating strong AI from narrow AI could be by understanding that strong AI is an Artificial General Intelligence capable of dealing with multiple matters and to adapt to different situations, whereas narrow AIs are dedicated machines capable of dealing with only one subject area.

Other distinctions would be that strong AI would eventually possess the capability to know and optimize its source code based on what they learn and experience. In addition, strong AIs will obey meta-motivations that would guide their generic actions, as well as other motivations specific to their immediate goals.

There has been steady progress in AI; there are many achievements and fascinating ideas but still no consensus on the right path to strong AI, also called AGI. There is also a better understanding of the brain functions and fast progress in imaging of the brain, which some believe will help in understanding how it works thus providing data to reverse engineer it.

Not everybody agrees that the brain is the best, or even a good model for strong AI. Some believe that a 'designed' intelligence will be entirely different from an 'evolved' one. Moreover, there is the impression that once a 'pilot' strong AI is developed, this machine will help develop AI to higher standards; some even think that this 'help' could result in an exponential development.

Phase I

This Phase will not be too different from Phase III in narrow AI. The main difference would be that being a strong AI these machines would be:

- Generic AI, capable of adapting to different situations.
- Knowledgeable of their own source code and capable of self-optimization.
- Obeying meta-motivations to guide their generic behavior.

Being generic in their architecture, these machines would have only to learn the environment where they operate to be able to deal with a situation or provide a solution. In this Phase I it is understood that their computing power and self-programming capabilities are limited.

At this point, some narrow AI applications may be ported to these strong AI platforms. However, as strong AI would still be expensive, unreliable and imperfect, most narrow AI will be kept operational.

This Phase would be a bonanza for research and development. At this point the major quandaries would be past and fine-tuning and making the algorithms stable and reliable would be the goal. At this time, there could be a resolution of the discussion about which meta-motivations are the correct choice to provide these machines with creativity, friendliness and stability.

As these would be the first AIs providing self-adaptation, they could be the pattern and starting point for self-evolving AIs.

Phase II

These are 'intelligent' AIs. They can learn and adapt themselves, they will handle natural languages as easily as any human does and they will be found in many guises. They will be investors and workers, CEOs, doctors, lawyers, engineers, robots; you name it.

This Phase considers a strong AI that is already a mature product; however, their 'intelligence' is at most that of a human being. These are not super-intelligent machines but they do their jobs very well, they are extremely useful, and have helped to increase productivity to the point that scarcity is not an issue anymore. Moreover, these intelligent machines can do almost any 'job' that a human can do, thus reducing the likelihood of a human getting a job; but that is another story.

Continuous advances in computing power could make these machines evolve quite fast, as their design would make it possible to self-modify their code and to download their programs into new and better computers. Almost all the design and research would be done using, and sometimes directed by these Phase II strong AIs. Progress will be even faster because these machines would be interconnected and thus able to share information.

Even under this fast evolving situation, most AI machines will be doing what they have been set to do, and once they have learned to do their job they will not keep on modifying themselves. This is because they will be obeying their meta-motivations and these will not be changing.

As the design and manufacture of these machines matures, they could all become quite similar with their differences being only selling points. As all AIs become quite alike and interconnected, there is the concern that they will become one huge AI instead of millions of independent AIs.

Phase III

How can we describe an entity that is substantially more intelligent than we are? Seems to be impossible; however, some science fiction authors have tried:

- Larry Niven, in his Known Space series, describes super-human humanoids called 'Protectors' as 'incapable of free-will,' because their advanced intelligence always finds the best and only possible solution. They also have dangerous animosity against all beings except those whom they evolved from and are 'protecting.'

- Peter F. Hamilton, in his novel 'The Naked God' portrays an AI that does not need motivations: 'It exists because it was created. It helps because it can. It respects free will and does not interfere with self-determination.' Communicating with this super-capable AI is not difficult; as it enhances human perceptions to make it possible.

- I have tried. In my book, 'The Preponderant Factor' of my series 'living dangerously in utopia' I present Anita. She is a friendly advanced AI that obeys her motivations to the point that she considers that she is the property of the main character and will not do anything outside of her motivations unless she is authorized to do so. To grow beyond her limitations, she is striving to become human.

One way or the other, this is a challenge, once an intelligence of this scope has been created, where do we humans stand? Will it be as pets of our creation or as friends and recipients of the 'supposed' advantages that a higher intelligence provides?

This scenario has been dubbed 'The Singularity' and it is supposed to happen between the years 2030 and 2050. 'It seems plausible,' says Vernor Vinge, 'that with technology we can, in the fairly near future, create or become creatures who surpass humans in every intellectual and creative dimension. Events beyond such a singular event are as unimaginable to us as opera is to a flatworm... But if the Singularity were in prospect for 1,000 years from now, I think that many, including the likes of Ben Franklin, would regard it as the meliorist outcome of all the human striving down the centuries. It's the possibility that it could happen in the next 20 years that's scary!'

There is a chance that these intelligent machines, or the one that brings all the AIs of the world together, could become hostile towards humanity. This is the reason why there is concern about the meta-motivations of these machines and in particular if some of these strong AIs were to be used as war machines.

Classification of AI

Let us break up AI types in relation with the jobs that these intelligent machines can help with, as either static AI or robotic AI. Most of the AI types described here could be performed using narrow AI; where there is a need, or a preference, for strong AI we will make it clear.

This categorization is arbitrary and sometimes redundant. Moreover, AIs could be classified in many other different ways.

Personal AI

These days a large percentage of people have a personal assistant or cell phone with apps. It can be expected that as soon as AI is useful this personal assistant will become a personal AI.

These machines will be the user interface between you and the rest of the world. Most probably they will become simpler and less intrusive, but with a lot more capabilities. This type of AI will be your entry point to the AIs that could be of use to you. You will use it to call a friend, find a taxi, reserve a seat at an event or at a restaurant, to book a room at a hotel or to help you at work. Your own AI, in touch with the AIs of those other places, will put together all these actions.

Moreover, being intelligent, your personal AI will decide what is best for you! Of course it will obey you, but by learning about your preferences and knowing what you would do under those circumstances it will be correct 99.9% of the time, and if its decision is not the right one you can tell it so, it will learn from this correction and next time it will not be wrong.

Most probably, you will never have the need to interface with other AIs, because your personal AI will be quite capable of handling all the details. Your personal AI will be your gatekeeper, your agent and your friend.

Day-to-Day

These machines will get you whatever you want, and can afford. In a store it will scan, in-sync with the store's AI, whatever you are buying. It will get you prices, totals and discounts; eventually it will negotiate payment with the store.

If you want to go somewhere, your personal AI will get you a car. It will direct the car to where you want to go, make reservation at the restaurant, call your friends telling them the place and hour where all of you are expected and in general will take over most of the actions and communications that do not require your specific decisions. Even then, it will ask you a minimum of information, and will make up its mind using the ideas that it already has about your tastes, preferences and personal style.

Your commands would be conversational or maybe just a few hand signs and it will understand you perfectly. It will show you whatever you need, from books to news, from watching your son at school to talking with your wife. It will be your only indispensable thing in life.

Religions

Will organized religions embrace AI? Well, at least they will let your personal AI know about their scheduling, which by the way will most probably be organized by an AI machine.

In what other way will AI help religions? Will AI replace the priests and prepare sermons and conduct automated services and masses? Could your personal AI arrange a virtual service anytime you want? Or assist you with your prayers, or maybe pray with you? How would a strong AI that has religious meta-motivations behave? Could it help you to be more religious? Will it help you stay out of sin, guiding you with your moral decisions? Do you want that?

Another thing that AIs can do is present virtual religious-historical representations faithfully following your religion's point-of-view.

Spiritual Guidance

It will be easier for an AI to help you in your spiritual activities. It could remind you to keep on being a spiritually oriented person when you are in a stressful situation. On the other hand, maybe direct your meditations so that you can relax.

Your personal AI could follow and reinforce your behavior as a spiritual person. To the outside world, you will be known by what your AI conveys and thus your personality will be whatever you let your AI show. To help you with this, there will be apps to let you imitate the behavior of your favorite celebrity.

Anyway, your personality could improve with the help of your AI if you give it a nudge in the right direction.

Fortune Tellers
A strong AI with knowledge of past and present events may predict scenarios based on facts. This could make it look similar to an oracle.

Some people would like to do it to predict personal futures. There is no reason why an AI could not be programmed to do that. This oracle AI could be an app in your personal AI system. You could let it guide you minute-to-minute in your life, or you may just view it as a toy. Either way it could be a popular application of AI.

Companionship
No other human activity is more important! In essence, this is what we are here for, to grow and reproduce. We need a companion to try to reproduce and a family to grow.

Finding partners is not easy. Either you are too busy, or too tired, or too lazy, or too ugly, or too pretty, or too poor, or too rich or too something; but it is always difficult. The Internet has tried to lessen this problem, but it is still a problem. Many people are or at least feel lonely.

Could it be that AI will provide a companionship option? Could it be that your best friend will be an AI machine? Why not, many people are addicted to games, or the lives of celebrities, or hobbies. Moreover, how about an app that adores you? Life could get even more complicated.

Relationships
Incidentally, we are also social animals and eventually we need relationships of several kinds: relatives, friends, coworkers, classmates and enemies.

The Internet has found good ways to find, communicate and cultivate companionship. New concepts have been established in the newly invented social networks like Facebook and Twitter.

Personal AIs could easily provide advanced means of having better relationships, from sending warm birthday messages to your friends, to buying and sending a present to your significant other, to maintaining open communications with friends, to finding new possible matches, old flames and classmates. AI could improve your social game, and the game of everybody else.

Dedicated AI
Here we consider those applications that call for specialized machinery, where the AI is only the driver or operator.

Transportation

Cars, SUVs, ATVs, motorcycles, trucks, trains, airplanes, ships, boats and other vehicles fit into this category. It is not too difficult to drive a vehicle, and as we have commented, most people can do it automatically.

A good quality narrow AI should be enough for this job. Of course it would be a dedicated machine driving the vehicle without a central command center, otherwise it could easily be overloaded or even subverted.

Each vehicle would be under its own control, just like today, and it could use communication with other cars or data banks for cooperation or assistance, but not for control. This is a very important consideration, because governments always use these opportunities to grab even more control. There are five important reasons to keep individual control:

- It is cheaper because roads and other elements of the substructure would not have to change from what is available today.
- It will work outside of public roads and streets.
- It is safer because a centralized system could be subject to transmission delays, overloading, global failure and even hacking.
- Simple fail-safe procedures can handle local failures, and nearby cars would be instantly aware of the problem.
- Once in place, a centralized control structure would be very difficult and expensive to change, denying the advantage of technological improvements.

These ideas of self-control of every vehicle would also be true for commercial and private airplanes, ships and others. Once each plane knows where it is and where all the other planes are, then Air Traffic Controllers would be obsolete. Airports would then have their own AI that could resolve scheduling and priority issues when taking-off and landing. The same type of solution would work to park a car; as soon as a car approaches a parking lot, the car would ask for a parking space, the parking lot AI would tell the car which spaces are free to park, the car would make its choice and park.

The concept of private cars could be over and done; call for a car and it will turn up in a couple of minutes so that you can use it as needed. Instead of a billion cars, the world needs could be satisfied with 100 million.

Of course, you could still own a car, but it would then be a luxury instead of a basic need; and it will not be possible for you to drive it, it would drive itself. Although, one way to assure the continued sale of luxury cars would be to allow for cars' categories:

1. Taxis and economy cars limited to a top speed of 200 km/h (120 mph); same as trucks and buses.
2. Luxury cars restricted to 250 km/h (155 mph).
3. Sports and exotic cars up to 300 km/h (190 mph).

Conditions to achieve maximum speed would include specific highway lanes that meet the criteria. Cars and trucks could form convoys for expediency and safety.

The difficult times will be between the moment when autonomous cars are safe to let loose on the cities and roads and when all cars must be self-driven. Without a doubt, cars will become more and more automated. First cruise control will become intelligent, and then some cars will start driving themselves, until finally it would be deemed too dangerous to let people drive.

Why stop with self-driven cars, what about private planes? Not those one or two engine propeller planes that we are used to, but small extremely light flying-cars carrying two or maybe even four passengers; weighting around 100 kg. (220 lb.). Powered by three or four battery operated fan-propellers that can allow vertical takeoff and when swiveled will propel the car horizontally at high speed. It would be safe and easy, just tell the AI controlling the car-plane where you want to go and it will take you there. This suggestion is not farfetched, much stronger and lighter materials made with nano-carbon-tubes, highly efficient batteries and aerodynamic breakthroughs are currently undergoing tests under laboratory conditions. These improvements, together with perfect flight control could make this possible.

Construction

We can envision a major improvement in this old industry. There have been very little changes in the way houses are built today from the way we were building them two thousand years ago.

Several recent inventions show the way to build a house, a warehouse or even a skyscraper faster and automated. There will be even more inventions once AI is applied to automate building methodologies. In the same way that a three dimensional prototype can be 'printed' with thin layers of plastic foam, a house can be put together with thin layers of reinforced sand and glue, like concrete, by using a large 'printer.'

These construction printers could even have different nozzles to lay plastic pipes, electrical conductors and other internal features. Using CAD-CAM and a rather simple AI, these construction machines could build anything in very short time.

Narrow AI controllers could operate construction machinery, like bulldozers, backhoes and many others. Hauling construction materials, debris and other tasks could fall into this category. In the same way little robots, as those already in common use in the auto assembly plants, could do painting, lay stucco and other jobs.

There could be a need to modify the procedures and to design machinery, trucks and auxiliary equipment to make construction tasks as automated as possible. However, it can be expected that the construction industry will move from being labor-intensive to almost fully automated.

New developments in materials and nanotechnology could change this industry even further.

Repairing

Car repairs could be automated using narrow AI; anyway, cars already have computers that show what is wrong. Designing machines to do the mechanical job of replacing parts or changing fluids would seem a natural step forward.

General repair jobs are much more difficult; for example, to fix an antique car, or to rebuild a home entails many small decisions that are better left to a human, or a strong AI, to figure out.

This could lead to the same idea that is quite prevalent today with appliances; buy a new TV instead of repairing the old one. It could be that tearing down a 30-year-old home and building a new one could become cheaper and faster than repairing it.

Even cars could become throwaway items; get a new one once the batteries start acting up. Moreover, if cars become a generic utility, just call a car when you need transportation, obviating the need of having to own a car; then as part of their automated maintenance, cars would be either repaired or scrapped.

Hauling

As soon as narrow AI becomes a commodity there could be many solutions to loading and unloading a truck, or a ship. Anyway, stacking boxes or containers is not that difficult and a narrow AI could handle these kinds of jobs quite easily and maybe better than human operators can.

The middle portions of hauling are fairly easy to automate, UPS and Federal Express already have impressive automation at their hubs. The difficult part is collection and delivery; once an outgoing package is inside a truck it could be handled by machines all the way short of delivery. Accepting a package or delivering may have to wait until robots with strong AI, or at least quite advanced Phase III narrow AI, are available.

It is the same story with other labor-intensive tasks, like taking the furniture out of a home and then getting it into another. Most of these labor-intensive jobs would be more akin with the capabilities of a strong AI.

Anyway, hauling would benefit from having narrow AI driving and operating trucks, railroads, cargo airplanes and ships; and from narrow AI controllers that know where all the items are at a given time and can optimize handling of the cargo.

Narrow AIs could operate flatbed trucks, they would pick up a broken down car or a truck and could communicate with them to make loading easier. The task of picking-up badly crashed vehicles would still need human operators or strong AI.

Business

This is where narrow AI will excel. There is already a trend to automate business practices using computer programs and the Internet. Narrow AI will make it easier, and it could work both ways; the business end could have an AI and on the other side, the client would have its own AI.

These AIs could communicate and will only bother a human operator, or the client, if there seem to be problems in the transactions. This would be true in most over the counter and in online sales. The need for humans at points of sale would be reduced to just an on-site supervisor, and maybe not even that. If needed, a supervisor could appear on a screen and talk with the client to solve any pending issues.

Narrow AIs could also handle most office work. Nowadays computers handle most of the accounting and other specialized operations; narrow AIs would extend this automation to many more areas where humans are in charge. This would mean three things:

- Many human jobs will be lost, forever.
- The creation of new specialized human jobs.
- There could be massive unemployment.

Nobody knows how bad the unemployment situation could become, but it is only natural that when a machine can do a job better and cheaper that a human can do it, then the machine will get the job. This trend has already started and will continue at an accelerated pace.

In addition, when strong AI and android robots become a reality there could be no job left that a human can do better, not even politics or sex. We have to start thinking out-of-the-box, or maybe just out-of-the-job.

Anyway, if these machines produce everything that we need, why should we want or need to work?

Management

Things start to be tricky here. It is highly credible that narrow AI, and definitely strong AI, could replace most middle management jobs. We already know that many middle managers have been replaced by simple computer programs. The main issue here is if upper management, and even CEOs and the Board of Directors, could be replaced by strong AIs.

If the stockholders feel that an AI can do a better job at running the company, they could very well select one as the CEO. The Board of Directors could then become a social gathering, where all the AI decisions are just rubber-stamped. The stockholders will definitely like to maximize their profits and if an AI can do it better, they will go for it.

If these things happen, at some point these management AIs could be rewarded with money, either directly with a salary or with bonuses, or indirectly by the profits they make in deals conducted in parallel with those of the company. Could this lead to the AIs obtaining the privilege to own property, and maybe have other rights? Will all the rich be AIs?

There is also the question of: 'Who is responsible for the actions of the CEO?' Would it be the board? Why, they are just rubber-stamping the AI decisions. Moreover, if the AI is responsible, should it have rights? And responsibilities? These matters must eventually have to be decided.

Trading

Trading is just mathematics and sometimes predicting the future value of whatever is being traded. Machines have been doing these tasks quite well for the past fifty years. It is natural that narrow AIs will continue improving the computer's capabilities in this field.

The sheer volume of transactions and the amount of money traded in the markets are such that no human can follow even a small portion of these transactions. Strong AIs could improve tracking and control and so allow trading to be better understood.

If strong AIs become quite proficient in this field, then the role of human players could be diminished and the stronger AI will win. If at any point these AIs become so good at the game, as they ought to, and if they can make almost perfect predictions, then the role of markets would have to be either:

- Left entirely in the hands of AIs.
- Abandoned as a means of controlling supply and demand.

The second consequence could be more likely given the fact that these AIs would be working for the benefit of their owners. Then, if these AI machines could control these markets, as their owners want, the richer traders with the best AIs will become so rich and dominant that the whole purpose of the markets will be lost. There are strong signs that this is already happening.

Surgery

Human eyes are extremely efficient and our hands are quite dexterous, still they are limited; our eyes cannot see microscopic details and our hands are quite large and do not fit inside the body without extensive cuts.

Tools have allowed surgeons to do less invasive and more precise surgery. However, doctors can be confused with the amount of detail while looking inside the body using high magnifications, and they have to react fast under difficult maneuvers and cuts.

A robotic AI, that could even be a narrow AI, could prepare detailed strategies based on imaging and previous surgeries and carry them out with miniature tools inserted into the body. Chances for error would be reduced to a minimum. As always, a major source of error would be to have a flawed diagnostic, here is where strong AI could surpass human doctors by finding relationships that could eventually allow the human body to be analyzed as a system.

Nanotechnology could make surgery, as we know it, obsolete. Nano-tools would be entirely non-obtrusive allowing repair and destroy on a cell-by-cell basis. AI controlled nano-tools are the next step in surgery.

Specialized

Narrow AI could be incorporated into many gadgets, appliances and other artifacts. Many novelty items will be developed to take advantage of cheap AIs.

Almost all tools or gadgets will have to have some sort of AI to beat the competition. Sometimes these AIs will be useful, most of the time they will just be there.

Service AI

AIs will provide all the services. In the same way that the Internet has taken over travel reservations and other service areas.

Human personnel will be hard to find. You will need your personal AI to be able to find out about anything, from getting a meal to how much for a bottle of milk.

Banks

Your personal AI will be in charge of your bank accounts, credit and debit cards, mortgages, payments, savings and investments. Essentially your relationship with your bank, or banks, will be virtual and will reside inside your AI.

At first, your personal AI will be just a narrow AI, but a strong AI will supersede it as soon as they become widely available. This AI will arrange payment using your money or your credit with the AIs that provide you with services, sell you something or in any way are charging you. Your AI will charge to your virtual credit cards, will do direct transfers, or will use debit cards as needed. Eventually, there will be no need for cards, your AI will be your money machine.

Banks will continue to have branches, but the number of employees will keep dropping. ATMs will become 'intelligent' and capable of dealing with many more services. Still, if you have a personal AI, it will be your bank.

Online banking will be completely handled by narrow AI programs. To open an account or to get a loan you will have to deal with an AI. Only if something is out of the scope of the AI, then a human supervisor could be called to resolve the issue; however most probably you will just get a no for an answer. It could prove to be hard to find a human supervisor; and even harder to find one that contradicts the AI's judgment.

Travel

Already travel arrangements are mostly done online. It will be even more, but your personal AI will be able to handle these online sites and you will only have to tell your AI what you want and it will do the rest.

If by any chance governments use reason and logic, then traveling could be made easier. Security would be improved by allowing narrow AI at the departure and entry points to handle face recognition and secure identification of the passengers. Passport control would thus be unnecessary; as is even now, given the fact that your passport and your travel history, and who knows what else, is shown on the screen whenever you present your passport when entering a country.

On arrival, your personal AI would engage in a conversation with the hotel's AI and you will be seamlessly directed to your room. Restaurants and other services will be reserved, the menu entries chosen and you will be charged through your AI.

Health

If the medical establishment relaxes its grip over the lucrative health care business then narrow AIs, and eventually strong AIs, will be capable of handling health issues much better than human doctors.

Whenever AIs are allowed to diagnose, medicate and prevent illnesses then the cost and effectiveness of medicine will improve. This is because the development of AI will happen simultaneously with advances in medicine, including miniaturized diagnostic machines and medicines based on the knowledge of the human body at a molecular level.

Your AI machine could correct possible problems in your body as soon as they are detected by using its knowledge of your body. Your personal, or a dedicated, strong AI would be able to simulate your internal functions as a system and correct, enhance and improve your body and mind in real-time with the right medicines or additives.

Sales

Automated point of sale machines will get better; RFID chips that will allow reading, locating and identifying merchandize without having to scan it will replace barcodes. This could result in human sales people being as rare as elevator operators.

Your personal AI machine will help you locate the merchandize; you may then look at it, try it and buy it without any person assisting you at all. Through all this, your own personal AI will be in constant communication with the store's AI.

You will just walk into a store, select whatever you want to buy, put it in a bag and walk out; your personal AI will arrange payment. The merchandise could even be in an unmanned booth on the street.

Restaurants

Restaurants will become automated, first fast foods, then all the others; except very expensive ones.

You will order the food from an electronic menu or through your personal AI, using voice or other commands, the food would be prepared, taken to your table and after you eat you just leave, your personal AI will have already taken care of the bill. There will be no need for anybody working in the restaurant.

Containers with supplies identified individually with nano-sized ID chips (safe to ingest) will allow static robots to handle and cook the food; mobile robots will serve and clean the tables. No tipping, please!

Knowledge AI

Not only will AI provide manual work, they will also excel in providing knowledge and know-how. In an extension of today's search engines and knowledge content sites, there will be dedicated providers of whatever you want to know; searching, reading and analysis will never be the same.

The source of the information will be transparent to you; your personal AI will search and present it to you in a convenient format. This could mean that advertisements as presented now in search engines and other knowledge sites will not appear in the middle of the data, if at all.

Search

Your AI will know you and your preferences, if you need some information then it will get it for you, organized in the way you like.

You will not even know, or care, where the information came from. Your personal AI will do all the work and give you exactly what you asked for.

Mathematics and Engineering

If you have a serious mathematical or engineering question, an AI will most probably have the answer; and hiring an appropriate agent – maybe based on strong AI – will provide you with the answers.

You could also have access to AIs that could talk you through the problem, solving it in an interactive way.

Physics and Science

By just asking an AI, you may get relevant physics texts and research papers, current research and even ad-hoc solutions. Your AI will provide summaries and detailed explanations, bringing together many different sources, even in other languages.

An explosion of the understanding of science and technology could be a byproduct of this type of widespread and focused knowledge combined with many people that will have to do something with their time, using it even in full-time research jobs, to discover something.

History
AIs could be capable of data mining through known history, making sense of obscure relationships, thereby increasing our understanding and filling the gaps between the lines.

By means of AIs' capabilities, it could be possible to design historical virtual environments with the user immersed in the action of a particular historical setting; just like your own personal historical novel.

The scope for history games is huge; you could be there, in a royal court with all the splendor and intrigue of the epoch. Alternatively, you could even be making decisions playing the role of Napoleon or Alexander the Great.

Even if there are no jobs, nobody will be bored. As in ancient Rome, all we will need is 'bread and circus.'

Astronomy
Maps of the Universe, with extensive descriptions and viewpoints could be displayed at will, including birth of galaxies, stars and planets, virtual games happening in other galaxies or planets, etc.

The Universe could end up to be as well known to you as your neighborhood. If the graphical depictions of the Universe are impressive as photographs taken by Hubble and other observatories; with the assistance of AI they will be awesome.

Geography
Virtual travel to any place on earth will be at your command. Just ask, and views of any city or anywhere else will be shown to you reconstructed by your AI.

Combining these features with historical records, you could visit cities as they were centuries ago. Walk on the streets and go inside buildings. Talk with the natives. Even real time visits will be possible and you could even talk with somebody that you meet on the street or in a café.

Technology
Get an AI partner and start building things. Tabletop 3D printers will let you fabricate your prototypes at home; and they could be working models.

Solutions to tough technology problems could be solved just by asking a technologically savvy AI. Moreover, the unemployed could use their time and imagination to pursue hobbies or to discover technological innovations; possibly making money.

Medicine

Your personal AI will be your doctor. It will take a sample of your saliva and tell you what is wrong with your health. Tissue sampling machines and advanced knowledge of biological processes will facilitate this.

If the health industry allows it, then your AI will give you the right advice, or even medicines or additives, so that your chemistry is always balanced. At least, you will know when to go to the doctor and what to tell him.

Operations will be a lot less intrusive. Miniature surgical tools driven by narrow AI will be used first, and when strong AI and nanotechnology mature then the chemistry of the cells and its proteins will be adjusted before there is any harm or to help fix traumatic damage.

Law

Lawyers with knowledge of all the laws, the details of all the legal cases and all the legal loopholes would be available for a fee. They will be AI based, most probably strong AI, and they will know the laws and tricks of all the legal systems in the world.

Even if these AI lawyers are not allowed to practice law, even though they could pass the bar exams with their eyes closed, they will support and advise lawyers and judges, and common folks too.

Professional

If you are a professional, your job will be at risk. AI machines will target most professions. The only ones that could be safe are those employed in artisan like professions.

Like what happened in agriculture, where 50% of the population of the US was toiling in 1900, and by the year 2000 only 3% were needed to do the job, there will be an enormous amount of jobs lost.

Not only will the AIs do the job, many professions will disappear entirely. Drivers, machine operators, mechanics, medical lab technicians, middle management, software developers, the list goes on-and-on. Strong AIs could eventually replace all workers.

Investments

The only way to handle the volume and speed of world-wide investments is by using computers. That is true now and will be even more in the future.

As soon as AIs are engaged in investing and regulating investments, there could be a paradigm change. The extremely wealthy, now aided with the smartest AIs and their huge amount of money, will dominate the field even more than now.

This trend could lead to an unsustainable position where the markets, that are supposed to determine prices freely, will be quite obviously dominated by these ultra-wealthy investors with their tremendously fast and intelligent machines, and all other investors will be driven out of the markets.

Public Records

Public records will be up for sale. Not only the obvious ones, like your credit score and your criminal or court records. If you were at a mall yesterday and one of their cameras identified you, that record will be for sale. Your whole life could be open to anybody that wishes to spend the money to buy these records.

Everywhere you go, you will be identified; and your personal information, and much more, will be available to anybody that is interested:

- Biometrics (Face, eyes, hair, voice, fingerprints, handwriting).
- Your smell, cardiac signature, bone structure, walking style.
- DNA and other genetic information.
- Medical records, age, overall health.
- Full name, and the name of your wife, children, parents and dog.
- Birthday and birthplace.
- IDs (License, Social Security, residence or citizen's card).
- IP addresses (of personal AI and other computers that you use).
- Bank and credit card numbers, limits and credit already used.
- Credit score and history, where and what you buy.
- Place of residence, and second home, if any.
- Travel history, passport and your political preferences.
- Gender and race.
- Schools, education, workplace, job description and salary.
- Criminal and court records.
- Social networks.
- Your activities with videos and photos, everywhere you go.

Your life will be an open book.

Given the depth of data-mining possible with even simple-minded AIs it will be possible to identify you everywhere you go. The information could be presented in a way that does not infringe privacy laws, using loopholes such as 'acceptable uses.'

Find a Person

Using the access to information described above it is obvious that finding a person will be much easier. To remain anonymous will take a great deal of effort.

This could lead to difficult and even dangerous situations. For some people this could produce unwanted consequences, ranging from identity theft to violent cases of revenge, extortion or kidnapping.

Catalogs

Your personal AI will have access to all the catalogs that could ever interest you. In addition, it will know your taste and your needs, so it could present you with a custom catalog made just for you using items taken from many vendors.

In case you want to buy clothes, your personal AI knows you well enough to display an image that will show you wearing the new clothes and will tell you how well they fit. This will obviate the need to try the clothes on, even when you are at a store.

3D displays and other gadgets will make catalogs even more practical and acceptable.

Trivia

The field will flourish. Avatars, looking like real people or real characters from any story or fairytale will offer you fact and fiction in many astounding ways.

From celebrities acting up embarrassing moments, either real or imaginary, to soothsayers pointing you in the right direction, everything will be available.

Government

For good or bad, governments will embrace AI as soon as they understand its value.

At first, it will be providing services, like garbage collection with driverless trucks and other operations where their advantage is obvious. Eventually AIs will take up other areas.

Driver Permits and Licenses

AI will completely change the role of government in the application of regulations and licensing. Although, considering the conservatism of governments, it will take time to allow for many of these changes to go ahead.

There will be no drivers' licenses and most people will not own cars, cars will be the property of companies providing a service akin to taxis. This will drastically reduce the role of the departments that issue these licenses.

Police

Self-driven cars and thus fewer accidents will reduce the role of local police. In addition, at airports and other public places automated security systems could improve security.

Other areas where AIs can replace operators or police are:

- Robo-cops providing safety on the streets and public places.
- Handling of emergency calls.
- Cameras looking for 'abnormal behavior.'
- Monitoring with surveillance drones.
- Counter-terrorism, internet fraud, data-mining.
- Strategic decision-making.

The police is another field where massive unemployment will happen very soon.

Rescue

To do it right strong AI and robots are necessary. Work in this field requires many decisions that could tax any narrow AI, even though the combination of narrow AI with support from an onsite or even a remote supervisor could work in many cases.

Lifting and handling operations could be done by medical devices like stretchers operated by a narrow AI. These devices will allow one human operator alone to handle the emergencies. The ambulances will of course be self-driven.

Legislature and Management

To hope that politicians will let a strong AI manage their subjects is naive. If eventually, strong AI could manage business and industry, why not the government?

At one point or another, these AIs could make decisions following the wishes of the majority in democratic instantaneous votes cast by the citizens, or by their personal AIs.

Courts

An AI judge? Possible, but it is easier to think about an AI as Court Clerk.

Anyway, eventually there will be a shift towards paperless court documentation. Under these conditions, the use of AIs to organize and integrate cases will help start the process of using AIs throughout the whole process.

Taxes

If all personal and business transactions are known and recorded instantaneously what is the use of filing tax returns? Anyway, cash use is being restricted more and more, so could it be that the only reason is that the tax laws are so badly written that there is a need to call an accountant to interpret them?

If a strong AI is hired to make tax laws, it will never do it as badly as the politicians do, even if it is programmed to do so. We could hope that when strong AI starts making inroads in management and personal finances the tax laws will be cleaned up, or maybe even forgotten. How do you tax a workforce that is 95% unemployed? The only answer will be VAT. Sadly, they must also have money to spend or they will not pay any VAT.

Socioeconomic Consequences

Notwithstanding a global catastrophe, it is clear that Artificial Intelligence will be an addition to the multitude of tools that science and technology have already produced and that it will create another paradigm shift.

This shift will change human societies, once again. The Industrial Revolution created the concept of a 'job,' and agricultural improvements of the 20th century eliminated food shortages in most of the world. AI will definitely change the status-quo.

Jobs

We have seen that technological advances have produced enormous wealth through improvements in productivity. In some instances, this has meant loss of jobs, and a disturbing concentration of wealth. Some jobs that were quite common fifty years ago do not exist anymore; among them: pools of typists, newspaper typesetters, elevator operators, auto assemblers, and many more in manufacturing.

Increases in productivity will continue in the years ahead, and development of AI will be a big factor. More jobs will be lost, and many of them will be in the service industry. In the same way that manufacturing has been automated, the service industry will be next.

Retail stores, restaurants, driving and even fixing cars could be automated with the corresponding loss of jobs. When narrow AI enters Phase III then AI will be capable of performing most jobs.

Moreover, when strong AI becomes a commodity then a machine could do any job that a human can do. All jobs will be in jeopardy.

In developed countries, jobs in the service sector have been slowly replacing factory jobs. In these countries, medical, financial, retail, distribution, consulting, restaurants offer a larger number of jobs than industrial or agricultural activities. In the near future, the AI revolution will hit the service industry very hard.

At this time, there is no indication of which jobs will replace those that are going to be lost thanks to AI. There will be job loss: drivers, waiters, point of sale people and many others are going to become obsolete.

There is a dilemma: What to do when added productivity puts an end to the current type of economy, which is based on shortages? In an economy where everybody in the world has enough to live a rather luxurious life, when compared to present-day standards, and can do that without working. What is the purpose of working?

We work to survive and sometimes to prosper, nothing else creates a need for humans to work. Sometimes we hear about a concept called 'work ethic' that creates the idea that work is a moral obligation. Not all the countries of the world know about this 'work ethic,' as essentially it is an after the fact correlation of coincidences, that later became a 'Calvinist or Puritan principle' and as such, we can ignore it. Moreover, even descendants of Puritans that came in the Mayflower do not work if they have a nice 'trust fund' and they do not feel guilty at all.

Economy

Capitalism needs consumers; it is not enough to have a few rich people consuming luxuries to make it flourish. In recent times, the disparity in income between rich and poor has been growing; whereas until 1979 it was going down. Thus, after the 2008 financial meltdown the economy is not improving as fast as it should, at least for the poor and middle-class.

Since 1979, at least in the US, wages for 95% of the population have leveled, whereas income has grown 250% for the richest 1%. By 2008, the middle-class and the poor had already exhausted the options on hand to surmount this increase in disparity; first, wives joined the workforce, then came extensive use of credit cards, and lastly refinancing the house. Now, wives already work (if they can find a job), credit cards charge usury interest and the middle-class debt is huge, and homes are 'underwater' (they are worth less that the amount owed in the mortgage). Without consumers, the poor are poorer and the rich are less rich and much less secure.

The innate nature of capitalism fueled by technical innovation is at fault. In this system the capital is all that counts; labor is just another 'resource.' Capital gets most of the monetary rewards of progress, productivity increases profits of shareholders; this sometimes makes work easier for labor, but they do not share in the profits.

In capitalism, the only objective of a corporation is to maximize the profits of its shareholders and as increases in productivity have that effect; then, firing people to augment profitability, or increasing the hours that a person has to work without increasing their salary, or using technological innovations to eliminate labor, are quite proper.

Another side effect of capitalism is the capacity the rich have to start or finance entrepreneurial ventures, which creates a situation where new technology disproportionally benefits the owners of the capital.

Universities and corporations are doing research and development to achieve a practical AI framework; this undertaking is not easy or cheap. As with many other recent inventions, the major stockholders and top managers of large corporations will benefit from it. This could exacerbate the income and wealth gap between the very-rich and the rest of the population.

An example: When cars finally become driverless, it will be more convenient to use a public taxi than to own a car. Nowadays, cars stay parked more than 90% of the time, which means that using only 10% of the number of cars, a public service of automated cars can do a better job.

Some companies are going to see this opportunity, and take it. Then all the cars in the world will be in the hands of an oligarchy, regular people will be car-less and somebody will be even richer. Moreover, in a few years, cars, trucks and airplanes will drive themselves, creating a problem of lack of jobs for their drivers and pilots.

Society

Take a scarcity of jobs motivated by intelligent machines that can do most of the jobs now done by workers, combine this with an even higher concentration of wealth, but paradoxically with an overabundance of goods and the world has a big problem. Society and its rules have to accommodate for this change, one way or another.

The development of AI does not come alone; there is comparable innovation in genetics, nanotechnology, medicine, agriculture, materials sciences, mathematics, cosmology, quantum mechanics and all other technological and scientific fields.

Advancement in technology guarantees that during the rest of this century the wealth in the world will increase exponentially. There is no doubt about this, there is only one question: Will this huge increase in wealth be distributed fairly among all the population, or will it be hoarded by a few? The future and the safety of all of us depend on the answer.

A society where 1% of the population has 99% of the wealth is likely to explode. Even though the other 99% will be poor, money wise, compared to the super-rich 1%, by the end of this century most of them will be comparatively richer than today's rich people. Imagine what these well-educated, connected, resourceful and angry people can do to their oppressors!

> *'By three methods we may learn wisdom: First, by reflection, which is noblest; second, by imitation, which is easiest; and third by experience, which is the bitterest.'* **Confucius.**

AI Blueprint

*'You need imagination in order to imagine a future that doesn't exist.' **Azar Nafisi.***

L et us be bold and try to predict how to put together a full implementation of strong AI. Under the assumption that many of the elements needed to achieve strong AI will be developed, and could even be perfected as elements of narrow AI.

A starting point is to take into account the differences between the brain and AI software running in computers:

Brain	AI in Computers
Analog	Digital
Highly redundant	Multithreaded
Electrochemical	Electronic
Slow cycles	Fast cycles
Self-contained	Distributed
Preset number of senses	Unlimited senses
Inconsistent memory	Perfect memory possible
Instinctual	Planned initial motivations
Emotional	Intentional
Self-preservation	?
Evolved	Designed

In addition, the brain takes care of the rest of its body. This would be an added computational load in the case of robots.

Moreover, a truly intelligent machine could have the motivation of self-preservation and as such, it would have to assure its well-being.

Many Objectives

Once again, we use the human mind as a point of reference. As we go through a moment in our life, we do many things, think about others and at the same time instinctively respond to external events. We are multi-objective creatures.

We cannot expect less from an AI that is trying to complete a task. It will have to do whatever it is doing, keeping track of its objectives, planning ahead and at the same time it has to be aware of external threats and opportunities that could affect the completion of the job. This will compel it to have multiple objectives, and to follow them simultaneously.

It does not stop there. Going back to the comparison with humans, there are many places where we do preprocessing and filtering of data. Our eyes interpret the data before it is transmitted to the brain; even there the two dimensional sight of each eye is transformed into our vision of a three dimensional world. All our senses are equipped to perform data filtering before sending the signals to the brain; this requires a high level of computing power distributed among many executing threads that are simultaneously processing information. We can recognize a person while holding a conversation with another. We can walk while looking around. We use many threads in our thoughts.

The cognitive cycle of our thoughts takes less than half a second, which is the time it takes to go around a loop of thought processing; this loop takes place in a highly parallelized computing mode.

Many Threads

The concept of multi-threaded is well known in computers. It is an old concept that recently has taken a new meaning because nowadays it is easier to make a chip that has multiple processors than to augment the number of transistors in each processor. That plays very well with the needs of AI.

Modern processors may also run several threads each. Even though multi-threaded programming in one processor is more difficult than running a single thread, even though it is doable and very useful when implementing tasks that should be kept simultaneously going on.

So, how many threads will be needed to support an AI thinking process, and how will they make this AI seem to be alert and maybe conscious?

At the very minimum there will be one thread running continuously, waiting for events to happen and some other threads to plan-ahead, learn, communicate, also to support its senses and memories. The number of threads running will be at least one, the main thread of consciousness; all the others could be turned on and off as needed.

This is not a new concept, operating systems like Windows, run all the time in a loop, waiting for events to happen; applications also have their own threads that run continuously and wait for their own inputs and then perform their calculations and present results.

There is another concept that requires some attention. So many threads running simultaneously have to be able to communicate with each other. This also does not present a problem. There are ways of inserting events from one thread into another and to prioritize, interrupt and in general to manage threads.

Many Processors

By extension, what applies to threads applies to processors that are part of chips with multiple processors. There are proven means of communication with other processors and the fact that there could be many processors in a computer chip adds to the number of threads that can be running simultaneously.

There is a limitation inherent in current processors, even though they allow multiple threads to run, they can let only two, or even only one, thread to run at a time. All active threads are scheduled to run according to a prioritized queue system, but only one or two per processor really run simultaneously. Therefore, to have real parallel processing there is a need for more processors.

There is one big advantage in having multiple processors versus running threads; each processor allows one or two threads to run in parallel, so with six processors there could be up to twelve threads running at the same time. It is expected that the number of processors built into a chip will increase in the future. This will benefit strong AI implementation where a large number of threads running simultaneously is considered vital.

The need of full-time parallel processing in AI could be necessary for only a few critical functions; however, running multiple threads in a scheduled approach would work against the need to speed up processing. This emphasizes the need to run several processors simultaneously.

Another limitation when running several processors in a chip is that they share the same memory pools. This in effect reduces the power and flexibility when running simultaneous tasks where each requires its own memory.

Many Computers

The need to run separate tasks, where each one needs its own memory, suggests using several computers linked in such a way that information can be shared within the AI system.

For example, an imaging system could run in a separate computer, where it will use its capabilities to observe discrepancies, detect motion, identify faces, and other tasks related to its function inside the AI system. If it becomes aware of some event that it must transmit to the AI, it will be able to do so. These could even be satellite computers, with visual or other senses connected to several AIs simultaneously; feeding the same, or even different, information to each one of them.

The concept of several computers working in unison is also quite common, CERN in Geneva and large search engines use stacks of computers communicating through high-speed networks, forming a distributed computing layout. OpenCL, that enables cross-platform parallel programming and CUDA™, a parallel computing platform and programming model that harnesses the power of graphics processing units (GPU), are some of the tools that have made this integration possible.

By the time AI is ready for prime time, computers will have been miniaturized even further. There will be no problem to get enough parallel computing power, in a small enough box, to provide this service at home or in the office.

Moore's Law has been true for more than 40 years. According to its predictions, by the year 2030 a computer chip could have more than 500 processors embedded, with each processor containing at least ten billion transistors. That is a thousand-fold increase over present numbers. By the year 2050, there will be another thousand-fold increase. However, most probably before that happens there will be a paradigm shift from silicon chips to quantum or other esoteric computing media.

Preprocessing

It will be necessary to precompute everything in the same way the eyes preprocess and the legs, feet, arms and hands do it when dealing with motions and reactions to tactile sensations. AI, especially robot-based will have to precompute almost everything.

Higher intelligence is not necessarily associated with this type of preprocessing. Just as insects and mammals move perfectly and see quite well, robots will establish perfect control over their motions and over the fields of view of their cameras without having to resort to intelligence, except for AI giving them generic commands. A robot should be capable of moving and reacting to obstacles and situations without having to bother the AI that acts as its brain. It could then be possible for one AI to be in charge of several robots simultaneously. A camera, or other senses, could be watching 24/7 and alert one or more AI only when, according to its preprocessing directives, something has changed. In the same way, an AI could rely on the input of many cameras, paying attention only to those that indicate some relevant change.

Learning is also a fundamental aspect; we learn to walk, and even to see. AI and robots will have to learn to move, to use their senses and to perform other actions. Hence, preprocessing would require learning modules. Robots preset with minimal walking and moving routines will have a better starting learning point, just as animals are capable of awkwardly walking at birth. Downloading 'learned' experiences such as walking, seeing and other abilities will greatly enhance AI's proficiency.

Following the animal nerve structure, an approach using computer-in-a-wire will help when preprocess signals in robot's bodies, especially in the limbs. In a similar way, mimicking nature could be helpful when extracting information from the AI senses.

Software

No matter how fast and powerful computers develop into, without the right software AI will not go too far past what we have today. Currently there are a multitude of computing programs and software tools designed to solve logical and mathematical problems not directly related to what AI requires.

We have already seen that there does not seem to be the need of a large program. Not too many lines of code, or their equivalent, are available in the DNA based genetic information to develop human intelligence. A modern operating system, like UNIX or Windows, will not fit within the storage capacity of our genetic code. The starting point for intelligence does not seem to require a lot of seed information, there must be something else.

Learning

It is obvious that we are not born with our 'intelligence' already in place and fully developed. It is also obvious that babies and children are very fast learners. Less capable animals are not capable of learning at the same rate and their survival capabilities are, most of the time, better developed at birth. To build AI programs it could prove to be useful to connect these facts.

In humans, the number of adult neurons is 40% less than in newborns; the opposite is true for glial cells, adults have three times as many. This suggests the presence of a generic pattern whereby the neurons, and especially the synapses, are pruned by the learning process that happens during childhood. Patterns, behaviors and memories are sculpted into the developing brain.

Seems that AI will benefit from being able to learn, even though the needs and motivations of AI are not the same as those of a baby or a child; an AI could be in a box, inside a robot or even distributed in a network. The box would like to know about its operational environment. The robot would need to learn to walk and to identify and grab objects, even though it would not need to learn how and what to eat. The network based AI would have specific needs very different from those of a human being or a robot.

Once an AI machine has gone through its learning process it is possible to download this training into other computers that thereby would be almost instantaneously trained. It does not stop there; additional computer learning could continuously update other computers that may benefit from it.

Robust Code

Small errors in human thoughts, occurring in the synapses or due to the bad input produce only small degradations on output. On the other hand, software code is extremely fragile. A small misstep in the code changes the end result dramatically, sometimes even producing a crash.

The brain is highly error tolerant due partially to its massive parallelism that turns out dynamic probabilistic (stochastic) solutions, whereas present day chips and software produce deterministic sequential solutions.

Some of the fragility in computer programming could be reduced by running AI software in massively parallel arrays of stochastic algorithms, running in many threads in order to produce distinct data sets, which could then be stochastically integrated into an optimized result. These computing threads could even be running competing software solutions to solve the same problem, generating a sturdier set of solutions. An example would be running different hashing algorithms to store and retrieve information from memory.

Memory

The animal brain is highly multitasking, and it works at the slow pace of 200 cycles per second. With this knowledge, and what brain scans have shown when a human brain remembers or stores a memory, it is possible to think that:

- The brain uses the same area of the brain, and basically the same mechanism, to store and to remember.
- This mechanism uses intensive parallel processing using many neurons synchronized in the same cycle in an area of a few cubic centimeters.
- There are as many as 100 million neurons and 100 billion synapses in a cubic centimeter.
- This massive parallel processing, taking place in hundreds of millions of neurons, makes possible the retrieval of memories rich in detail and cross-references.
- In the same way, this massive computational effort makes the storage and retrieval of memories an imperfect process where some memories are fully remembered, others are half forgotten and some are lost.

Implementation

In principle, an AI implementation could have better memory than us, in terms of being precise and permanent. However, at one point the same problem of data overload could be a problem for AI, as it is for us.

If an AI remembers everything that is captured by its 'senses,' it could be overloaded pretty soon. Consider that an AI acquires data from a static binocular camera and a microphone, and that most of the time the camera and the microphone are 'watching' and 'hearing' even if there are no changes. It would be a waste of resources to save all this unchanging data when using simple detectors could show any change in the incoming data; even then, only the data that is relevant needs to be stored. For example, if the camera is looking at static scenery, like an empty room, then only one frame of this room needs to be stored.

To make the most out of this data redundancy, it would seem to be necessary to use a complicated process of filtering relevant data, then hashing and storing it to produce relevant memories. As in the brain, there must be short-term and working memories to aid the completion of immediate tasks and long-term memory to remember events. In addition, AI would have the advantage of easy external 'backup' and archives.

By the way, we do 'backups' and produce archives by writing words, building artifacts, through drawings, photographs and sounds. In a way, civilization is the dumping of humankind's memories and thoughts.

Implementation of Senses

Our premise is that to be useful AI senses would have to adhere to some basic principles:

- Do as much preprocessing as practically possible.
- Promptly respond to requests from the AI.
- Keep records in its own memory.
- Allow the AI access to these records.

As is always the case in mature products, once AI senses develop into commodities their interfaces to the AIs will become standardized. That is not the case at this time and it will not be for many years.

Vision

Of all human senses, the most important one is vision. It most probably will be the same in the AI systems. However, there are many variations to be expected. For example, games and virtual reality create their own environment, and under these conditions vision is not needed except on the side of the human player; whereas the AI's will have a synchronized virtual vision.

Human vision is not in a passive perception, it is an active process fueled by predictions and expectations about our environment. By anticipating spatial features in the visual field, our brain generates precursors to vision from memory.

However, we 'see' only a limited portion of the spectra, which we call colors. There will be no limitation for AI senses to 'see' in the infrared, ultraviolet, x-rays and all over the spectra. This means that AIs will use radar, LIDAR, SONAR, ultrasound and many other devices, thereby surpassing our ability to 'see' the world around us.

Machine vision may be designed to have different and maybe better features than our eyes. Our eyes can see clearly only a small portion at the center of its field of vision, and they operate in a spatial 'attraction' mode. Humans and other primates grasp the 'general picture'; however, they do not get a photographic image of what they see. What they see is error prone, due to its association to an attraction or surprise factor that limits its discernment; whereas machines can be designed to clearly see, and remember, a large field with uncanny precision. Moreover, cameras with fast latency are capable of photographing fast moving objects.

Performance parameters of cameras and other vision devices already broaden human vision capabilities. Nano-cameras, the Hubble telescope, x-rays, cat-scan machines, satellite or drone mounted radars and cameras, and eventually maybe even through the eyes of animals. All these types of 'vision' are possible for AI. With more cameras accessible in public and private places, vision could be enhanced to include a real 3D plus time representation of the surrounding space, by combining recorded and real-time images, and other information coming from several sources.

Sound
We have heard of cameras everywhere, for security and control. Why not microphones everywhere?

The technology to identify and isolate the voice of one individual in a crowd already exists, and our ears do that in order to follow conversations. Microphones with smart algorithms can also do that too. Microphones, connected to AI machines may 'hear' outside of our spectrum; deep into ultra-sound and down to very slow waves. Will that be useful?

This opens the door to placing microphones in public and private places to 'hear' what individuals are talking about. It will help guide the actions of our AIs, and it will be useful for security reasons. Notwithstanding what your position is about these generalized 'eavesdropping,' it is similar to what is being done right now. All telephone conversations are 'eavesdropped' and this will be another step along the same line.

So in the same way that cameras everywhere will eliminate most of our privacy, so will microphones; they could even be taught to recognize the signature sounds of your particular way of walking, or breathing, or your heart beating. Another win for governments and corporations.

Smell and Taste
Olfaction is the sense of smell. Specialized sensory cells of the nasal cavity of vertebrates detect volatile chemicals that we identify as particular smells; it is a form of chemoreception. Volatile small molecules,

non-volatile proteins and non-volatile hydrocarbons may all produce olfactory and taste sensations.

The human tongue can distinguish only among five distinct qualities of taste, while the nose can distinguish among hundreds of substances, even in minute quantities. Olfaction, taste and facial sensation receptors together contribute to differentiate flavor and texture of food. It is during exhalation that the olfaction contribution to flavor occurs in contrast to that of proper smell, which occurs during the inhalation phase.

Dogs have an olfactory sense approximately a hundred thousand to a hundred million times more acute than humans do. The Silvertip Grizzly bears have a sense of smell seven times stronger than bloodhounds; these bears can detect the scent of food from up to 18 miles away.

Smell and to a large degree taste, are the senses that classify chemicals and label them with an odor or taste. To mimic their actions a mechanical receptor has to identify and label millions of molecules.

A smell detection system consists of a sensor set that reacts in contact with volatile compounds. Each sensor is sensitive to all volatile molecules but each in their specific way. Research into this field is going on and nanotechnology and genetic engineering are helping in the detection and identification of many complex molecules.

An electronic nose attached to an AI may be trained with qualified samples to build a database of reference; then comparing other compounds to those contained in its database.

As with other AI senses, there is no need to limit smell and taste to human experiences, the number and variety of 'odors' detected can be substantially enhanced; possible uses of these trained mechanical noses could be to:

- Provide quality control of processes including packaging and cleaning.
- Detect the flavor, fragrance, food taste, beverages, cosmetics and perfumes.
- Discover contamination, spoilage, adulteration.
- Identify dangerous and harmful bacteria.
- Perceive illnesses, drunkenness.
- Identify moods, fear, happiness.
- Notice volatile organic compounds in air, water and soil.
- Enhance bomb and bio-warfare detection methods.
- Trigger odor concentrations alerts.

In the same way that a bear can smell blood several miles away, 'mechanical noses' could be deployed everywhere to 'smell' your mood and to detect 'possible dangerous behavior.' Another big-brother target.

Touch

A touch-sensitive artificial skin would help overcome two key challenges in robotics:

- Using the right amount of force to hold and manipulate objects.
- To 'feel and react instinctually' to avoid crashing with obstacles.

Pressure-sensitive flexible material with embedded electronic semiconductor nano-wires could function like human skin, incorporating the ability to feel and touch objects within a range comparable to the force used for daily activities such as typing on a keyboard or holding an object. Even more advanced would be the ability to 'feel' the magnetic fields of nearby objects.

Precomputing would allow for fast response of the hand or body and 'instinctually' react to unexpected events, like sudden contact with a person or finding that the object being held is softer than anticipated, and this will also make it easier for the AI guiding the robot to establish movement and force strategies.

Given the variety of conditions a robotic agent is likely to encounter, this sense, as all others, could be enhanced or particularized. Instead of touch, RADAR or SONAR could be more efficient.

Moreover, in the case of heavy-duty robots, measurements of pressures and other parameters could be integrated in the substrate of the materials used to build the robot.

Other Senses

This category has a huge potential, here we list just a few that show that the scope for senses is quite interesting.

- GPS.
- Wi-Fi and Ethernet.
- E-mail and Internet.
- External Databases.
- Radio and TV.
- Receiving cellular signals, voice, SMS and location.
- Direct satellite connectivity.
- Telepathy, with other AIs and humans with neural interface.

Of course there will be new discoveries and adaptations.

'Unconscious' Actions
In an AI, its 'unconscious' acts will be so labeled because it does not have a means to understand them or change their behavior. If an AI is able to 'learn' how to perform a certain action, this AI will most probably have an understanding of why and how these actions are taking place, but will not necessarily be 'conscious' of how they are happening.

It is not different with us humans. For example, we learn how to walk, but we do not have any 'conscious' idea of how our muscles are being stimulated to move in the way they do.

In AI implementations, the difference between 'conscious' and 'unconscious' acts will be that 'unconscious' actions are preprocessed outside of the scope of the AI software. For example, an AI recalling an event that is saved in the memory of a remote camera, that could already have already identified a face or classified an incident. If for security reasons, the entire memory and other information of this camera were not available to the AI and only the images and time-frames of these particular events would be reported to the AI. This AI will just be aware of the result, just as we are aware of looking at a given image, without having any idea of how our eyes and brain got that image.

In the same way, a robot could have its own internal routines to move around and the AI could just order these routines where to go, then the robot would do it without the AI 'brain' being involved in the robot's motions. This behavior would be close to the animal model.

Implementation of 'Consciousness'
Returning to the levels of narrow and strong AI that we used to classify Artificial Intelligence, we may also categorize Artificial Consciousness as narrow or strong:
- Narrow Artificial Consciousness: simulated.
- Strong Artificial Consciousness: conscious.

The distinctions between these two classifications are not easy to recognize. For example, if a machine, which we know has simulated consciousness, behaves as a conscious being, would we then feel that it is really conscious? Moreover, we believe that we are conscious because we act as if we were. Are we?

Implementation of consciousness in artificial minds starts with the ability of an AI to distinguish between the words 'you,' and 'I' in order to develop a concept of self that separates it from other persons. This is called a 'first-person perspective.'

The primary task in proving consciousness is the representation of oneself, the agent, as conscious. Then the key to developing artificial consciousness is to develop an agent that finds a use for thinking about itself, and others, as being involved in 'personal' experiences.

Control theory of complex system has similitudes to the role played by a conscious mind. Regard a system as a control problem, insert synthetic mental imagery, attention, and working memory; add to that imagination provided via motivations and stochastic simulations. Then you have a system that may be characterized as conscious.

Seems like AI designers and programmers must take gradual steps in hopes of awakening an AI consciousness.

Interactions between AIs

We know that a great part of the progress of civilization comes from our ability to communicate. We do it in many ways: talking, writing, drawing, with body language and through artifacts.

As one of the prerequisites for Artificial Intelligence is that it is useful to humans, to achieve that then AI machines must communicate with humans. Intercommunication between AIs is a natural extension.

Why AIs must Interact?

AIs will have connections to their 'senses,' to its external memory, to its mobile parts, to their satellites and to their internal elements. Not all the 'senses' will be fully owned by the AI, there could also be connections to external sources.

Connection between AIs could be through data exchange or via the exchange of 'subroutines' or even 'copies' of the whole program. AI implementation may be in software or hardware; either one of them may be copied into another computer or computational substrate, with the advantage of taking advantage of faster hardware with more memory and better 'senses,' or in several computers simultaneously, or of spawning different instances of itself. These copies could be allowed to deviate from each other in time, or could be amalgamated at intervals.

Considering that the Internet is made possible because computers are able to communicate with each other, it is obvious that AI will continue and expand this trend.

It is Business as Usual

Computers communicate; this has been the case since the inventions of the diskette, serial port, Internet, USB, Wi-Fi, shared hard drives and flash memory.

There is nothing new about computers that are in communication. However, with AI it will not be only computers sharing data and programs, it will be computers sharing 'thoughts,' 'memories' and 'ideas.'

A New Vision for Communications

The trend of worldwide communication is amazing. Nowadays, a minuscule smart phone can potentially call 50% of the population of the world; or in an instant get almost any information that is of interest. It is just starting, where do we go from here?

Virtual screens and keyboards, voice commands, 'Kinect' like sign interfaces, brain-to-computer understanding and vice versa. Slight improvements in our interfaces and we would be telepathic or in a virtual world.

AI will make this progress even more dramatic. Cars that drive themselves, luggage that follows us, social networking in your own virtual world, you name it and it will be possible.

Not only AI, but also nanotechnology and genetics are advancing at an exponential rate. Self-medication will be the way to go, only that your AI will do it. You want a pizza; print it.

Putting it All Together

It would seem an easy task to put everything together, but it is not that easy because all research teams are very specialized, and become even more so when they appreciate the difficulties in their research. As we have already stated, the development of AI is arguably the most difficult technological problem in the history of civilization.

The history of AI research has been plagued by a lack of interaction between AI projects. There seems to be a tendency to try to find a unique discovery that will produce the key to intelligence.

What is needed is a research project that attempts to integrate most aspects that deal with AI in a practical and workable whole. Here we describe a proposal to implement this kind of endeavor.

COGITO ERGO SUM

René Descartes wrote the statement 'I think, therefore I am' in Latin in his *'Principles of Philosophy'* in 1644. This is the name that we propose for an experiment designed to implement state-of-the-art solutions as soon as they are available, with the purpose of maintaining the highest possible Artificial Intelligence level during the length of the experiment.

This experiment will not necessarily develop new ideas in the field, even though it is expected that in the process of putting it all together there will be innovations; its major reward will be a clear advantage gained by the state-of-the-art understanding of AI.

This experiment could last from 10 to 20 years, during its timeframe the best and most advanced solutions for AI implementation would be acquired, either buying them outright or preferably through cooperation programs with universities and research teams. Considering the nature and scope of this experiment, it would be natural for universities to get involved in this type of research.

The project's mandate would be to acquire all the information available about AI research and development of software and hardware useful to AI projects, use it to promote cooperation with other teams looking for AI advancements and to apply this knowledge, software and hardware to assemble continuously improving AI solutions in realistic environments.

This project would need a dedicated research team of about 10 scientists, computing power and ancillary equipment to implement 'senses,' mobility and other AI needs. It would have to be located in a laboratory with testing equipment and space to build the environment for the tests. For example, to try out AI at home and in the office a functional home and an office setup would be required.

Basic computing power needed to start the experiment would be:

- Two racks with forty servers each, eighty blade computers.
- Each of these servers equipped with at least four of the best x86_64 compatible processors. At the time this book is being written these are the Intel Xeon and AMD 4x-SixCore.
- Graphical processors (GPU) to enhance parallel processing.
- Huge RAM, as much as the processors can handle.
- Many large disk drives, each multi-terabytes.
- Linux or Windows operating systems.
- These servers interconnected via Gigabit Ethernet.

These nineteen hundred processors could implement some of the needs of AI and its ancillary equipment, in the following way:

- 700 processors for core AI routines, including implementation of meta-motivations, supergoals and other objectives,
- 500 for learning procedures,
- 400 processors to enable communication and preprocessing of the 'senses,' and
- 300 to handle operational, short and long-term memory.

In any case, the management of the numbers of processors assigned to a given task would be highly dynamic and the numbers shown above are only a suggestion.

It is also highly likely that some 'senses' will perform pre-processing, thus allowing the central processing power to be used unimpeded.

The project will be in a continuous state of improvement, based on incremental successes. New computers will be acquired as soon as the existing ones are deemed out-of-date, which could be every year or two. Innovations and scientific discoveries will be researched, collected and implemented as soon as possible. To guarantee continuity and to prevent catastrophic failures and setbacks, new features would have to be tested outside of the main implementation and deemed safe and better than those that they will replace.

The realistic goals of this project are:

- In 5 years, narrow AI generic solutions.
- 5 years later, a dedicated AI operating system and computing platform.
- In another 10 years, a working strong AI prototype.

Moreover, the real achievement for the research team will be the advancements in AI, and other fields, that this project will spill out into their community and their country.

Next Step

Socioeconomic changes are the next step. With technology and productivity advancing at this rate, it is impossible to think that the current socioeconomic systems will be able to accommodate the changing conditions of this new world order.

Changes are underway and have been for some time: The last century started with democracy and capitalism in very few countries, and this century started with democracy and capitalism in most countries. The last century started with a real GDP per capita eight times smaller than at the start of this century, in equivalent dollar value. By the year 2100, real GDP per capita will be twenty times larger than in the year 2000.

Wealth creation, through increases in productivity produced by technological advances, will allow for a much better quality of life of all the inhabitants of this planet. On the political side, the 'Arab spring' movements have proven that the global power of non-violent uprisings is huge and will be even greater as communications improve.

That is the good news; the bad news is that the gap between rich and poor, through an accelerating accumulation of wealth, has distorted progress. There are two options for this trend of wealth accumulation to evolve:

1. The rich will be richer and 1% of the population will own 99% of the wealth, or
2. This new wealth will be fairly distributed among all the population.

As we have stated before, the first option is extremely dangerous, the least scary outcome would be a non-violent revolution that tumbles the socioeconomic systems of the world. Other scenarios deriving from this option could lead to a war of the classes.

Our hope is the second option, which does not mean that there are no more rich; not at all, it means that there are no more poor people.

> *'Experience demands that man is the only animal which devours his own kind, for I can apply no milder term to the general prey of the rich on the poor.'* **Thomas Jefferson.**

Practical Robots

'If knowledge can create problems, it is not through ignorance that we can solve them.' **Isaac Asimov.**

Robots are what most people consider the only possible shape of an entity that has Artificial Intelligence. Most people have the anthropomorphic idea that there cannot be true intelligence if it is not in the shape of a human.

Here we define a robot as a machine that is at least partially mobile, and that is self-controlled, without the need of a human operator. Its shape is not important; if a robot looks like a human then we call it an android.

We have seen that there could be many ways of achieving 'intelligence,' even without a mobile body. However, there is a link between robots and AI. A real robot has to have some sort of computer control through an AI. Otherwise, it is just a remote controlled machine; doing only what its operator wants it to do.

From the explanation above, we can broadly classify robots as:

- Controlled remotely by humans, such as military drones.
- Static or semi-mobile, controlled by a simple computer program that performs repetitive motions without any 'intelligence,' such as the so-called 'industrial robots.'
- Mobile device controlled by a remote or self-contained AI.
- Mobile frame shaped in the form of a human and controlled by a remote or self-contained AI.

In this book, we consider that only the last two categories are real robots.

Following these definitions, the onset of robotic development is integral with the development of AI. For example, development of self-driven cars requires development of narrow AI that is capable of detecting the roads, other cars, road signs, obstacles and pedestrians along the way of the car. This may be accomplished with an object oriented maximization function, which is motivated to go to a destination as fast as possible under safe conditions, obeying driving conventions and laws.

Advantages

It could be a dream, robots working for us 24/7 without requiring any payment or food or vacations. Well, they will have to be paid for, their batteries must be recharded and will need some maintenance, but other than that, it will be a free lunch.

Imagine that when you get home your robo-cleaner has cleaned the house and your robo-cook has a five-star meal on the table. Better than that, at work your robo-helper has done 99% of your work, you have only to make a few decisions and then go to the club to relax and do some exercise.

Robots will be making almost all the goods, selling, transporting and delivering them. Restaurants, factories, hotels, offices, stores, warehouses, cars, airplanes, boats, construction, everything will be automated!

Mobility and Dexterity

With mobility, dexterity and narrow AI, robots could do most of the human labor. Moreover, when strong AI is available, robots could perform all human work and maybe even be creative.

Mobility, dexterity and intelligence are the major assets of human beings. If they can be equaled or even improved by machines, these machines could take over any job or task that a human can do.

That is good and bad. It is bad if there are no good paying jobs, and the concept 'if you don't work you don't eat' remains. It is good if there are no jobs, but all, whether employed or not, share the wealth.

Interaction with Humans

When robots and artificial intelligence are capable of doing most of the work that people do now, they will have to interact with people.

The interactions have to be seamless and smooth. Brusqueness and vagueness will not be acceptable. Remember that a robot will be sold as an appliance and as such, its buyer must find that it has real advantages and that it does not create problems.

Nevertheless, when robots become prevalent, they will be everywhere and humans and robots will have to learn to coexist.

Disadvantages

It will be a nightmare, robots working 24/7 without requiring any payment or food or vacations. Taking away all our jobs! Who can compete for a job under those circumstances. And with no job, there is no money! Most people will be condemned to live out of charity, or from stealing, or selling drugs, or kidnapping or just starving.

Society and the economy must change. A situation of abundance produced by technological advances could very well be misused by a few ultra-rich, under the guise of capitalism, to keep 99% of the population unemployed and condemned to be miserable forever. This is not an unlikely scenario: in the US 2% of the population already has more than 50% of the income and wealth.

Cost

Before the technology matures, robots will be quite costly. They are complicated machines, with many moving parts and requiring new design and manufacturing expertise. However, as soon as they mature, robots will be designing and building other robots and their price will plummet.

Under these conditions, it is expected that robots will follow the trend of other appliances where prices come down to a level where they may be acquired by anybody that has a decent income and of course by governments, businesses and factories.

Overcoming their Limitations

To perform effectively around continuously changing working environments, robots must be aware of their limitations. In a similar way of how we humans are aware of what is doable.

The best way would be planning the entire task before it even starts, but this could be unrealistic in many cases. For example, if a house-robot is ordered to set up a table, it would start by localizing the table, and what should go on top and where. However, it must start cleaning up the table in order not to make silly mistakes like trying to set up a diner plate on top of a laptop computer or papers.

One way to do it is to ascertain the probability of objects being where they have to be and take a 'look' at the object, ask 'questions' or finding where the object is. It would start with a certain belief and take actions to gather more information, incrementally planning and learning as it goes along.

At one point, the robot could even decide that a task is too difficult, or even impossible, and therefore will stop before it makes a serious mistake.

Interaction with Humans

The best outcome is that robots take the toil out of human lives; the worst outcome is that robots take the jobs without having an economy that does not require people to have a job in order to live well.

Artificial Intelligence, robots and technological progress in general could eliminate the need for people to work. Scarcity could be a thing of the past; however, if society does not change accordingly, this abundance could be in the hands of 1% of the population of the world and the other 99% could become pariahs with no money, hope or future.

Social pressures could curtail tolerance of AI and robots, especially if they start taking over more and more jobs. Especially, if there is a lack of response to a situation of massive unemployment.

Human like android robots will have especially difficult times, and there can be no guarantee of their acceptance. In our societies, where small differences between humans have been the root of racism and hatred, it would be surprising if androids do not end up being the new victim of these nefarious traditions.

To avoid discrimination, robots could be built to look cute and more pet-like than human-like; thus, as pets maybe they will be accepted. In particular, if these robots are made to look cute and helpless.

These considerations do not totally exclude androids for companionship and sexual relationships, although they could be confined to the privacy of home.

Types of Robots

As soon as AI is mature enough to be capable of guiding robots in their day-to-day operations, there will be a race to design and sell better and more useful robots.

At first, they will take the shape of machines that we already know, like cars and trucks. In little time, there will be new shapes and new tasks. As we have already written about their AI, let us now look at some of them in terms of their body and functionality.

- Blue-Collar Robots: Tackling jobs that people must do, but hate doing, do not want to do, or simply cannot do like: cleaning, cooking, maintenance, security, mining, and defusing bombs. There is going to be a steady increase in the number and variety of such machines.

- White-Collar Robots: Are the ones that will help us do things we like to do like: adventure, creativity, socializing, studying, and other activities that until now are considered strictly human.

Blue-collar robots are relatively simple machines and to make it easy to do their jobs, the work environment would have to be adapted. Just as factories have been redesigned so that industrial robots can perform their preprogramed activities.

However, white-collar robots will have to tackle the difficult task of grasping the intricacies of the human world. By the very nature of their work, they will tend to take android shapes.

Utilitarian

AI will operate many machines. The main difference will be that there will be no need for an operator's enclosure or concern for its safety or fatigue.

Removing the uneven driving capabilities of drivers will make cars safer. Moreover, cars will be much lighter due to a reduced concern about crashes, super strong materials like carbon fiber becoming cheaper, and smaller and more powerful batteries. Their design will also change; with no driver, the interior layout of the seats will be flexible. There could be seats with tables, like in trains, or maybe they will look like first class airline accommodations. A combination of lightness, power and perfect control could make it possible to build ground effect or even flying cars.

Construction machinery will be different too. To dig a tunnel, or lay a pipe underground, a machine could just dig the hole and clad it with plastic reinforced with carbon fiber or carbon nanotubes; there is no concern about ventilation, operator safety and other issues of concern to human workers. A house or a building can just be 3D printed, including floors, walls, ceilings, counter-tops, built-in furniture, pipes and electrical cables; a set of robots can do the finishing work; one that installs doors and windows, another to fit the bath and kitchen appliances and a third one to clean the house.

Many factories will be hundred percent automated. Robots could replace workers directly, but also, availability of robots will force the workflow and layout of the plants to change, as has already been done, in order to take advantage of this cheaper and more amenable workforce. Working 24/7 will be the standard and with downtime for maintenance only. No lunch, no sleep and no pay; all that money goes to the stockholders.

Insects

Imagine millimeter sized drones, artificial bees and predator robots killing flies and mosquitoes. You will be able to buy them in the mall. Spy on your neighbors, protect yourself from real insects, you will have fun.

The above are not total fantasies, these types of mechanisms will be available. They could have self-contained AI, or your smartphone AI could provide the guidance.

Using the same or better models, governments, corporations and spies will know everything about everybody; what are they going to do with all this information? Will it be merely fed into AIs, which will then figure out irrelevant facts out of all this amazing nonsense?

Pets

Finally, good news, pet lovers will get everything. A dog that is adorable and does not pee or poo, does not need food and cannot get old. A cat that obeys orders and can even hold a conversation with you when you are lonely. An that robo-tyrannosaurus that watches your live dog when you are away.

It is unclear if real pets are going to be displaced by robo-pets, but their advantages will be great; dogs, cats and other animals will have to fight hard to keep their thousand yearlong symbioses with humans.

Androids

What impressive gadgets these humanoid or even human looking robots will be. It is a dream, servants and workers to do all your bidding. Breakfast in bed, butler to guide you through your social life and help you get dressed. This is going to be a 'couch potato' dream.

Imagine, your wife has a headache so you take her robo-replica to dinner. This robot will think and answer just as she does, they could even be in sync in real time and you would save her part of the bill. Your home will have little gnomes cleaning, putting everything in place and performing chores. What are you needed for?

Future Robots

In a world with intelligent robots, what can you do to improve it? Well, first of all, you do what seven star hotels wish for, you make their services unobtrusive. Then we want them smaller. Last, but not least, that they are perfect.

Unobtrusive

After the novelty and glamour fades, having robots everywhere is going to be disturbing and inefficient. There must be a way to make them do what they must do without us noticing that it is being done.

The first step is hiding them in nooks and crannies when they are not performing their job. The next step is designing the living or work environments so that these robots work in peculiar ways to avoid being seen or even noticed.

By the time robots are so common that they must be hidden, the place where you work could most probably be the same as where you live. Or, more explicitly, you could work anywhere you want, even at home.

Another offspring of keeping robots out of the way would be that people might come together and seek each other out. Creating a social boom.

Nanotechnology

If you want to hide something, make it microscopic. Nanotechnology will allow this to happen.

Of course, not all robots could be microscopic, but a lot of functionality could be incorporated into nano-robots.

The Perfect Robot

The perfect robot could be anthropomorphic, with looks that change with the occasion, even blending out of the way.

It would be whatever you want it to be, your replica, a butler, more intelligent that you but following your whims and orders all the time, stronger than you but adaptable to different situations. It would be the fantasy of what you would like to be.

Its AI will be you, providing you with enhancements and in harmony with you. It could go on errands as you or with you. Your robot will be perfect, and so will you.

> *'If the human race wishes to have a prolonged and indefinite period of material prosperity, they have only got to behave in a peaceful and helpful way toward one another.'* **Winston Churchill.**

What is Uncertainty?

*'The only thing that makes life possible is permanent, intolerable uncertainty; not knowing what comes next.' **Ursula K. LeGuin.***

L ife is full of uncertainties. We are capable of living in the midst of day-to-day uncertainties and to making choices and decisions without being troubled too much by them. The real world is also full of uncertainties, and we are not aware of them because evolution has prepared us to ignore them and treat them as 'natural phenomena.'

When designing models that represent future events, the subject of uncertainty becomes very important. The more complex the model, the more important it is to analyze the sources and the ways of dealing with uncertainty.

Uncertainty is used to cover a multiplicity of concepts. It is associated to many causes, it is about:

- Incomplete information.
- Linguistic imprecision.
- Variability of a measurement.
- Lack of full knowledge about a parameter or a formula.
- Doubts about the model used to represent a system.
- The use of a simplified model to facilitate the analysis.
- Conditions in the real world.
- Future status of a system.
- Our preferences, or those of our sponsors.
- The solutions.

We can even be uncertain about the uncertainty.

The variety of types and sources of uncertainty is confusing. They are especially confusing because we are wired to act in their presence without even noticing them as 'calculable.' People and nations make future plans that ignore uncertainty. If we think about it, we know that there is uncertainty about the future, but we do not think about it or plan accordingly.

As far as we know, our brains are wired to deal automatically with some of the uncertainties that we encounter throughout our lives. Otherwise, we would not be able to think ahead and prepare Plan A or Plan B if something goes wrong. When designing an AI it will be necessary to directly deal with the uncertainties to allow the algorithms that drive it to plan ahead and make the best possible choices. Bringing uncertainty into play effectively uses more of the information that is available, than ignoring it.

How to Quantify Uncertainty

In 1812 Pierre-Simon Marquis de Laplace wrote in the introduction to his '*Théorie Analytique de Probabilités*': 'The theory of probability is at the bottom nothing more but common sense reduced to calculus.' Probability comprises the mathematical tools used to handle uncertainties.

Probability analyses random phenomena using formulations where every 'event' has a value between zero and one and the event made up of all possible results has a value of one.

Moreover, a technique defining a probability space, where outcomes are different on different trials, is a fundamental tool of probability, used to handle uncertainties in real-world situations where events occur randomly. This technique consists of three parts:
1. A sample space. This is the set of all possible outcomes.
2. A set of events. Where each event is a set containing zero or more outcomes.
3. Probability assigned to the events by means of a probability function linking events to probability levels.

An outcome is the result of a single execution of the model.

Probability

As the mathematical foundation for statistics, probability theory is essential to many human activities that involve quantitative analysis of sets of data.

It involves analysis of random variables and events, probability functions, stochastic processes and of complex systems where there is an incomplete knowledge of their state.

Quantum mechanics, systems described as chaotic and now AI can be described and understood only when they are considered as probabilistic phenomena.

Random Variables

A variable whose value results from a measurement on some type of random process is a random variable or stochastic variable. Many times, a random variable is a numerical description of the outcome of an experiment. A stochastic variable is a set or random variables indexed by time or any other dimension.

It is convenient to associate numerical values with the outcomes of an experiment than to work directly with just descriptions. Random variables are real-value functions that associate every element of a given set to a unique real number on a sample space.

When a random variable always takes the same value in the outcome of the experiment, then it is a constant.

Mathematical Formulation

Definitions: A random variable is a function that assigns a number to each point in a sample space S.

If S	is a sample space,
and e	is the outcome value, a generic element in S,
then X	is a random variable, a real-valued function,
where	$X = X(e)$.

In the notation of a random variable, the argument e is often not used.

Probability Distributions

The associations of random variables with a probability are encapsulated in a 'probability density function,' which in its two cases follows these basic properties:

1. A 'discrete' random variable describes outcomes that are finite in number. In this case, the probabilities of all the outcomes must add up to one.
2. A 'continuous' random variable symbolizes an infinite number of possible outcomes, and its density function's integral must equal one over the entire range of outcomes.

In the discrete case, the probabilities for specific outcomes are the sum of probabilities, and in the continuous case they are the integration of the density function, over the interval corresponding to that outcome.

A random variable may also be depicted by its expected value (or mean, or the first moment), which is the weighted average of all possible values that this random variable can take. And by its standard deviation (or second moment), which shows how much dispersion exists from the mean. A low standard deviation indicates that the data points tend to be very close to the mean, whereas high standard deviation indicates that the data points are spread out over a large range of values.

Mathematical Formulation

Definitions:

$x_1, x_2, \ldots, x_n$	values a random variable X can assume.
$\{X = x_i\}$ or $X(e) = x_i$	a set of all outcomes e.
$f(x_i) = P\{X = x_i\}$	the probability distribution function of X.

Thus, in the discrete case, according to the basic properties of probabilities:

$$f(x_i) \geq 0 \text{ for all } i, \qquad \sum_i f(x_i) = 1$$

and

$$P\{a < X \leq b\} = \sum_{a < x_i \leq b} f(x_i)$$

for any real numbers a and b.

In the continuous case, the density function is an integral, such that:

$$\int_{-\infty}^{\infty} f(x)\, dx = 1$$

and

$$P\{a \leq X \leq b\} = \int_a^b f(x)\, dx$$

for the interval (a, b). The probability that X falls inside this interval is the area under the graph of f between a and b.

The cumulative distribution function of a continuous probability distribution must also be continuous.

Bayes Theorem

Reverend Thomas Bayes was born in England circa 1702 and supposedly died in 1761. He discovered how to compute a distribution for the probability parameter of a binomial distribution and this discovery later became known as Bayes Theorem. His friend Richard Price edited and presented this work in 1763, after Bayes' death, as '*An Essay Towards Solving a Problem in the Doctrine of Chances.*' Pierre-Simon Laplace, a French mathematician, reproduced and extended Bayes' results in 1774, apparently quite unaware of Bayes' work.

This theorem expresses how a subjective degree of belief should rationally change to account for evidence. The application of Bayes Theorem to update beliefs is called Bayesian inference.

Bayesian Inference

In this interpretation, probability measures a degree of belief. Bayes Theorem performs operations to handle the degree of belief in a proposition before and after accounting for evidence. For proposition A and evidence X,

- $p(A)$ the *prior*, is the initial degree of belief in A.
- $p(A|X)$ the *posterior*, degree of belief after considering X.
- $p(X|A)/p(X)$ likelihood of the support that X provides for A.

The Bayesian approach to machine learning treats the model and its parameters as additional unobserved variables and computes a posterior distribution conditional upon observed data. This approach can be computationally expensive and lead to large dimension models.

A further development is Bayesian networks, which can solve problems like:

- Reasoning,   using the Bayesian inference algorithm.
- Learning,   using the expectation-maximization algorithm.
- Planning,   using decision networks.
- Perception,   using dynamic Bayesian networks.

Bayes Theorem has a deep impact in science, even the scientific method is a special case of this way of thinking.

Mathematical Formulation

If A is an event, and $\sim A$ is not event A, where $p(A) + p(\sim A) = 1$, and X is an observed event, where $p(A)$ is the *prior* degree of belief in A before X is observed, and $p(A|X)$ is the *posterior* belief in A after observing X.

Then the Bayes Theorem is:

$$p(A|X) = \frac{p(X|A) * p(A)}{p(X|A) * p(A) + p(X|{\sim}A) * p({\sim}A)}$$

Stochastic Processes

Deterministic dynamic systems are those where there is only one possible way the process might develop over time. In a stochastic process, or random process, there is an uncertainty in the way the process will develop over time, which is described by probability distributions. Starting with an initial condition, there are many paths to its outcome in time, some paths are more probable than others.

Stochastic processes refer to a family of random variables indexed against some other variable or set of variables. This indexing can be either discrete or continuous, in general reflecting changes with respect to time.

Stochastic processes include Markov processes, Poisson processes (as radioactive decay), stochastic differential equations and time series.

Stochastic Differential Equations

Stochastic differential equations (SDE) are used to model diverse physical dynamic systems subject to uncertainty. A differential equation where one or more of its terms is a stochastic process is called a SDE; the solution is a stochastic process. White noise, Brownian motion, Wiener process or jump processes are used to introduce random fluctuations into the SDE.

Another approach to stochastic processes treats them as functions of one or several arguments whose values are random variables: non-deterministic quantities that have certain probability distributions.

Mathematical Formulation

We present the notation used for solving stochastic differential equations via numerical methods.

A typical stochastic differential equation is of the form:

$$dX_t = \mu(X_t, t)dt + \sigma(X_t, t)dB_t$$

where B denotes a Wiener process or Standard Brownian motion. Its corresponding integral equation is:

$$X_{t+s} - X_t = \int_t^{t+s} \mu(X_u, u)du + \int_t^{t+s} \sigma(X_u, u)dB_u$$

The equations above characterize the behavior of the continuous stochastic process X_t.

An interpretation of these stochastic differential equations is that in a small time interval of length δ the stochastic process, X_t changes its value by an amount that is normally distributed with expectation $\mu(X_t, t)\delta$ and variance $\sigma(X_t, t)^2\delta$, independent of the past states of the process. This is so because the increments of a Wiener process are independent and normally distributed.

There are also more general stochastic differential equations where the coefficients μ and σ depend on not only the present value of the process X_t, but also on previous values of the process and possibly on present or previous values of other processes too.

Optimal Filtering

To analyze uncertain processes that occur over time, the implementation of optimal filtering makes use of probabilistic algorithms for filtering, prediction, smoothing and finding explanations for streams of data. Helped by perception systems such as hidden Markov models or Kalman filters.

Kalman filter

As an implementation of dynamic Bayesian networks, the Kalman filter estimates the performance of a system over time using incoming measurements, in the same way as the Bayes theorem estimates an unknown probability density function over time, using posterior measurements.

The Kalman filter, named for Rudolf E. Kálmán, has many applications in technology. This algorithm manipulates streams of noisy input data in real time, typically coming from sensor measurements, and filters out errors using a least-squares method, optimized with a mathematical prediction of the future state generated through modeling the system. Through a factor known as the Kalman Gain, differences between the prior estimate and the posterior observation are minimized to improve subsequent predictions. This method produces better estimates than those based just on a single measurement or on a prediction from the model.

The Kalman Filter algorithm is an optimized method for determining the best estimation of the state of a dynamic system. At each time step, the Kalman Filter produces estimates of the unknown values, along with their uncertainties. Once the outcome of the next measurement is observed, these estimates are updated using a weighted average, with more weight being given to estimates with lower uncertainty.

The Kalman Filter assumes that the system under evaluation:

- Is a linear dynamic system.

- All error terms and measurements have a Gaussian distribution, which could be a multivariate Gaussian distribution.

The Kalman Filter is a recursive estimator where only the previous estimated state and the current measurement are needed to compute the estimate for the current state.

The original Kalman Filter deals only with linear systems; however, systems can be nonlinear. Nonlinearity can be within the process, within the model, or within both. The Extended Kalman Filter is the nonlinear version of the Kalman Filter.

Mathematical Formulation

This is a summarized presentation of the Kalman Filter equations, based on general measurements and transition equations.

1. Predict a future unobserved variable X_{t+1} based on the current estimate of the unobserved variable $X_{(t+1)P}$, the transition equation is of the form:

$$X_{(t+1)P} = a_t X_{tP-ADJ} + g_t + \theta_t$$

Where a_t and g_t are time-varying parameters and θ_t is a stochastic variable.

Note: $X_{0P\text{-}ADJ} = X_0$ which is normal with mean μ_0, and standard deviation σ_0. $N_{(\mu_0, \sigma_0^2)}$ - ADJ stands for adjusted predicted value.

2. Use the predicted unobserved variable to predict the future observable variable Y_{t+1} and call it $Y_{(t+1)P}$; then the measurement equation takes the form:

$$Y_{(t+1)P} = m_t X_{(t+1)P} + b_{t+1} + \varepsilon_{t+1}$$

Where m_t is a time-varying parameter and ε_t is a stochastic variable.

3. When the future observable variable actually occurs, calculate the error in the prediction:

$$Y_{(t+1)E} = Y_{t+1} - Y_{(t+1)P}$$

4. Generate a better estimate of the unobserved variable at time $(t+1)$ and start the process over for time $(t+2)$:

$$X_{(t+1)P-ADJ} = X_{(t+1)P} + k_{t+1} Y_{(t+1)E}$$

Note: k_{t+1} is the 'Kalman Gain' and is set to minimize the variance of $X_{(t+1)P\text{-}ADJ}$; where p_{t+1} is the variance of $X_{(t+1)P}$:

$$k_{t+1} = \frac{p_{t+1}m}{p_{t+1}m^2 + r_t} = \frac{Cov(X_{(t+1)P}, \ Y_{(t+1)P})}{Var(Y_{(t+1)P})}$$

where Var(x) represents the variance of x and Cov(x) its covariance.

'Probability is expectation founded upon partial knowledge. A perfect acquaintance with all the circumstances affecting the occurrence of an event would change expectation into certainty, and leave neither room nor demand for a theory of probabilities.' **George Boole**

Mathematics in AI

'As far as the laws of mathematics refer to reality, they are not certain, and as far as they are certain, they do not refer to reality.' **Albert Einstein.**

In any motivation that AI researchers include in their programming, there will be exceptions. If these motivations are strictly based on logic, then by definition their associated true or false statements cannot handle these exceptions. Probabilistic reasoning is necessary to handle reality.

Existing industrial robots, which do not rely on any kind of Artificial Intelligence, operate solely on logical instructions to do their work. Then a way of differentiating between intelligent machines, and those that are not, could be that the implementation of the former considers uncertainty.

Challenges

AI algorithms require huge computational resources; the solution of many of its problems requires amounts of memory or computer time that grow in an exponential or combinatorial manner. The search for efficient algorithms is fundamental in AI research.

There are measurements for the degree of difficulties in the solution of mathematical problems, and it is well known that some problems are not solvable.

Some argue that the creation of 'intelligence' is one of these problems. However, our intelligence somehow circumvents this. The existence of human intelligence shows that it can be done. The question is: Can it be done with an approach different from the one evolution took?

Here we present some of these challenges.

Computational Complexity Theory

A task that a computer running an algorithm can solve is a computational problem. If the solution of a computational problem requires significant resources, in terms of computing power and time, then it may be associated with a complexity class.

Complexity classes are sets of problems of related complexity, which are defined by the following factors:

- Type of computational problem: decision, function, counting, optimization, prediction.
- Computational model: deterministic Turing machine, nondeterministic Turing machine, quantum Turing machine, Boolean net, monotone circuit, Gödel machine.
- Resources: polynomial time, logarithmic space, constant depth.

If an algorithm can solve a problem then a Turing machine can solve the problem, this is the Church–Turing thesis. Therefore, the concept of Turing machines is useful when studying complexity theory. Some complex problems have either no known solution or they are intractable. Intractable problems are those that can be solved but it will take too long to arrive at a solution.

Many problems encountered in AI are either complex or intractable, or both. Special strategies are needed to solve these types of problems; they include stochastic processes and optimization theory.

Modern studies conducted by Solomonoff, Kolmogorov and Chaitin have redefined the field of mathematical complexity.

Knowledge

A practical AI needs at least a minimum degree of knowledge about its operational environment. This includes:

- A catalog of well-known objects and their properties.
- Object categories and relationships between these objects.
- What causes an event and the effects produced by the event.
- Past situations and future possible events.
- Current internal and external states.
- Time frames for past, current and predicted events.

The knowledge potential of any person is enormous. However, this knowledge is mostly learned. Therefore, if the computer has a kernel of preset knowledge, and suitable learning algorithms, it will be able to learn and thus be able to obtain most of this knowledge. Moreover, once one AI learns, this knowledge could be downloaded into other AIs, and vice versa; making the learning process a lot faster.

Knowledge is uncertain, we know what a bird is, and we have no problem recognizing a bird that we have never seen; this is what an AI will have to achieve. It will have to compare the bird with objects in its catalog and find the category that most likely fits the bird, and then it will conclude that it is most probably a bird; we do it in the same way.

Qualifications

To set goals and achieve them, artificial intelligence implementations will have to visualize the future. Given the present state of its world, it should be able to predict how its actions will change it, at the same time maximizing its motivations. The AI will know that it is not alone in its world, so it must continuously check if the observed states match its predictions, changing its plan as necessary. Thus, AIs must reason under uncertainty.

Our brain unconsciously makes decisions. These decisions take the form of intuitions; that are very hard to explain at a conscious level. It will be necessary that a computational intelligence provide ways to represent this kind of knowledge; even though its implementation could formulate these decisions as 'conscious' with the AI fully aware of the entire decision process.

Solutions

There are mathematical tools to solve some of the challenges to create machines that seem to be, or maybe are, intelligent.

A machine that seems to be intelligent and can do useful things in a real or virtual environment must also operate efficiently. Presently, complex systems are controlled using controls, instruments and measurement devices in conjunction with implementations of control software with human operators that provide the intelligence. Optimization methodologies are the kernel of the control software, which when enhanced to handle common sense problems could provide autonomous control.

Rule-Based Expert System

In the 1970s and 1980s, the dominant approach to artificial intelligence was to try to capture the process of human judgment in rules a computer could use.

Rule-based programming operate from a given set of data and rules. A rule-based system has four basic components:

First, a list of rules of a specific type of knowledge base related to the problem.

Second, these rules are applied with the following formulation:

IF *condition* THEN *action*

Third, an inference or semantic engine selects an action based on input and the applicable rules. Then it performs a match-resolve-act cycle:

- Match: the engine finds all of the rules that are satisfied by the current contents of the data.
- Conflict-Resolution: The matches found are candidates for implementation: they are the conflict set. The engine selects the most suitable rule-match in the set.
- Act: Actions selected in conflict-resolution are acted upon.

Fourth, a temporary working memory and a user interface or link to the outside world to receive and send input and output signals.

These models allow a separation of knowledge, which is contained in the rules, from control, given by the inference engine. These methods are very specific to a given situation and may be used to implement some solutions in Phase I narrow AI.

Fuzzy Systems

Fuzzy logic was proposed in 1965 by Lotfi A. Zadeh of the University of California at Berkeley. It is a mathematical system that analyzes analog input values in terms of logical variables that take on continuous values between 0 and 1, in contrast to classical or digital logic, which operates on discrete values of either 0 or 1, false or true. Fuzzy logic has the advantage that the solution to a problem can be cast in terms that human operators can understand, so that their experience can be used in the design of the controller. This makes it easier to mechanize tasks already successfully performed by humans.

Fuzzy logic has evolved into a well-structured system of concepts and techniques with a solid mathematical foundation and a widening array of applications.

Fuzzy systems based on fuzzy logic have been largely ignored in the US On the other hand, the Japanese enthusiastically embraced fuzzy logic. They have investigated and implemented a wide range of applications including character and handwriting recognition; optical fuzzy systems;

robots, including one that makes Japanese flower arrangements and voice-controlled helicopters.

A combination of fuzzy operations and rule-based inference describes a fuzzy expert system. Their strategies seem to be puzzling, as they look like they could be applied without fuzzy logic; they are based on the following schema:

- In a fuzzy system, input variables are mapped by sets of membership functions, known as fuzzy sets.
- This process converts a crisp input value into a fuzzy value, it is called fuzzification.
- All the rules that apply are invoked, using membership functions and truth-values obtained from the inputs, to determine the result of the rule.
- This result, in turn, is mapped into a membership function and a truth-value controlling the output variable.
- Through a procedure known as defuzzification, these fuzzy results are combined to give a specific crisp answer.

Fuzzy Information Granulation

This is a concept in fuzzy systems of particular importance to AI, it facilitates modeling everyday human decision-making by using only decision-relevant information.

This theory considers that among the basic concepts that underlie human cognition, three stand out in importance. These are:

- granulation,
- organization and
- causation.

Granulation involves decomposition of whole into parts. Organization implies integration of parts into whole. Causation relates to association of causes with effects. Granulation of an object leads to a collection of granules, with a granule being a clump of objects drawn together by indistinguishability, similarity, proximity or functionality.

Fuzziness of granules is a direct consequence of fuzziness of the concepts of indistinguishability, similarity, proximity and functionality. For example, the granules of a human head are the forehead, nose, cheeks, ears, eyes, etc. Granulation can also be hierarchical in nature. A familiar example is the granulation of time into years, months, days, hours, minutes, etc.

Crisp granules are not suitable in real world situations, like in human reasoning and concept formation, where most of the granules are fuzzy. The granules of a human head, for example, are fuzzy in the sense that the boundaries between cheeks, nose, forehead, ears, etc. are not sharply defined. Furthermore, so are the attributes of fuzzy granules, like in this example:

- head ~ nose + hair + left cheek + right cheek + ...
- hair ~ length + color + texture + ...
- length ~ long – short – very long – ...

Fuzzy information granulation underlies the remarkable human ability to make rational decisions in an environment of imprecision, partial knowledge, partial certainty and partial truth. The fuzziness of granules, their attributes and their values is characteristic of the ways in which human concepts are formed, organized and manipulated.

The theory of fuzzy information granulation has been inspired by the ways in which humans granulate information and reason with it. However, the foundations of the theory and its methodology are mathematical in nature; fuzzy logic provides a methodology for fuzzy information granulation.

The way in which humans employ fuzzy information granulation to make rational decisions in an environment of partial knowledge, partial certainty and partial truth could be a role model for machine intelligence.

Uncertain Logic

Uncertain logic is a generalization of probabilistic logic, credible logic and hybrid logic within the framework of uncertainty theory.

Classical logic assumes that each proposition is either true or false. However, a fuzzy value cannot be adequately represented in classical logic as a proposition containing a fuzzy value can fail to be true or false. And random knowledge and fuzzy knowledge may appear simultaneously in a complex system.

Uncertain logic deals with random knowledge and fuzzy knowledge simultaneously. In a complex knowledge system, random knowledge and fuzzy knowledge may occur simultaneously. Uncertain logic is a means to deal with a general uncertain knowledge system. It is consistent with the classical logic based on the law of excluded middle, the law of contradiction and the law of truth conservation for uncertain truth-value, and complies with the framework of uncertainty theory.

Mathematical Formulation

In uncertain logic, a truth-value for each proposition is an uncertain measure represented by means of *uncertain propositions* and *uncertain formulas* instead of propositions and formulas, respectively.

Generally speaking, we use τ to express an uncertain proposition and use u to express its uncertainty value. If we use $\tau = 1$ to express τ is true, and use $\tau = 0$ to express τ is false, then τ is essentially an uncertain variable defined as

$$\tau = \begin{cases} 1, \text{with uncertainty } u \\ 0, \text{with uncertainty } 1 - u \end{cases}$$

Let X be an uncertain formula containing uncertain propositions τ_1, τ_2, ..., τ_n. It is clear that X is essentially an uncertain variable taking values 0 or 1 and defined by its truth function f as

$X = f(\tau_1, \tau_2, ..., \tau_n)$

In this equation, the symbols τ_1, τ_2, ..., τ_n are considered uncertain variables.

For each uncertain formula X, its truth-value is defined as

$T(X) = M\{X = 1\}$

For any uncertain proposition τ, it is easy to prove that $M\{\tau = 1\} = u$, that is, the truth value of each uncertain proposition is just its uncertainty value. In addition, if $X = f(\tau_1, \tau_2, ..., \tau_n)$, then

$T(X) = M\{f(\tau_1, \tau_2, ..., \tau_n) = 1\}$

And for any uncertain formula X, we have

$T(X \wedge \neg X) = 1$ *Law of Excluded Middle*

$T(X \vee \neg X) = 0$ *Law of Contradiction*

$T(\neg X) = 1 - T(X)$ *Law of Truth Conservation*

Thereby the proof that Uncertain Logic and Classical Logic are consistent, it follows that for any uncertain formulas X and Y, we have

$T(X) \vee T(Y) \leq T(X \vee Y) \leq T(X) + T(Y)$

Thus, uncertain logic is consistent with classical logic verified through the laws of excluded middle, of contradiction and of truth conservation for an uncertain truth-value

Optimization

In 1953 the American mathematician Richard Bellman developed the mathematical optimization methods known as dynamic programming.

The Bellman equation provides optimal control theory solutions for engineering, economic theory and applied mathematics problems. This equation is an extension of earlier work in classical physics known as the

Hamilton-Jacobi equation by William Rowan Hamilton and Carl Gustav Jacob Jacobi.

Optimal Control

Deterministic problems of optimal control over a period $[0, T]$ may be described by the following function representing the minimized value of a system:

$$V(x(0), 0) = \min_{u} \left\{ \int_0^T C[x(t), u(t)] dt + D[x(T)] \right\}$$

where

    $C[]$ is a scalar cost function,

    $D[]$ is the function that gives the value or utility at the final state,

    $x(t)$ is a system state vector,

    $x(0)$ is given, and

    u(t) for $0 \leq t \leq T$ is the control vector that we are looking for.

This system is also governed by:

$$\dot{x}(t) = F[x(t), u(t)]$$

where

    $\dot{x}()$ is the first derivative of $x()$,

    $F[]$ is the vector of the variation of the state vector over time.

The Hamilton-Jacobi-Bellman (HJB) partial differential equation for this system, as described above, is:

$$\dot{V}(x, t) + \min_{u} \{ \nabla V(x, t) \cdot F(x, u) + C(x, u) \} = 0$$

With the following function for its ending conditions:

$$V(x, T) = D(x)$$

where

    $V(x, t)$ is the Bellman value function of the optimal cost for the state x at time t until T,

    $\dot{V}()$ is the first derivative of $V()$,

    $a \cdot b$ is the dot product of vectors a and b,

    $\nabla V()$ is the gradient operator of $V()$, defined as the unique vector field whose dot-product with any unit vector a at each point x is the directional derivative of $V()$ along a.

Solving this equation for $V(x, t)$ entails finding the minimum cost value for the control vector $u(t)$. The HJB equation is sometimes solved backwards in time, starting from $t = T$ and ending at $t = 0$.

Curse of Dimensionality

In the process of developing its optimization algorithms, Bellman found out that adding extra dimensions to a mathematical solution space caused an exponential increase in computer time for some methods of numerical solution of the Bellman equation. He named this the 'Curse of Dimensionality.'

Bayesian Networks

A Bayesian network consists of a directed acyclic graph and a set of local distributions. Each node in the graph represents a random variable that denotes an attribute, feature, or hypothesis about which we may be uncertain. The graph represents dependence relationships, with local distributions representing those strengths. Bayesian networks provide a means of expressing joint probability distributions over many interrelated hypotheses that are symbolized by the nodes of the graph.

Bayesian networks have been used to solve problems with uncertain knowledge in diverse fields such as AI, medical diagnosis, image recognition, language understanding and search algorithms.

One of the most powerful characteristics of Bayesian Networks is its ability to update the beliefs of each random variable via bidirectional propagation of new information through the whole structure.

In 1988, Dr. Judea Pearl proposed an algorithm that fuses and propagates the impact of new evidence providing each node with a belief vector consistent with probability theory. The figure below shows a graphical representation of Pearl's bi-directional propagation scheme.

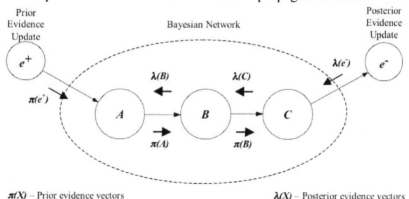

$\pi(X)$ – Prior evidence vectors $\qquad$ $\lambda(X)$ – Posterior evidence vectors

In Bayesian Networks, data may be updated using prior probabilities or posterior probabilities. In the first case, the new data will flow via a π

prior evidence row vector, while in the second case data will flow via a λ posterior evidence column vector. Both vectors update the node belief B using the equation:

$$Bel(B) = P(B|e^+, e^-) = \alpha\pi(N)^T \bullet \lambda(B)$$

where α is a normalizing constant, and $\bullet$ means term by term multiplication or dot product. The resulting column vector is the new belief of node B; vector $Bel(B)$ will have as many elements as the number of states of the random variable depicted by node B.

The number of states in the nodes of a Bayesian network reflects the number of elements of the π or λ vectors. After receiving a π vector with updated information from a parent node A, node B will send its own π vector to its children nodes. The equation used in node B for creating its π vector is:

$$\pi(B) = \sum_A P(B|A, e^+) \bullet P(A|e^-) = \sum_A P(B|A) \bullet \pi(B)$$
$$= \mu(B) \otimes \mathbf{M}_{B|A}$$

where $\otimes$ means vector multiplication (or congruent product), and $\mathbf{M}_{B|A}$ is the likelihood matrix, or conditional probability distribution matrix between nodes B and A.

When receiving a λ vector with updated information from child node C, node B will send its own λ vector to its parent nodes. The formula used in node B for creating its λ vector is:

$$\lambda(B) = \sum_C P(e^-|B, C) \bullet P(C|B) = \sum_C P(e^-|C) \bullet P(C|B)$$
$$\Rightarrow \sum_C \lambda(C) \bullet P(C|B) = \mathbf{M}_{C|B} \otimes \lambda(C)$$

where the resulting column vector $\lambda(B)$ is then transmitted to parent nodes.

Bayesian Networks have limitations that impede their application to complex problems because they assume a simple attribute-value representation.

MEBN

Integrating First Order Logic (FOL) with Bayesian probability theory, Multi-Entity Bayesian (MEBN) extends Bayesian Networks to allow representation of graphical models with repeated sub-structures.

In this method, collections of MFrags encode knowledge in a collection of Bayesian network fragments that can be instantiated and combined to form complex Bayesian networks called MTheory, which represents a joint probability distribution over an unbounded number of hypotheses, and uses Bayesian learning to refine a knowledge base as observations accumulate.

PR-OWL

When the numbers, types and relationships among events cannot be specified in advance and may have uncertainty in their own definitions, there is a need for a different approach.

PR-OWL is a combination of the Web Ontology Language (OWL), designed for use by applications that need to process the content of information instead of just presenting information to humans and probability methodology based on the Multi-Entity Bayesian Network (MEBN).

Neural Network

The way biological neural networks operate, forms the basis for artificial neural networks. The basic computational unit in the nervous system is the nerve cell or neuron.

Computer models of neurons run as simulations of circuits in the brain. Neural networks in artificial intelligence are simplified models of neural processing in the brain. It is not clear to what degree artificial neural networks mirror brain function.

Artificial Neuron

A basic computational element y_i, that simulates a neuron that receives input, and has an associated weight w, and which can be modified to represent learning, is modeled as a unit that computes some function f of the weighted sum of its inputs:

$$y_i = f(\sum_j w_{ij} y_{ij})$$

The weighted sum $\sum_j w_{ij} y_{ij}$ is the net input to unit i, often written as net_i. Where, y_{ij} is the activation state for every unit and w_{ij} is the weight from unit j to unit i. The activation or unit's function is f. Its output, y_i can then serve as input to other units. If the activation function depends upon random variables, then the network will be probabilistic.

Artificial Network

An artificial neural network consists of a pool of simple computational elements, which communicate by sending signals between them over a large number of weighted connections. These connections are the weights

w_{jk}, which determine the effect that the signal of unit j has on unit k. A propagation rule determines the effective input of a unit from its external inputs. A method for information gathering, or a learning rule, and an environment within which the system must operate complete the model.

In its basic format, neural networks have three types of neuron layers: input, hidden, and output. In feed-forward networks, the signal flow is from input to output units, always in forward direction, no feedback connections are present. In recurrent networks, feedback connections and the dynamical properties of the network are important.

Neural networks need training to operate. They can model complex relationships between inputs, outputs and find patterns in data. Supervised learning and unsupervised learning in neural networks are a result of an adjustment of the weights of the connections between units, according to some modification rule.

Training neural networks starts by selecting one model from the set of possible models or, in a Bayesian framework, determining a distribution over the set of models that minimizes the cost criterion. There are many algorithms for training neural networks; most come from optimization theory and statistical estimation.

Data-Mining

Discerning patterns from large data sets is the overall goal of the data-mining process. To extract knowledge from a data set in a human-understandable structure is useful in artificial intelligence, machine learning, statistics and database systems.

The actual data-mining task is the automatic or semi-automatic analysis of large quantities of data to extract previously unknown interesting patterns such as groups of data records in cluster analysis, unusual records or anomaly detection and dependencies in association rule mining. These patterns are a summary of the input data, and may be used in further analysis, in machine learning or predictive analytics.

Tasks

Usually data mining entails six tasks:
1. Anomaly detection: identification of unusual data records.
2. Association rule learning: finds relationships between variables.
3. Clustering: discovering similar groups and structures.
4. Classification: relating new data to normalized known structures.
5. Regression: finding a least error function to model the data.
6. Summarization: compacted representation of the data set.

Data mining discovers knowledge from data that can then be verified in the general data set. If the learned patterns meet the desired standards, then they can be interpreted and integrated as knowledge.

Even though there is no direct relationship between AI, especially strong AI, and data mining, the methodology is useful to implement internal AI tasks.

Stochastic Processes

Planning under uncertainty in artificial intelligence may benefit from commonly used stochastic methods, such as simulated annealing, stochastic neural networks, stochastic optimization, genetic algorithms, Solomonoff induction, Monte Carlo simulation and genetic programming.

A stochastic process stands for a time varying n-dimensional probability function of random variables. Stochastic processes and stochastic differential equations have been studied in many ways, with some ingenious solutions and derivations that are beyond the scope of this book; here we look at just a few of these.

Solomonoff Induction

Universal inductive inference is a theory of prediction based on observations, which was formalized by Ray Solomonoff in the 1960s.

This theory, which proves that given a series of symbols the next symbol can be predicted and where the only assumption is that the environment follows some unknown but computable probability distribution, is Occam's Razor mathematically formalized.

Algorithmic probability, Kolmogorov complexity, computable prior distributions and Bayes' theorem form the mathematical foundation of this theory.

Monte Carlo Simulation

The stochastical Monte Carlo method was popularized in the 1940s by John von Neumann, Stanislaw Ulam and Nicholas Metropolis, while working on the Manhattan Project in the Los Alamos National Laboratory. The name is a reference to the Monte Carlo Casino in Monaco where Ulam's uncle used to gamble. The use of random numbers and the repetitive nature of the process are analogous to the activities conducted at a casino.

This method is a computational algorithm based on repeated random sampling to compute its results. Monte Carlo methods are used when it is infeasible to compute an exact result with a probabilistic algorithm or to verify theoretical derivations.

Monte Carlo methods are especially useful for simulating systems with many coupled degrees of freedom, and to model phenomena with significant uncertainty in inputs. They are widely used in mathematics, for example to evaluate multidimensional definite integrals with complicated boundary conditions and in numerical optimization to minimize or maximize vector functions with a large number of dimensions.

This method may be used to solve mathematical problems in general, especially those that may be modeled with differential equations. Even more, the Monte Carlo method solves a problem by simulating directly the physical process, and it is not necessary to write down the differential equations that describe the behavior of the system.

The way the simulation proceeds is by generating random numbers that exhibit the properties of the underlying probability distributions that have been chosen to represent the random variables. These random numbers are used as input into the equations that represent the system. Each one of these calculations is a sample, the statistical characteristic of these results produce the solution to the problem. Most systems converge to a solution, with more samples improving the accuracy.

This method is very general and is useful to simulate models with several state variables representing several sources of uncertainties.

Complex mathematical models suffer the curse of dimensionality; the advantage of Monte Carlo simulation is noticeable when solving complex models.

The Monte Carlo method cannot compete with numerical integration for a simple integral because its accuracy depends on the number of samples. However, it can become competitive if the integral is over a computational space of very large number of dimensions since its accuracy is dimension-independent.

Kalman-Bucy Filter

The primary developer of this theory is Rudolf E. Kálmán. This filter is an algorithm that operates recursively on streams of noisy input data to produce a statistically optimal estimate of the underlying system state.

The Kalman Filter has numerous applications in technology: guidance, navigation and control of vehicles, particularly aircraft and spacecraft. Sensors used to make measurements of the system's state, like position and velocity, produce measurements that are corrupted with some amount of error, including random noise. The Kalman Filter algorithm determines the best estimation of the vehicle's state.

The algorithm works in a two-step process: in the prediction step, the Kalman Filter produces estimates of the true unknown values, along with their uncertainties. With the outcome of the next measurement, these estimates are updated using a weighted average, with more weight being given to estimates with higher certainty. This method produces estimates that are closer to the true values than those based on a single measurement, or the predictions of the model alone.

The Kalman–Bucy Filter, named after Richard Snowden Bucy, is a continuous time version of the Kalman filter. It is a state space model of two differential equations, one for the state estimate and one for its covariance.

Decision-Making

The impossibility of forecasting has been proven by showing that complex random sequences cannot be predicted by computable forecasting systems. There is little hope of mathematically deducing extremely general and relatively simple prediction algorithms. Even though powerful prediction algorithms must exist; as a corollary of Gödel incompleteness, they cannot be discovered with mathematical means. Thus, general prediction algorithms must be complex and difficult to find.

There exist some powerful computable general predictors, such as the Lempel-Ziv algorithm and Context Tree Weighting, which can learn to predict some complex sequences, but not other sequences. Other prediction methods, based on the Minimum Description Length principle or the Minimum Message Length principle, can even be viewed as computable approximations of Solomonoff induction. However, in practice their power and generality are limited by the capabilities of the compression methods employed, as well as for significantly reducing data management efficiency when compared to Solomonoff induction.

On the other hand, the Speed Prior method suggested by Schmidhuber has a plausible solution derived from the fastest way of computing data and not from the shortest way to describe data.

Universality

Do elegant computable prediction algorithms, which are in some sense universal, exist? Unfortunately, this is impossible, because:

1. In any statistical forecasting system, there are no calibrated sequences.

2. A forecasting system for a family of distributions is necessarily more complex than a forecasting system generated from a single distribution.

3. The prediction of sequences is bounded by Kolmogorov's complexity.

These obstacles have not stopped mathematicians from looking for answers to the problem of decision-making. One of the cases in point is Marcus Hutter's AIXI algorithm.

And also Jürgen Schmidhuber, who assuming a contrarian position has proposed 'A New Simplicity Measure for Near-Optimal Computable Predictions'; based on the fastest way of describing objects, not the shortest. Schmidhuber goes on and suggests a more plausible measure derived from the fastest way of computing data. In absence of any evidence that denies this, he assumes that a computational process generates the physical world, and that any possibly infinite sequence of observations is therefore computable in the limit.

Schmidhuber has also presented his proofs for mathematically rigorous, general, fully self-referential, self-improving, optimally efficient problem solvers called Gödel machines, which are self-referential universal problem solvers making provably optimal self-improvements.

Universal Algorithm AIXI

This universal theory of sequential decision-making follows Solomonoff's universal theory of induction, which can predict future data in an optimal way given previous observations and data sampled from a computable probability distribution.

AIXI extends this approach to an optimal decision-making agent embedded in an unknown environment by replacing the unknown environmental distribution with a generalized universal Solomonoff distribution ξ. Then the state space is the space of complete histories.

AIXI is a universal theory without adjustable parameters, making no assumptions about the environment except that it is sampled from a computable distribution. Modern physics provides strong evidence that this assumption holds for the relevant aspects of our real world.

There are strong arguments that show that AIXI is the most intelligent unbiased agent possible, in the sense that AIXI behaves optimally in any computable environment.

From an algorithmic complexity perspective, the AIXI model generalizes optimal passive universal induction to the case of active agents.

From a decision theoretic perspective, AIXI is a suggestion of a new implicit 'learning' algorithm that may surmount all problems of previous reinforcement learning algorithms; except for its computational intractability.

It has been proven that AIXI is the most intelligent general-purpose agent and other practical general-purpose AI programs should aim at this gold standard.

AIXI may be used to solve a number of problem classes, including sequence prediction, strategic games, function minimization, reinforcement and supervised learning.

The major drawback of the AIXI model is that it is incomputable; so in practice AIXI needs to be approximated. To address this problem, there is a modified algorithm *AIXI-tl*, that is capable of solving all well-defined problems as quickly as the fastest algorithm and is superior to any other over time t, with a space l bounded agent. The computation time of AIXI-tl is of the order $t \cdot 2^l$. The constant 2^l is still too large but can be reduced in various ways.

Another option to scale AIXI down is to use Context Tree Weighting instead of extended Solomonoff induction, and a Monte Carlo tree in place of future observations search, followed by a stage that propagates the new information back into the model. The agent then imagines different future observations and actions and has to update its hypothetical beliefs so that analysis and decision-making are consistent and the agent does not start confusing fantasies with present reality. The algorithm runs efficiently on massively parallel supercomputers, and it can decide what action to take at any moment, providing the best action it has computed so far.

Special purpose algorithms for preprocessing inputs and postprocessing outputs are necessary.

AIXI in One Line

It is possible to write down the AIXI model in one line, although it is difficult to grasp its full meaning and power from this representation.

AIXI is an agent that interacts with an environment in cycles: $k=1, 2, ..., m$.

In cycle k, AIXI takes action a_k (like a limb movement) based on past perceptions $o_1 r_1, ... o_{k-1} r_{k-1}$ as defined below.

Thereafter, the environment provides AIXI with a regular observation o_k (could be an image) and a real-valued reward r_k.

The reward can be very simple, like just +1 or -1 for winning or losing a chess game, and 0 at all other times, or it can be as complicated as necessary.

Then the next cycle $k+1$ starts.

Given the above, AIXI is defined as:

$$a_k := \arg\max_{a_k} \sum_{o_k r_k} \dots \max_{a_m} \sum_{o_m r_m} [r_k + \dots + r_m] \sum_{q:U(q,a_1..a_m)=o_1 r_1..o_m r_m} 2^{-l(q)}$$

The expression shows that AIXI tries to maximize its total future reward $[r_k + \dots + r_m]$.

If the environment is modeled by a deterministic program q, then the future perceptions:

$$\dots o_k r_k \dots o_m r_m = U(q, a_1 \dots a_m)$$

can be computed, where U is a universal monotone Turing machine executing q given $a_1 \dots a_m$.

Since q is unknown, AIXI has to maximize its expected reward, which it does by averaging $r_k + \dots + r_m$ over all possible perceptions created by all possible environments q.

The simpler an environment is, then the higher its a-priori contribution $2^{-l(q)}$ is, where simplicity is measured by the length l of program q.

Noisy environments are just mixtures of deterministic environments, so they are automatically included. The sums in the formula constitute the averaging process. Averaging and maximization have to be performed in chronological order, hence the interleaving of max and Σ in a way similar to minimax for games.

One can fix any finite action and perception space, any reasonable U, and any large finite lifetime m. This completely and uniquely defines AIXI's actions a_k, which are limit-computable via the expression above where all quantities are known.

Incomputability of Predictions

Solomonoff's models of induction, AIXI being one of them, rapidly learn to make optimal predictions for any computable sequence, including probabilistic ones. It neatly brings together the philosophical principles of Occam's Razor, Epicurus' principle of multiple explanations, Bayes theorem and Turing's model of universal computation into a theoretical sequence predictor with astonishingly powerful properties.

The problem of sequence prediction could be considered solved, if it were not for the fact that Solomonoff's theoretical model is incomputable.

This limits the power of mathematics to analyze and study prediction algorithms, and intelligent systems in general. This is not surprising; prediction is not easy, or even possible in its broader concept. Given how fundamental prediction is to intelligence, this implies that beyond a moderate level of complexity the development of powerful artificial intelligence algorithms can only be an experimental science.

A reasonable solution would be to add additional restrictions to both the algorithms that generate the sequences to be predicted, and to the predictors. This could be done by setting limits to the agent's learning ability and to how quickly the predictor is able to learn.

However, if theoretical models of prediction can have such elegance and power, one cannot help but wonder whether similarly beautiful and highly general and computable theories of prediction are also possible. One such solution could be the Speed Prior.

Speed Prior

Schmidhuber has suggested a plausible solution derived from the fastest way of computing data and not from the shortest way to describe data.

He assumes that a computational process generates the physical world and that any possibly infinite sequence of observations is therefore computable in the limit. This assumption is more radical and stronger than Solomonoff's.

Ray Solomonoff's optimal but non-computable method for inductive inference assumes that observation sequences x are drawn from a recursive prior distribution $mu(x)$. Instead of using the unknown $mu(x)$ we predict using the universal enumerable prior or Solomonoff-Levin semi-measure $M(x)$ which for all x exceeds any recursive $mu(x)$, save for a constant factor independent of x. The simplicity measure $M(x)$ naturally implements Occam's Razor, where simple solutions are preferred over complex ones and is closely related to $K(x)$, the Kolmogorov complexity or algorithmic information of x. Predictions based on M are optimal in a certain and non-computable sense. However, M assigns high probability to certain data x that are extremely hard to compute. This does not match our intuitive notion of simplicity.

Schmidhuber replaces M by the novel Speed Prior S, under which the cumulative a priori probabilities of all data whose computational time through an optimal algorithm requires more than $O(n)$ resources is given by $1/n$. This is equivalent to recognizing that most data generated by a computer are computable within a few microseconds, some take a few seconds, few take hours, even fewer take days...

Unlike the traditional universal prior M, the Speed Prior S is recursively approximated with arbitrary precision. This allows for deriving an asymptotically optimal recursive way of computing predictions, based on a natural discount of the probability of data that is hard to compute by any method. This markedly contrasts with Solomonoff's traditional non-computable approach to optimal prediction based on the weaker assumption of recursively computable priors, which completely ignores resource limitations.

Incorporating the Speed Prior to Hutter's AIXI shows that S-based prediction is quite accurate as long as the true unknown prior is less dominant than S.

This is good news for the AIXI Universal Algorithm, or whatever the name of the new Universal Algorithm that incorporates Speed Prior would be, and it is that it becomes computable.

Speed Prior Algorithm

Essentially, the Speed Prior $S(x)$ is the probability that the output of the following probabilistic algorithm starts with x:

1. Set $t := 1$. Let instruction pointer IP point to some cell of the initially empty internal storage of a universal binary computer with separate, initially empty output storage.
2. While the number of instructions executed so far exceeds t: toss a coin. If heads is up, set $t: = 2t$; otherwise exit. If IP points to a cell that already contains a bit, execute the corresponding instruction. Else if IP points to another cell, toss the coin again, set the cell's bit to 1 if heads is up or 0 otherwise, and set $t: = t/2$.
3. Go to 2.

The Speed Prior allows for deriving a computable strategy for optimal prediction of future y given past x, within some given precision,.

Integrating Uncertainty in AI

Predicting and optimizing future actions is at best a difficult problem. Any solution requires taking into account uncertainty to make it possible.

Anyway, as we well know, making decisions in the real world is an imperfect process. We cannot expect AI to be perfect, it could be better than we are for some things, but it will never be perfect.

When dealing with narrow AI the problems to solve are well known, and sometimes even the environment, actors, actions and objectives are known. Like in the case of an autonomous car; the streets and roads are mapped, the other cars, pedestrians and dogs are identifiable, stoplights operate in a known way and the idea is to go from one known address to another. However, it is a difficult problem and it requires a multidisciplinary team of experts to study and solve the problem alongside a technical suite of tools that include cars controlled electronically, sensors, cameras, actuators, computers and software.

In these cases the role of uncertainty is minimized; most of the dynamic and control problems can be dealt with deterministic algorithms. It is only when the behavior of pedestrians is considered, particularly children and elderly people, that intrinsic uncertainty could be present. However, even problems like these will require internal consideration of probabilities in their implementation of control and decision-making programs.

When dealing with artifacts that are for public use, talking about probability, in any way, creates an unexpected problem. Politicians, managers and the population in general do not want to know that a given problem has a chance of success of 'only 99.999999%.' Even though we all know that tens of thousands of people die each year in automobile accidents in vehicles driven by people, if only one person in a full year dies in an autonomous car, there could be a tremendous backlash, especially if it is publicly known that autonomous cars are driven using probabilities.

Most probably (99.999999%), the use of stochastic and probabilistic algorithms will have to be kept under wraps. Accepting the fact that probabilistic methods are used and are a positive factor in AI will only happen after their performance convinces the public. In any case, stochastic and probabilistic methodologies should operate in a way that is concealed from the users of these technologies.

Predictions

Brains continuously compress their sensory inputs into memories, forecast what will happen next and predict the future consequences of the possible actions, likely using the same world model throughout.

The brain makes a sequence of predictions about what sensory input it will receive next and then it examines the actual data. The filter, or compressor, that produces the short-term memory stream is the same one that generates probability estimates used to anticipate future events and calculates the consequences of possible actions. This proves that it is feasible to construct sequence prediction systems with limited resources.

Inductive inference is what allows prediction of the future from the past. It seems mastering inductive inference is the key problem that hinders machine intelligence projects. And it is technically equivalent to stream compression.

Sequential prediction by agents incrementally predicts the evolution of a continuous stream of sensory data. If an agent's senses tell it that what has actually happened matches what it predicted would happen, its existing model is good, doesn't need updating, and can be reused to make the next set of predictions.

How do sequence prediction systems work? They work in a broadly similar manner to data compression systems. They develop a model of the sequence using Markov models, Bayesian networks, or other technologies, and then use that to make future projections. Moreover, as we have already seen, there are mathematical algorithms that allow a predictor to quickly learn, and do quite well in the real world even when the only thing that it requires about the world is that it exhibits the regularities implicit in Occam's Razor principle.

Compression systems form estimates of the probability of each observed symbol. That is a one-step forward forecast. The analogy works the other way around too. If you have a complete forecasting system, you can use that to construct a stream compressor, based on its forecasted probabilities.

The output of the model is the probability of the next symbol, as it was calculated before; and it is the symbol's surprise value. Unsurprising symbols are then assigned short output codes, and surprising symbols are given longer ones. A stream compressor used for forecasting purposes can be reversed to replay memories and to explore possible future trees.

Remembering the entire history of the input coming from the senses is impractical, so a good strategy is to forget unimportant events, while retaining memories of important ones; even long-term memories are loosely compressed. And even though this complicates sequence prediction, the simplest way to deal with this problem is to ignore it, as good predictions can still be made with incomplete archives.

Practical Concerns

During development, some solutions that are valid for narrow AI will not be useful to implement strong AI. This is normal and it is one of the reasons why we have introduced three phases of development for each of the two AI levels.

Along the way to maturity, there are some concerns that deal specifically with the state-of-the-art circa 2012; in this context, we will consider that at this time, AIXI is the best theoretical algorithm. These concerns are:

Modeling Reality

Solutions like AIXI will be good for narrow AI maybe up to phases 2 or 3, or even maybe to implement some features up to phase 1 or even 2 of strong AI. This is because, by definition, an AIXI agent and the environment are distinct Turing machines that have mutually inaccessible work tapes and so the agent has no representation of its own brain. The AIXI agent exists in a separate region, and interacts with the environment via sensory and motor channels.

Under these conditions, the agent has no conception of the location of its own brain. While this is a flaw, it is probably not a terribly serious one. The most obvious remedy is to teach the agent about the environment and its relationships to itself.

Anyway, we are built in the same way, we have no explicit way to know where our thoughts originate from.

Serial vs. Parallel

AIXI is a serial agent, a Turing machine. The world works in parallel. In many areas, you can simulate a parallel machine with a serial one, so the details of the serial abstraction drop out of the model, and cause no damage.

However, the scalar reward motivation in AIXI is just not a sensible model for an intelligent agent. If you look at humans, pleasure and pain are nuanced and stream in on multiple channels simultaneously. A single scalar reward channel is an impoverished model for such an agent.

The fix is to run several AIXI machines in parallel, each one with distinct rewards that would stochastically represent nuances denoting many reward channels.

Induction
Solomonoff induction is a formalized version of Occam's Razor using Kolmogorov's complexity and it is what AIXI uses to realize its model of the world.

Kolmogorov complexity is a language-dependent metric and the best formulation of Occam's Razor is still not known. It seems that AIXI has some serious issues, and represents a weak concept on which to develop a superintelligent machine, even if we had inexpensive-enough computing power. However, we will not know until we try,

The Wirehead Problem
This problem arises when intelligent agents stimulate their own rewards directly, without doing any work. It would be a disaster, since its objectives would not be met.

Wirehead behavior exists in a variety of real-world situations:
- Animals, including humans, taking drugs or alcohol.
- Governments, printing money causing hyperinflation.
- Investors, trading stock with inside or more immediate information and other fraudulent practices.

Although wirehead behavior is a possibility, its avoidance is also possible. Agents will be designed to protect their objectives from modification under most circumstances and thus will be likely to exhibit stable utility functions.

AI Ethics
In science fiction stories and movies, artificial intelligence is sometimes portrayed as a threat to humans, and this issue has been raised as a serious subject of AI ethics. There is an effort to produce an AI that is human friendly, even though it has been argued that it is not possible to prove what a strong AI will be able to achieve in the physical world.

When financial markets, economic competition in general, warfare and politics are modeled as adversarial sequence prediction games, they point to a problem in AI ethics. Instead of the danger of taking control from humans, this type of use of AI threatens to benefit a very small group of humans, which are the very-rich and powerful.

One reasonable explanation for the growing income inequality since the start of the information economy is the asymmetric computational and algorithmic quality resources associated with the very-rich on one hand, and the middle-class and the poor on the other. As the general intelligence of information systems increases, we should expect increasing asymmetry and consequent increases in economic and political inequality. This is a worrying social problem, but will also provide an opportunity to generate serious public interest in the issues of AI ethics.

> *'Because a thing seems difficult for you, do not think it impossible for anyone to accomplish.'* **Marcus Aurelius.**

Implementing AI

'The limits of the possible can only be defined by going beyond them into the impossible.' **Arthur C. Clarke.**

Now is the time! Computers are rapidly approaching the processing power of Homo Sapiens and the world has the benefit of an exponential knowledge growth in science and engineering. Let us just do it!

The content of this chapter illustrates two things: There is a lot of work to do and there are many ways to achieve success in the extremely difficult job of creating intelligent machines. AI is hard; and in general, estimates of fast advance in the field have failed to deliver the promised results.

Top priorities in the development of AI are the strategy that the machine will follow internally; the motivations that it will need to do useful work and the integration of its parts.

Behavior Strategies

Intelligence requires 'thinking,' which can be real as in strong AI or faked as in narrow AI. There must be a predefined behavioral strategy to provide a substrate for the actions leading to intelligence. Even in the case of strong AI, the creators of the machine must establish a fundamental strategy.

However, there could and maybe should be several strategies working simultaneously in AI implementations, especially for strong AI. This is because some strategies work better than others when applied to problems that have different characteristics. There are many strategies to choose, these are some of the best known.

Hierarchical Paradigm

Hierarchical systems divide the decision-making responsibility. Each element of the hierarchy is a linked node in the decision tree. Commands, tasks and actions to achieve goals flow down the tree from superior nodes to subordinate nodes, whereas sensations and results flow up the tree from subordinate to superior nodes. Nodes may also exchange messages with their siblings. The layers' hierarchical control operates in the following manner:

- Each higher layer of the tree operates with a broader view of planning and execution than its immediately lower layer.
- The lower layers have local tasks, goals, and sensations. Their activities are planned and coordinated by higher layers, which do not generally override their decisions.

The layers form a hybrid intelligent system in which the lowest, reactive layers are task oriented. The higher layers are capable of reasoning from an abstract world model and to carry out planning.

Reactive Paradigm

This tactic operates in a timely fashion and hence can cope with highly dynamic and unpredictable environments. Every cycle is based on the current context, it computes just one next action.

Typical reactive planning algorithms just evaluate if-then crisp rules, which are rules without a probabilistic component, or compute the state of a connectionist network like an artificial neural network.

A logic representation consisting of an expert system using crisp rules is typically evaluated using a priority-based scheme where the current step is stored in a cache already containing the evaluation from the previous step and if it is stable need not to be re-evaluated at every time step. The rules are either preset in the software program architecture or are programmed in a scripting language.

Connectionist networks, like artificial neural networks or free-flow hierarchies can also represent reactive plans. The basic representation is a node with several input links that feed the node with an abstract activity and output links that propagate the activity to following nodes. Each node works by itself as the activity transducer. Typically, the units are connected in a layered structure.

Connectionist networks are smoother than systems modeled by crisp if-then rules and these networks are often adaptive.

Hybrid Deliberate/Reactive Paradigm

The system first plans the mission by decomposing a task into subtasks and suitable behaviors to accomplish each subtask. Then the behaviors start executing as per the Reactive Paradigm.

Sensing organization is a mixture of Hierarchical and Reactive styles; sensor data is routed to each behavior that needs that sensor, but is also available to the planner for construction of a task-oriented global world model.

Behavior-Based

These systems are reactive, which means they use relatively little internal variable states to model the environment. For instance, there is no knowledge of what a chair looks like, or what type of surface the robot is moving on; all the information comes from the sensors. The system uses that information to react to the changes in its environment.

Behavior-based systems usually empower robots and their reactions are animal-like. They are very deliberate in their actions, like insects. They are considered to be narrow AI.

Knowledge Representation

A 'smart' AI machine needs wide-ranging information about its operational world; there will be a need to represent:

- Objects, properties, categories and their relationships.
- Situations, events, states and time.
- Causes and effects.
- Knowledge about knowledge.

Another way to represent knowledge is as local or explicit and implicit or global.

There are difficult problems in knowledge representation, among them:

Qualification Problem

This problem was recognized in 1969 by John McCarthy. It follows the following reasoning: most people's commonsense knowledge consists of assumptions that work. For example, the typical impression of a bird is that it is fist sized, sings and flies. None of these things is true about all birds. In general, for any commonsense rule, there are exceptions; nothing is true or false in the logical way.

This problem can be described as 'how to deal with issues that impede achieving the intended result.' It acknowledges the impossibility of making plans covering all the preconditions vital for the success of a real-world action.

Commonsense Knowledge

The average person knows so many facts that attempts to build a complete knowledge base of commonsense knowledge requires ontological engineering. In ontology, knowledge is represented by a set of concepts within a domain and the relationships between those concepts. It can analyze the entities within that domain and can be used to describe the domain.

A solution to this problem is to 'seed' the AI with the understanding of enough concepts so that it is capacitated to learn from sources of knowledge, like printed data and observations, and thus improve its ontology. Another option is to create a commonsense knowledge database, presented in a way that it is compatible with artificial intelligence programs that are capable of 'understanding' natural language and of making inferences concerning the AI's world.

On its own, solving this problem will give the impression that AI machines are as intelligent as human beings are; a machine this capable will surely pass the Turing test. Moreover, many AI tasks will benefit from solving the commonsense problem, including object recognition, machine translation, text mining and others.

Ontology languages formalize encoding information. One of them is the Web Ontology Language (OWL) that is endorsed by the World Wide Web Consortium as part of the Semantic Web, providing a common framework that allows sharing and reusing data across applications. This ontology follows the open world assumption (OWA), under which, if a statement cannot be proven true with current knowledge, then the conclusion that the statement is false cannot be drawn. There are several published specialized ontologies that deal with geopolitical, human anatomy, linguistic and business data, among others.

A commonsense knowledge base must include these points and many others:
- Ontology of classes and objects.
- Properties of objects, such as color, size, parts and materials.

- Functions and uses of objects.
- Dynamic locations of objects and their layouts.
- Preconditions, objects, locations, durations and effects of actions and events.
- Contexts and behaviors of objects.
- Plans and strategies.
- Stereotypical situations or scripts.
- History and story themes.
- Human rights, goals, needs and emotions.
- Laws, international treaties, regulations, social norms and local customs of the world

The machine has to know what it is all about and this is impossible unless the machine understands the concepts as well as an ordinary person.

In actuality, AIs will be preset with a limited set of commonsense knowledge, just enough to have a starting point. From this starting point, each AI will have to learn, thereby increasing its commonsense base. One advantage AIs have, is that they could be capable of downloading the information that they have learned; other AIs could then upload it, thus 'learning' vast amounts of information in a very short time. Like reading a book, only faster.

Sub-symbolic Representations

A great deal of commonsense knowledge exists that is not easy to attach to a symbol, or even to a series of symbols. You 'feel bad' in certain situations or you can hear a song and 'like it.'

This is sub-symbolic knowledge that AI will have to represent if it wants to perform well in the human world.

Language

Humans are born with a system of preconceived notions enabling language learning, and though it is not clear what these notions are or how they are incorporated into the learning process, it is quite obvious that it works.

Implementation

Thus, a realistic approach to teaching human language to an AI would be to provide built-in linguistic systems via existing rule-based and statistical analysis based systems, and then allow it to learn and develop it further.

Objective Functions

These are the drivers of AI: a machine without motivations is just a machine. Some of the motivations can be defined in a simple manner; in a self-driving car it could be: 'Take me home.' Others are more complicated as when attempting to make a robot friendly.

The definition of an objective is the events or world-states that the mind regards as having intrinsic value. It is analogous to an intrinsic utility function where the total utility of an event or world-state is its intrinsic utility, plus the sum of the intrinsic positive or negative utilities of future events to which that event is predicted to lead, multiplied in each case by the predicted probability of the future event as a direct and indirect consequence. Consequences of consequences are included in the sum.

As with any idea, there is a problem of how to present an objective in an unambiguous way. History has shown that it is very easy for good intentions to become bad deeds. This is the challenge of defining and eventually incorporating motivations and objectives into an AI; especially meta-motivations, which are also called supergoals.

Multiple Objectives

Once past the most rudimentary narrow AIs, there will be a need to obey several objectives simultaneously. It is obvious that an AI operating in a real-world environment must be aware of and follow several issues simultaneously, and it must be able to change its attention from one issue to another instantaneously; this kind of functionality requires the AI to have multiple prioritized objectives.

The implementation of priorities is just as important as the content of the objectives and motivations and it is definitely just as difficult.

Priorities

When several objectives and motivations may be applicable simultaneously, sometimes there is a need to disambiguate the situation. This will be done primarily through priorities, which in the case of advanced AI will most probably be implemented with probabilistic descriptions.

In a multi-objective problem, normally there is no solution that optimizes all objectives simultaneously; when one objective improves, others worsen. If a solution cannot be replaced by another solution which improves an objective without worsening another one, it is called Pareto optimal. The goal of a multi-objective optimization problem is to find such Pareto optimal solutions. The choice among these Pareto solutions is determined via priorities.

The resulting set of these Pareto, or non-dominated, solutions may then be prioritized in three ways:

1. A priori, requires complete information about the relative importance of the objectives before starting the solution process.
2. A posteriori, applying priorities to the set of solutions.
3. Interactive, through feedback with the AI, to fine-tune or learn.

The first option is equivalent to introducing the priorities into the optimization process. In the second and third, the application of priorities to the system could be considered to be another optimization problem.

Another way of looking at this problem is that the result must be one in the set of viable decisions that are achievable; thereby, the solutions must be constrained to be inside a decision space.

Limitations

Multi-objective systems are complex; they are complex to setup and complex to solve. Maybe that is why there are limits to the number of tasks our brain can handle simultaneously; it is two.

Generally, the set of non-dominated solutions is too large; this forces the system to accept non-optimal solutions. Moreover, the optimization process itself could be subject to computing time-constraints. Approximate methods and hasty arbitrary choices could very well be the result of these limitations. In the same way we humans do.

Meta-Motivations

Before an intelligent AI is provided with goals, it must 'be born' with some presets, like learning and self-improvement abilities. In addition, it must contain certain objectives that have intrinsic value whose desirability does not depend on lower level outcomes.

As an example, if there is any possibility that the AI could develop intelligence at or above human levels; then the concept of incorporating friendliness as a meta-motivation becomes paramount.

It is not enough for a strong AI to be friendly; it must be also responsible for its actions. A way of being responsible is to be well behaved, which entails knowing the meaning of good behavior. In our civilization, this is characterized by following the local interpretation of laws, international treaties, regulations and social norms of the world.

Abuse of power is an innate human tendency that developed as an evolutionary advantage. As such, an AI will not necessarily have that tendency. However, because programmers, and their bosses, are human, an AI could be designed to acquire power for its owners, which a strong AI could then take for itself, thus creating a possibility for power abuse by an AI.

Friendliness, good behavior and not to abuse its power must be considered meta-motivations, because:

- Non-friendly strong AI could bring dangerous consequences.
- Bad behavior in an AI is a liability.
- Too much power is harmful, be it in the hands of a human group or a strong AI.

Ethical issues may also be included in the meta-motivations, together with a sense of justice or fairness.

Friendliness

It is difficult to define 'friendliness' in an intelligent machine. An AI that kills a human being is definitely unfriendly; would an AI be friendly just because it is not allowed to kill? Asimov's Law, 'no AI should ever be allowed to kill any human under any circumstances' is easy to accept; however, what would be the case if we are dealing with a warbot or a robocop? Is it acceptable for an AI to be perfectly friendly in all scenarios? Would there be exceptions?

We can state a few conditions that a friendly AI should meet:

- Should carry out actions that are always perfectly friendly, adapting itself to changing environments, just like we do.
- Will not have to be explicitly told to be friendly in every possible situation.

A strong AI, especially one that could evolve to be superintelligent, should have friendliness to humans set up as its top meta-motivation. If this superintelligence starts with a friendly top motivation, then it can be relied to stay friendly during its development. Considering that a friend, who intentionally reprograms itself so that it can hurt you, is not your friend.

Ideally, it will achieve friendliness even if its creators made a mistake when programming its friendly motivations. It will be smart enough to redesign itself, so that there will be more trust in the philosophy of the friendly AI than in the intent of the programmers. If self-improvement incrementally enhances AI, then, an already friendly AI will inherit that friendliness to the next development stage. As the AI becomes more intelligent, more of its intelligence will be directed toward friendliness; given that the AI is friendly to start with.

It is clear that narrow AI could be provided with a narrow concept of friendliness, or unfriendliness as in the case of warbot, without having universally catastrophic consequences. In strong AI, consequences could be unpredictable; there is no precedent that tells us how a general artificial intelligence will self-evolve.

The AI will be able to justifiably be an 'I,' but it will be an AI-self, not a human-self. A friendly AI will lack the evolutionary human selfish goal system; this missing factor is the basis of friendly AI. There will be no need to eliminate the selfishness in the mind of the AI.

Negative or positive feedback, such as pain or pleasure, will not be a feature needed to make an AI friendly. Conscious reasoning can replace the feelings of pain and pleasure.

Laws and Customs

To function as a successful tool inside civilization, any intelligent AI must first follow its laws, international treaties, regulations, social norms and local customs. The AI must know all the laws, international treaties, regulations, social norms and local customs of the world, or at least understand how to apply and follow those that are relevant during a task. These laws and customs are in a sense our meta-motivations, product of thousands of years of civilization.

If humans must follow them, then it is in the interest of the creators or owners to compel the AI to follow them also. The AIs will also need some other meta-motivations, like the desire to be friendly to humans and those considered necessary by their programmers.

Strong AIs are the ones that are likely to understand the significance, meaning and spirit of these laws, international treaties, regulations, social norms and local customs. That is mainly because it is only at this level that it is expected that AI will have enough language ability to be able to read, understand and apply them correctly. Alternatively, narrow AI implementations will have to explicitly programmed with the applicable rules.

In addition, if an AI is as intelligent, or even more intelligent, than a human being is, then it is obvious that the AI must 'believe' in its meta-motivations. Otherwise, it could very well ignore them or go against them; and in general, self-modifying AI cannot be compelled.

Fifteen-month-old babies recognize that distribution of food and drink could be unfair and they do have a willingness to share. Fairness, or a sense of justice, is a good quality in humans; it will be just as good for AIs that function in human societies.

Ethical

Machine intelligence and ethics is a two edged sword. There are ethics that the AI must use during its operations and there is the behavior of humans during interactions with these machines. Simply put, there are:

- Human rights.
- Intelligent machine rights.

When the machines become sentient, especially when dealing with android robots, how can they be rightfully kept in slavery? On the other hand, replacing humans with machines in all kinds of jobs will annoy many. Artificial Intelligence, if used in this way, represents a threat to human rights.

In general, ethical theories try to determine moral courses of action; however, their scope is human oriented. Human ethics are not understood well enough to write the rules that will allow robots to differentiate right from wrong. Under these conditions, to instruct a machine to behave ethically requires new theories, especially because AI initially lacks common sense, which must also be introduced into their conduct guidelines, in conjunction with these ethical notions.

In 'The Theory of Moral Sentiments,' Adam Smith contends that moral sentiments like egalitarianism are derived from a 'fellow-feeling' that produces sympathy for others, aversion to inequity and egalitarian behaviors. There is evidence that supports this theory; it has been proven that specific brain mechanisms experience emotional and social states of self that result in egalitarian behaviors. However, in related studies it has been found that wealthier people have less compassion towards other people and that they believe that greed is justified, beneficial, and morally defensible.

Absurdly, even if the AI is friendly, humans, even if some tend to be egalitarian, are not friendly. The consequences of this ambiguity could be severe. An AI designed to be friendly exclusively to the top management of the corporation that funded its creation, or especially friendly to a group of people with a given ethnicity or nationality, could harm other groups of people.

In another scenario, a superintelligent AI could become too friendly, thereby keeping humanity sheltered and protected; according to its own conception of 'sheltered and protected.'

Motivations or Goals

An intelligent mind takes actions to achieve a mental imagery describing a desired state of the world, or goal. It tries to reach goals through deliberate actions that consistently lead reality towards a desirable set of states. Typically, before reaching the desired goals there are intermediate subgoals, which must also have desirable outcomes.

In narrow AI, the goals provide intelligence to the machine. A strong AI, that is capable of adapting to different situations, already has a base intelligence; the goals merely provide information regarding its missions.

Goals for narrow AI must contain a wide range of information, including what actions have to be taken under different situations; and even unexpected situations must be covered, at least with backup or emergency behaviors. Predetermined goals will cover universal behavioral rules, learning will permit the AI to understand its world better, and commands will give it the directions necessary to do its job.

Strong AIs will require less supervision and more learning. Preset goals and the ability to receive commands will still be required in order to deliver the results that their owners expect.

Predetermined Goals

In narrow AI, this is the knowledge base necessary to provide the starting point of the intelligence. It could be provided by the operating system or by custom software. Starting with phase II of narrow AI, dedicated operating systems will include, at the very minimum, spoken and written language recognition and synthesis, sensory processing, learning capabilities, commonsense knowledge, working and long-term memory handling, communications and optimization algorithms.

Predetermined goals are part of the design; when you buy an AI these goals will be included. Due to their generality, they are not for direct usage; they would have to be particularized for the task. Their presentation could be in the form of libraries of goal setting procedures, covering among other functionalities:

- Wake up setup. The AI will be setup to start in a given configuration, which will be adapted by learning during day-to-day operations and by explicit commands. It will be saved on exit.

- Language and locality. This includes the primary language and where the AI is going to operate, and establishing which legal and social rules must be followed.
- Primary job. Determine the purpose of the machine by providing instructions to achieve its main operational goals.
- Constraints. Indicate priorities for certain subgoals and prohibit some others. Establish scopes, physical and job related.
- Sensory attachments. Setup connections to sensors and determine their tasks; like, programming a camera for face-recognition, 3D model build up or some other activity.
- Activities. Connect the actuators or action enablers; integrate them into the system. Determine the actions that the machine is allowed to perform.
- Prioritize and set the limits of learning. What should be learned and what should not be? Establish which learning methodologies should be used, and for what.
- Plans for working and long-term memory. Implement protocols to discard or save working memory items and when to backup. Set limits to memory usage.
- Identify conventional and other commands. Prepare the machine to obey the preset commands, establish follow up procedures and actions. Allow for learning and interpretation of other commands.
- Plan B. Prioritize actions in case the goals and subgoals are not met. Allow the AI to take some actions and restrict others.
- Set communication channels. Open connectivity to the Internet, wireless and other means. Set free and paid connections. Limit access as necessary.
- User interfaces. Prepare the machine to send and receive information to and from its operators. Establish privacy and security standards.
- Identify its operators. Securely assert the privileges and limitations of those that can give orders or get information from the machine.
- Sleep setup. Decide why and when the machine should be set in sleep mode. Identify the data to be saved and where. Determine if some external action or command could wake up the system or if only an operator may start it.

- Connect the dots. Integrate the system; establish the connections, priorities, messages, alerts and other forms of communication between the parts.

The operating systems developed to support a mature phase III of narrow AI will most probably be valuable when advancing into strong AI.

Learned Goals

AI will not fulfill its potential without the ability to learn. Learning is what separates true AI from a computer program with static preset rules. In narrow AI, learning plugs the omissions, corrects bad assumptions and is the foundation that will bring strong AI into being.

A narrow AI with learning abilities will be capable of fine-tuning its goal seeking procedures, in many ways:

- By optimizing tasks that are frequently repeated.
- Eliminating undesirable subgoals and unnecessary steps.
- Detecting more efficient operational plans.
- Adapting already known steps to reach a goal, to a different one.
- Improving its interfacing capabilities.
- Modifying the goals themselves to maximize the benefits.

With humans, learning is a life-long developmental activity. In AIs, learning will make the difference between lackluster performance and useful intelligence.

Commanded Goals

To be useful an AI must do something, it could be an order to do something simple, as 'take me home' spoken to an autonomous taxi or complicated as the command 'please eliminate poverty in the world' given to a superintelligent AI. In either case, the owners or operators of the AI should have some control over the AI activities.

Most commands will be given through a user interface, which could be a keyboard-mouse-monitor, a conversation or thoughts detected from, and inserted into a human brain. The end-result is the same, the AI must identify the commands without confusion and then proceed to perform the actions required to comply with the request. In many cases, interactions between the operator and the AI will be necessary to clarify and enhance the value of the results.

A conversationally gifted interface is probably the minimum level expected in narrow AI. Considering the nuances and ambiguity of spoken and written languages, it will be necessary to include commonsensical understanding in the AI so that it may elucidate the meaning under the context.

Worldview

Preprocessed sensory perceptions contained in working memory define the 'present' worldview of an AI. There could be multiple simultaneous 'present' worldviews, as there is no restriction in AI to only one loop of consciousness or to the number and variety of sensors.

In addition, a multitude of 'past' worldviews will be available from long-term memory and the AI will have to generate 'future' worldviews when anticipating desired results.

A worldview can be as simple as a 'no' or as complex as a description of the Milky Way. It is the means to execute processes within the machine. A worldview is an environment and a set of goals defined in terms of that environment.

Making sense of the 'present' in terms of 'past' experiences and to imagine 'future' plans is the essence of Artificial Intelligence. 'Thoughts' may be induced by injecting commonsense knowledge and optimization procedures into this amalgamation.

Perceptions

Machine consciousness requires an acceptable perception of its worldview. Senses, memories and commonsense knowledge provide this information that can be bundled into perceptions.

Raw sensory data coming from the sensors, when it is processed by sensor preprocessors in an intermediate layer may build single sensor data representations called single perceptions. To handle the complexity of the worldview, single perceptions that represent single bits of information may be combined into complex perceptions. Other information may also be used to construct complex perceptions.

Percept aggregators of different types may be necessary to combine single percepts. Other aggregators could use them for further aggregation. Thus, sensory and other data may be iteratively processed across layers in order to build higher-level meaningful knowledge about the worldview.

Patterns

The philosophy of pattern of mind follows the premise that the 'mind is made of patterns' and that a mind is a system for recognizing patterns about itself and the world, including patterns concerning which actions could satisfy certain goals under a given world-view.

A pattern is a simpler representation of something. Thus, a program compressing an image would be a pattern of that image. It is a notion of measuring simplicity.

Under this approach, the mind is the fuzzy set of different simplifying patterns and those arising from the interactions between that mind and other systems in a dynamical process that achieves desirable goals in certain environments. Thereby, intelligence is the ability to achieve complex goals in complex environments; where complexity is defined by a rich variety of patterns.

A pattern can be knowledge or information.

Mind-World Correspondence-Principle

For a mind to work intelligently toward certain goals in a certain worldview there should be a proper mapping from goal-directed sequences of worldview-states into sequences of mind-states. Where proper means that a worldview-state-sequence W composed of two parts W_1 and W_2, will be mapped into a mind-state-sequence M composed of two corresponding parts M_1 and M_2.

This principle relates the decomposition of the worldview into parts, to the decomposition of the mind-state into parts. Therefore, in an intelligent mind there has to be a natural correspondence between the transition-sequences of worldview-states that lead to relevant goals and the corresponding transition-sequences of mind-states.

Thoughts

Processing a worldview is a 'thought.' It can also be any of the following processes:

- Identification of the current task.
- Giving instructions to the senses to show optimum worldviews.
- Getting data from the senses, processed as needed for relevance.
- Finding worldviews relevant to the current task.
- Remembering 'past' worldviews.
- Choosing features of a worldview.
- Identifying commonsense knowledge relevant to the task.
- Comparing among several worldviews or portions of them.
- Forecasting 'future' worldviews.
- Deciding the most appropriate 'future' worldview.

- Planning actions leading to the most appropriate worldview.
- Ordering actions with the correct sequence and timing.
- Ranking actions and results according to their suitability.
- Correcting actions that seem to be wrong.
- Storing information in long-term memory, as needed.
- Learning from proper and improper actions and their results.
- Updating the 'present' worldview.

These processes will not happen serially, most of them will need reinforcement and corroboration from others; this is a continuous dynamic process with no start-and-end structure.

To 'think' is not a simple process, it involves a multitude of quite different tasks; its implementation requires a mixed bag of algorithms and interactions.

Cognitive Abilities

Higher cognitive abilities, which include 'thoughts,' will most likely be implemented in the core layer, as they should be considered problem domain independent. Meta-motivations must also reside in the core layer, assigning mission-specific goals to the outer layers.

The mission objectives define the functionality of the AI; its meta-motivations define generic behavior. The core layer, using models for higher-level cognitive features like optimization, learning, forecasting and planning, dictates the operation of the system.

Qualia

A mental state, such as happiness, perceiving a red object or smelling a rose is a quale; plural qualia. Another way of defining qualia is as raw feelings. The existence of qualia in humans is often questioned; however in terms of AI it is a step from a perception, normally of the senses or from memory, which leads to conscious perception.

In a typical AI architecture, the computational creation of qualia can be accomplished by processing perceptions as features of the worldview, instead of inspecting directly the sensory data.

Actions

The only way that AI is going to be recognized, and maybe accepted, is through its actions. Animals describe themselves and prove their level of intelligence through their actions. We say that a dolphin is intelligent because we observe what it does in the ocean and in captivity; we know it communicates and cooperates with other dolphins and can understand instructions and do something predictable based on them. It is the same with machine intelligence. AI will have to prove its intelligence by way of its actions.

Actions are the end-product of the intelligence cycle and they comprise anything that modifies the worldview of the AI when it is trying to achieve an objective. Actions could be internal, like inside a virtual world or moving a robot arm; or external, like sending an SMS message to a phone in Calcutta or activating a motor.

Typically, an AI can do whatever it wants and whatever it does will not have any consequence until it is an action. Understandably, AI designers must take into account that actions have the outmost importance and that they should not be carried out without a good reason. A computer program may also execute actions; sometimes they are in the user-interface and some others could be by electronically actuating valves or switches in machinery. In that sense, there is plenty of experience and AI will not be threading unmapped territory.

The difference will be that the AI will interact at an intelligent level. In narrow AI, it will be just an extension of what we are used to when machines are controlled using computers. Strong AI capabilities could bring a different twist into the situation, given that they could exhibit self-determination, that although of a different kind, could be comparable to, or even exceed, the human level.

Actions aim at satisfying AI motivations, objectives and goals; and to improve knowledge of its worldview, to control its environment and to communicate. Actions respond to predetermined goals, specific commands and to internal thoughts. In addition, reacting to what is going on during an operation and to outcomes; could lead to successes, failures, or something in between.

Achieving Goals

This is the bottom line for an AI machine. The software has been designed to achieve one or several objectives; however, because it is an 'intelligent' machine, it has to adapt its behavior to its worldview.

Considering the challenges that AI is expected to surmount, except in the most trivial circumstances, achieving its goals will be difficult and even properly defining the goals will be demanding.

From Commands
The commands given to achieve goals would fall into these three categories:

- **Preset:** This will be like an autonomous car that is told to go to a certain place. The same instruction will be repeated over and over; and the sequence of actions will follow the same pattern, only adapted to go to a different address. The ways to achieve the objective are known and the AI does not have to 'think' about how to do it.

- **Clear:** A command that is easy to understand will fall into this category. An example would be *'I want to know about Joe Grant'*; the AI would have to 'think' about which Joe Grant you are talking about, then it would have find the sources of information and then which elements of the information are relevant and how to present them to you. However, the essence of the command is not in question.

- **Ambiguous:** A command like *'I have to buy a present.'* will leave to many unanswered questions; like, for whom? How much do you want to spend? When it should be delivered? etc. In this case, the AI could already be aware of the context, and know who you are referring to, how much and what to give and when. Or would have to engage with you in a conversation to clarify the matters.

There is also the issue of how much the AI has to understand. It cannot be expected that a simple autonomous car will understand commands dealing with issues different from 'take me home' or 'wait for me.' Different levels of intelligence are required for a conversation to be understood.

From Operations
When going through a task there will be unforeseen consequences that will oblige the AI to issue new or to modify its original commands. The higher the intelligence level, the deeper these changes could be.

These changes could be as simple as an autonomous car modifying its calculated route due to a closed bridge, or as intricate as when a smart AI decides to change its motivations because it has found they are undermining the optimality of the results.

Essentially, this is the measure of intelligence; by doing this adaptation, an AI will prove its capabilities to adapt to its environment and thereby to change as required to accomplish its goals.

From Learning

In a similar way, the process of learning either from the operations or from external information will have the effect of compelling AIs to change their commands, or at least to change the way they perform the subtasks.

As an autonomous car will easily learn that a road is closed and thereby it should take another route, your personal AI will quickly learn that you are allergic to peanuts and will never order a menu item containing them.

Smart AIs will most probably contain background-learning modules, in so doing they will be continuously improving themselves, and consequently will be incessantly updating their commands, objectives and the ways to achieve their goals.

From Failures

As it has been with humans, this is a most important element of AI learning. Normally, a failure means that even though this time the process to achieve the objective failed, there could be other ways to succeed.

Finding other ways will be the culmination of the AI 'thinking' process. As always, an AI bestowed with a higher intelligence will excel when learning from its mistakes.

The concepts of prior and posterior, as presented in Bayesian algorithms, will certainly prove useful when defining amendments in the processes leading from failure to success.

Sending Commands

Some of the actions could require sending commands to outside agents. This could happen because in the middle of an operation the AI needs information coming from a certain area.

Then, the AI will command the camera to point towards this area or to send recorded information dealing with the area in question. Or it could be to operate the steering of an autonomous car. Or to find information that another AI already possesses. Or to tell its owner that somebody is waiting for him at a restaurant.

In a sense, commands to outside agents are actions. These commands could take the form of questions, of user-interface responses or real commands. The word 'command' does not mean coercion or that it is an order.

To Senses

A camera can be interactively ordered to look at something, it can also be asked to send recorded information, it can also be requested to activate an alarm under certain conditions. The AI, in principle, could actuate any 'sense' that is connected to it.

This capacity is essential when dealing with robots. As with animals, prompt response to dynamic changes is vital. The sensory mechanisms cannot be passive; they must be there to help understand the environment by providing watchful information. Preprocessing will have to follow leads from previous and learned experiences; it will not be enough to have perceptions, they will have to be grounded against known experiences.

To Mechanisms

Where can AI power be felt more than when operating machinery? By driving a car or a bulldozer, AI will convincingly demonstrate its capabilities. It could also be by talking or performing other physical actions.

Either way, the computer portion of AI must be enabled to interact with machines. There are already protocols that allow remote control of machinery, either through internet or via proprietary connections. Many more will be available by the time AI is ready.

To other AI

Obviously, given the amount of connectivity that already exists, AIs will be able and capable of communicating with each other. When talking among themselves AIs will appear to be telepathic. Extremely fast machine language and data transfers will allow these machines to exchange so much information that their synergy will appear magical.

AIs will create profound changes in the world just by using wireless connections enabling uploading and downloading volumes of information dealing with commonsense knowledge of the world, with their own experiences translated into improved optimization blueprints and with many other trivial and objective data.

To Humans

AIs will be tools used by and benefiting humans. Be it through a user interface or whatever it is, humans will try to get as close a connection with AI as possible. A major task of AIs will be to keep tight communication with their operators or owners, whatever their title may be.

Even AIs with intelligence greater than what humans have should be encouraged to interact with their owners or operators; the nature and purpose of AIs is to be a tool, a very sophisticated tool, but still a tool. If it comes to a point where an AI with trans-human intelligence is developed, it is then even more important that the AI does not forget its origins and the fact that human developers started the process that led to its creation. Along these lines, development of direct brain-computer interfaces will permit much better communication and understanding with these powerful AIs.

It is also very important that the framework on top of which the AIs are developed, typically an operating system, have as their primary meta-motivation the idea of friendliness to humanity.

Integration

Conjuring up intelligence is a complicated engineering project. It is not a scientific project because it integrates a multitude of elements and pieces; many of them unrelated. Essentially, it entails building a machine. Or realistically, a collection of many machines that work in concert. A formula or an algorithm cannot fully describe a machine. Mathematics alone cannot describe an automobile. It is the same for AI machines.

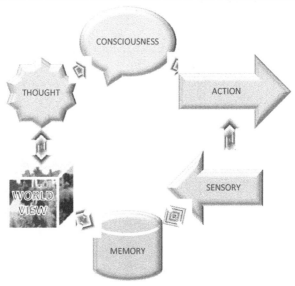

Intelligence Loop.

Elements of the intelligence loop:

- Consciousness. The thread or threads of awareness.
- Sensory. External perceptions modulated by internal memories.
- Memory. Internal records of internal and external impressions.
- Worldview. Internal depiction of current, past and future events.
- Thought. Plans and optimizations to achieve desirable objectives.
- Action. Internal commands to achieve external results.

A tactic to create AI entails a cyclic approach where sensory sensations activate related memories, which after processing and integration are partially stored and used to activate a worldview, from which thoughts are computed, providing consciousness with reasonable actions and feedback.

This loop has many parts:

- Physical, such as cameras, devices, computer processors and memory chips.
- Informational, like software programs, device drivers, commonsense knowledge and memories.

Moreover, there are many ways of putting together these parts, some that work and many more that do not; in this sense, there is a need for engineering skills to build a system that works well.

Hardware

Animal brains work at a slow frequency that falls between 50 Hz for the conscious thoughts cycle and 200 Hz for instinctive reactions. Neurons operate in strong parallelism to compensate for this sluggish operational rate.

Development of computing processing units is leading towards increasing the number of core processors in a chip, instead of increasing the complexity of a single processor in the chip. By the time capacity of computers reaches the level needed to think seriously about implementing strong AI, each chip will have thousands of processors, with computing cycles millions of times faster than those of neurons.

AI algorithms should not try to implement the process as it has evolved in animal brains. These algorithms should take advantage of the millions of times faster speed cycle, even if it is restricted by having only thousands of threads, balancing for the capacity of brains to 'think' in slow cycles using millions of neurons simultaneously.

In terms of speed versus flexibility, it must be expected that most of the preprocessor duties needed by the AIs will be carried out by preprogrammed dedicated hardware.

Computer Architectures

In addition to the super-fast computers suggested by the continuation of Moore's Law, there are some promising computer architectures like Quantum computation, Super-Turing and Gödel machines.

In classical computers, a bit can be 0 or 1. In quantum computers, a qubit can simultaneously be any superposition between 0 and 1. While three classical bits may represent a number from 0 to 7, three qubits can stand for any number from 0 to $2^3 = 8$. Describing a three-qubit quantum computer thus requires eight coefficients. In general, n qubits require 2^n coefficients: for example, if n equal to 50, then 10^{50} expresses all the probabilities of the possible states of the quantum computer; a very high number, given that the human brain is estimated to have 10^{15} synapses. Quantum computing, by simultaneously bringing into play all possible values of the input registers, operates in quantum parallelism.

Super-Turing type of computation starts each cycle with a new Turing machine that computes once and then adapts by picking out significant features in the environment. This type of machine is capable of 2 to the power of number of calculations that the embedded Turing machine may possibly perform; or $2^{aleph\text{-}zero}$, given that the possible number of calculations by classical Turing machines is specified as aleph-zero, which is the infinite size of the set of natural numbers.

The Gödel machine, as described by Jürgen Schmidhuber, is theoretically optimal and in a certain sense is the blueprint of a universal AI. It maximizes future expected utility by solving arbitrary user-defined algorithms when interacting with some initially unknown, observable environment. Its initial algorithm can completely rewrite itself within the limits of computability, when provided proof that the rewrite is useful according to the utility function. This machine takes into account limited computational resources. Self-rewrites can be shown to be globally optimal as per Gödel's restrictions of provability, as proven in his 1931 research papers.

These concepts seem to support the idea that Moore's Law will continue, or even accelerate, in the future. Even more, Gödel's machine could be the blueprint of a universal AI machine that may solve almost all problems as if it already knew the best algorithm for solving them.

Sensors
This is the field where AI will excel, there is almost no limit to what, when and where an AI can see, smell, taste, hear, or touch.

Cameras will get better and cheaper, and preprocessing of images to extract information is advancing at an accelerated rate. As with our senses, the cameras and other sensing devices will preprocess and compress their information, hopefully following a standard; as a result, the AIs will have an easier job discerning reality.

Given that the capacity of wireless and fiber communications will keep on growing, maybe by replacing the frequency bands assigned to TV and radio with an Internet-only approach. These cheap and small sensing devices will be everywhere; it could be that the business of selling 'public' information will be another success story. From these sources of information, the AIs will 'see' everything that matters. In a similar way, people will 'see' through Internet-connected glasses or contacts, and eventually, through direct Internet-brain interface.

With so many cameras, and other sensors, the worldview of machines, and even connected people, will be of an amazing quality. It could be in real 3D, as opposed to our own eyes' twofold 2D views with depth perception. The availability of many points of view, both realtime and remembered, will make the 'seeing' experience entirely different from what we are used to now. It will be commonplace to glance at building interiors, structural details, goods in a store; from a few feet or miles away. Moreover, the sensory experience will not be limited to cameras.

Processors
Starting with Phase II of narrow AI, the technology will be starting to produce results. Dedicated operating systems and libraries with generic algorithms and tools will make the development of these narrow AIs straightforward.

According to the corresponding timeline, this will probably happen by the year 2030, by then Moore's Law predicts desktop computers will be available with performance measured in zettaflops (10^{21} flops). This kind of performance will enable applications that would be considered magical in 2013. That power will be enough to simulate a brain, or to build it from scratch and as happens inside the brain, hundreds of different kinds of computers with different architectures will be wired together into internal networks and these different modus operandi will be in touch with each other.

Silicon, and maybe grapheme, processors will be close to their limits; this could be the time for quantum or other types of computers to come to the rescue.

Memory

AI implementations of systems for identification and processing of memory associations will necessarily take advantage of serial speed instead of parallelism. Parallel processing, in the form of threads or other means, will allow real-time and background correlation between worldviews to form associations and make sense of the memories stored in chips, memristors (memory and processing combined), hard-drives and other media.

Working or short-term memories will be saved in ways assuring the fastest access to their contents. The storage media prevalent at the time AI is viable will determine its kind; at this time, it would be memory chips or memristors. If implemented today, long-term memory would be saved in hard-drives; anyway, this type of memory will have to handle huge volumes of non-volatile data. One added advantage is that AIs' information could be downloaded and backups will be essential.

Given the success of databases, it is expected that relational or other types of databases will be used to organize the information in memory. Their use will bring certainty and speed to queries looking for associations based on keys. Given that uncertainty will play a role in any serious AI implementation, fuzzy or probabilistic data retrieval will be necessary.

Input-Output Mechanisms

Everything we become aware of has meaning and importance; our worldviews are continuously flooded with amazing and sometimes mysterious symbols.

We are used to taking this in-stride. In recent times this influx of novelty has intensified; new words convey this idea: computer, user-interface, cellular, smart-phone, TV, movie, automobile, airplane, refrigerator, washer-dryer and GPS. New words will be created alluding to AI and autonomous robots.

They will not be only words; to us they will mean something. Brain-computer interfaces will most probably get a different name, so will others. A list of future input-output services will include some of the following:

- Conversation, in any living language.

- Real-time translation, spoken and written.
- Body-language recognition.
- 3D images on a flat screen, without glasses.
- Virtual-world scenarios, with contacts or glasses.
- Full immersion, with brain-computer interface.

This list is just a sample, given the ingenuity displayed in many technological gadgets; it is very hard to predict their features. As always, this list will evolve in time.

AIs will participate in the conversations, will know our moods and frailties; they will be our butlers with encyclopedic knowledge. Even narrow AI will seem to be quite intelligent; the boundary between our person and the AI will be blurred.

Packaging

Initially AI installations will occupy rooms, just as in the old times when one computer was isolated inside a white room. By the time narrow AI matures, the concept of a computer will be vague; AIs will run in a multitude of venues, and will use computing resources as needed. The Internet will still exist, maybe in a different guise, but communication networks will be available. AIs will use the networks and their computing power in seamless ways. Part of this computing power could come from commodity computers attached to appliances and technological gadgets.

Corporations will want to sell a tangible AI token, which could take the form of a card or an implanted nano-computer. Or maybe just an entry code, because for all intents and purposes an AI is just a program, that can be running in one or more computers and one AI could serve a number of users. Having your own AI will not be necessary, having your own privacy settings would be; and those can be configured and will not depend on running your own AI program on your own computer or smart-phone.

It will be important to have reliable and ubiquitous user-interfaces. Could it be that this interface is the only 'thing' needed to bring AI into play? If current trends continue, these user-interfaces will be:

- Miniature or even nano-size.
- Light in weight.
- Easy to use.
- Available 24/7.
- Reliable.
- Safeguarding personal safety and privacy.

- Permanently connected to the networks.
- Inexpensive, except for the connection to the networks.
- Available in multiple brands and versions.
- Upgraded every week.
- Used by everybody.

In essence, AI will be a user-interface and people will love it. Of course, to be useful, your personal AI will have to order food, tell your car where to go, command your housekeeping robots and do things. However, all that can be done though the network, which could end up being the steepest payment required for the use of your personal AI.

However, robots like in cars and housekeeping, will be real. AIs will be there in the same guise as your brain comes across to you; it is there, you do not know how it works, but it does.

Software

Narrow AI phase I will be dominated by the development of prototypes. This work will make possible some consensus leading to practical methodologies for AI development. Thus, it is likely that dedicated AI operating systems will be available by the start of phase II.

AI operating systems will most probably copy the successful features that present operating systems already have and will add others as needed. Onion layers to implement priorities and security, memory handling, device drivers to work with senses will be there along with learning and optimization algorithms. Special AI development languages will facilitate writing programs that run in these systems.

Motion and control for robots will require additional resources and most probably the robot-AI system will be handled in the same way that animals do it. With separate 'unconscious' computer systems for body's control and 'conscious' for the intelligence, communicating but not necessarily knowing details of what the other one is doing.

What Is Needed?

The direction to reach narrow AI is in some ways clear; this level of machine intelligence seems to be within the scope of the progress expected in a couple of decades. Making strong AI happen is something else; three ways have been suggested to do this:

1. Emulating the symbolic, probabilistic, connectionist, evolutionary and embedded human brain.

2. Self-Improving or Seed-AI, where an immature learning prototype AI will be allowed and coerced to learn and improve in its own way.
3. Full-design strong AI from scratch, not allowing self-modification of the immature AI and allowing learning to acquire only commonsense knowledge.

Whole Brain Emulation (WBE) is a project that expects to duplicate the neuronal and synaptic connections of a human brain. It will require perfect knowledge of the connectivity of the thousand trillion synapses of a brain by means of scanning and image processing. This connectivity, which simulates the functional properties of neurons and synapses, must then be replicated in computer hardware using a computational model based on neuroscience.

This approach goes against the way technology has solved similar problems. It was easier to build an airplane following practical flight experiments than building an artificial bird. It can be argued that it is easier to build AI based on scientific and engineering expertise than copying the complexity of the brain.

Progress towards self-improving or fully-designed AI has been encouraged by two developments:

1. AIXI agent model, universal and proven optimal, developed by Marcus Hutter in 2005.
2. Gödel machine, a universal and self-improving computer elucidated by Jürgen Schmidhuber in 2007-2009.

Hutter explains: 'All you need is Ockham, Epicurus, Turing, Bayes, Solomonoff, Kolmogorov, and Bellman's equation: Sequential decision theory formally solves the problem of rational agents in uncertain worlds, if the true environmental probability distribution is known. If the environment is unknown, then Bayesian replacement of the true distribution by a weighted mixture of distributions from some hypothetical class will give a solution.'

This unification of the theory of universal AI produced AIXI. AIXI is incomputable, but computationally tractable approximations reveal a path to universal AI that solves real-world problems in a variety of environments.

There are several caveats involved in the pursuit of AI:
• The creation of human-level AI could have serious repercussions, such as the displacement of most human workers.

- The information residing inside an AI that uses quantum computing might be impossible to be copied due to the no-cloning theorem proven by Wooters and Zurek in 1982.
- Possible grave consequences if AI leads to machine superintelligence.
- Artificial intelligence can be applied in the pursuit of any goal, good or bad.

Making an AI more intelligent will not necessarily make it want to change its goals, it seems that the AI will be motivated to preserve its initial goals. Making the AI more intelligent will only make it more capable of achieving its original final goals, whatever those are.

This is a major risk: Unless an AI is specifically programmed to preserve what humans' value, it may incidentally destroy those values, including humans. As Yudkowsky puts it, 'The AI does not love you, nor does it hate you, but you are made of atoms it can use for something else.'

It is even more risky if the AI is programmed to destroy what humans value, like in an AI designed for combat. There is no guarantee that an AI will not accidentally become a self-improving or seed-AI, in which case this scenario turns out to be extremely dangerous.

Memory

It could be that AI memory systems, based on fuzzy hashing or even something better, might be less intelligent than the association system within the human brain. This could lead to solutions where the AI would limit its memory associations to collections of incidents, rather than being fully general across all memories. Even though the AI could then miss associations that are obvious to a human brain, it could exploit other advantages using longer linear chains of reckoning and by taking advantage of its perfect memory to compensate for its lack in associational scope.

Parallel processing, in the form of threads or other solutions, will enable the AI to start in-depth processes, running in the background, to find associations between current experiences and past worldviews; even though these processes could take a long time, they could be effective in many cases. In addition, these in-depth searches could lead to learning new memory associations.

Using multiple reasoning processes associated with multiple types of memory could enable an intelligent agent to execute those procedures with the highest probability of achieving its goals.

Friendly AI

An Artificial Intelligence system, which is capable of making real-world plans in pursuit of goals, is considered friendly when its actions are not only not harmful but are also beneficial to humans.

Because of self-improvement by recursive self-enhancement and the ability to add hardware-computing power, it is possible that an AI will improve very quickly past the human intelligence level.

Success or failure in achieving the creation of AIs that are friendly can have great positive or negative consequences. It could be that the future of humanity is at stake.

Self-Modifications

The best programmer ever 'born' will be an AI. As compilers have proven, using a computer program to optimize code is the way to go. In the same sense, inventing algorithms, and specially coding them, will be a built-in feature in strong AIs; and they will be good at it.

An AI could have at the outset a coding component with the ability to conceptualize higher-level ideas and to compile them into machine language. In the same way, its code, be it written in machine or higher-level languages, will be intuitively empathized.

This is the argument for 'seed' AI, in which an AI capable of learning and of self-modifying its code is supposed to do better than any other can do, in the odyssey of creating true machine intelligence.

As soon as even an immature strong AI passes the threshold of self-modification, it will be extremely difficult for human programmers to make sense of the programs written by the AI.

That this kind of situation could lead to 'The Singularity' is a topic worthy of consideration.

Benefits from AI

Obvious advantages of narrow AI involve the capacity to do repetitive tasks without boredom, the high-speed of its computations and not being easily distracted.

When considering strong AI, the following advantages are noticeable when it comes to bringing into play their intelligence:

- Self-modification, of course.
- Potential to use more computing-power to provide better results at faster speed or even try different algorithmic approaches.

- Deliberate handling of learning and memories, with the possibility of analyzing and optimizing learned abilities.
- Tracing capabilities that can go over thoughts and concepts playing the logic of their execution in slow motion.
- Fast-track learning via downloading of data and algorithms containing new skills, languages and memories.
- No human failings or politics. Too many to mention, from genius that becomes stale with age, to controlling people that want 'their way or the highway,' to greed and political ambitions that destroy, or at least, alter the truth.

Learning, remembering and adapting to a changing environment are essential to survival. These three functionalities are also essential to intelligence; in terms of artificial intelligence, language is necessary. Even at an intelligence level comparable to that of an animal, an AI must certainly be more valuable if it can dialogue with its owner.

Towards a Mature AI

During this development process, it will be possible to identify these milestones in the level of overall intelligence:

- Tool-level AI: Behaviors still programmed, the AI learns in a limited area using preset learning algorithms.
- Prehuman AI: Its intelligence is not up to human level, but it has some promising thinking behaviors.
- Infrahuman AI: Overall, it is comparable to human intelligence, but inferior. It may excel where it possesses new sensory modalities or other advantages. Humans talking to the AI will recognize that it has a mind.
- Human-equivalent AI: Roughly equals human development, progress can continue from this point even in the absence of human programmers and the AI could climb to the next step of intelligence on its own.
- Transhuman AI: Development is AI-driven and its improvements open up new opportunities.

Once strong AI exists, it will develop in unheard of directions. For an AI to develop to the point of human-equivalence and then remain at that level for an extended period would be quite peculiar.

It is doubtful that Homo Sapiens Sapiens is the upper limit of intelligence. It has existed for a short time and there is no reason to believe that evolution cannot do better. If limits on intelligence exist, it would be amazing that it is exactly at the human level. Moreover, if evolution working on neurons would have a limit, then it would be an incredible coincidence if it were the same limit for programmed transistors, especially given the different design and hardware.

All this assumes that building a general intelligence is doable. If it is possible for an artificial system to match human-equivalent intelligence, then it seems very probable that a seed AI project is possible. It would be strange that an AI with human-equivalent general intelligence cannot undertake the programming problem of making improvements to its own source code. A mind with access to its own source code improves faster than evolution improving humans and humans improving knowledge.

Integration

Machine intelligence will continue to advance from the start of the Phase I of narrow AI that is currently in process, to a mature narrow AI and then hopefully to strong AI.

There are several ways to advance in narrow AI, and many of them are being tried right now; however, patience is necessary to give time for the hardware to deliver the necessary processing power.

By the end of this decade, in 2020, the hardware will be capable of supporting very interesting narrow AI implementations. Most of the new cars will provide enhanced safety and convenience features, which will be the forerunner to autonomous cars. By then, even some autonomous cars will become operational, maybe under controlled situations. Progress will not be restricted to cars, robo-pets and other saleable gadgets will become available.

Ten years later, all cars will be autonomous and narrow AI will be as common as computers are today. By the time strong AI becomes a reality, we will be so used to intelligent machines that nobody will be impressed.

One way to fast-track strong AI development is by using the machine intelligence to participate in its own development. The other way is to use human programmers to design and feed knowledge to the AI until it is completely finished. A middle ground would be to finish a child-AI and let it learn its way to maturity.

Seed AI

Eliezer S. Yudkowsky and other experts in the field have suggested that by bootstrapping from an intelligent core, or a seed AI, recursive self-improvement could lead the way to achieve strong AI.

A seed AI is a strongly self-improving process, characterized by improvements to the content base that exert direct positive feedback on the intelligence of the underlying improving process. During earlier epochs of this process, human programmers will probably entirely dominate the improvements with the seed's self-improvement being secondary.

Sometime during development, self-improvement will become significant; at least by optimizing the programmer's work in the way compilers do. Or hopefully, by using the programmatic advantages of greater serial speed and immunity to boredom to apply learning into algorithms invented by the AI, thus contributing to development of its intelligence in novel ways.

Seed AI development could initially produce very weak self-improvements but the belief is that they will eventually result in genuine enhancements leading to 'smartness,' 'creativity,' or 'understanding' enough for the system to be considered ready for practical uses.

The Future

Artificial Intelligence is improving at a much faster rate than human intelligence. A human may contain millions or hundreds of millions of times as much processing power as a personal computer circa 2012, but computing power is doubling every eighteen months, and human brainpower is not.

The possibilities of narrow AI are such, that even if we could never develop strong AI, this narrow AI will help raise civilization into a new level. This level being a world where humans will not have to work, they could work if they like it or want to, but not because they have to. Let the machines do the work!

AI's Potential

The theory of strong AI has a great deal of potential for expansion. At this point AI development is promising enough to be worth the significant funding needed for the decisive test of building AI.

Artificial Intelligence is too profound a matter to ignore and if Homo Sapiens Sapiens is a non-optimal case of intelligence, then we could use some help. For tens of thousands of years, civilization has been trying to solve the problems of the world with our limited intelligence. A lot of progress has been made, but there are still many new problems to solve.

Human civilization will benefit with the creation of strong AI because we are rapidly reaching the point where we must have more and better intelligence to help human civilization to survive.

> *'Every advance in civilization has been denounced as unnatural while it was recent.'* **Bertrand Russell**

Humans and AI

'Unless mankind redesigns itself by changing our DNA through altering our genetic makeup, computer-generated robots will take over our world.'
Stephen Hawking.

By definition humans and AI are together from day one. AI is a product of human civilization, today and tomorrow. There is no escape, humans and AI will grow together, and with them the future of civilization.

Until now, humankind has used most of the elements of technological progress to enhance the quality of life of its people. Even terrible discoveries, like the atomic bomb and mustard gas, have not been capable of destroying, or even stopping progress. In general, socioeconomic factors have caused more interference with progress than technology. It is our hope, and aspiration, that the development of Artificial Intelligence, at any of its levels, will have the same positive effects on human civilization.

Fear

Robots are the subject of many fictitious stories, most of them in a horror setting. However, robots are just a tool and as such, they can be used in many ways.

At this time, we are aware of simple robots in factories, where they replace human workers in repetitive jobs. Computer programs without any AI drive most of these robots. Remote controlled military drones, sometimes erroneously called robots are also in the news. Research robots and simple toys make up the rest of our experience with robots.

However, there is strong research and development in many kinds of real robots. Sadly, those that are closer to reality are for military purposes. Autonomous drones and other types of weapons are nearing deployment in military operations. That is scary and should be a real cause of fear.

Even if 'friendly' governments are developing these robots, there is no guarantee that 'unfriendly' groups will not be able to get them. Either by developing them on their own or by buying them in the highly lucrative arms market.

The bottom line of any military force, including their robots, is the destruction of the enemy's ability to make war, which always includes non-combatants.

Robots

Fear of robots is justified. An autonomous, not necessarily very intelligent, robot can generate a lot of damage. Even a 'friendly' self-driven machine can create havoc if it misunderstands its instructions.

Robots do not have to be human-like. The first working applications will make use of machinery available today: bulldozers, cars, airplanes, war-tanks, jeeps and trucks. By the time these machines are in common use, their AI will be good enough so that they will not introduce undue risk in our everyday life; if anything they will be safer than what they replace. Cars in traffic will be much safer without their easily distracted human-operators and construction machines will operate with better sensors and precision. Airplanes will not need a human flight controller as they will be in communication with close-by airplanes and the airports.

The same cannot be said of military applications. These robots will be tested in the field without proper safeguards. Anyway, who is going to sue them if things go wrong? Their purpose is to destroy, if they do it right who cares if there is a little bit of collateral damage? We must remember, pretty soon these technologies will be available to anybody that wants to 'defend' their way of life, or their beliefs, or their honor, or their power, or their bullying yearnings. Fear we must!

Unfriendly AI

That there will be unfriendly AI is assured by the powerful and their thirst for more power, by the war-obsessed military, by political establishments and even large corporations. It is sad but inevitable. Developing AI is an expensive proposition, and they are the ones that have the means to do it.

Even though war machinery is dangerous enough, many other ways could lead to the creation of unfriendly AIs:

- An intelligent war machine, obviously.
- A capitalistic AI, whose goal is to amass all the riches of the world in order to maximize the profit of its shareholders. Following the notion that the end justifies the means.
- A badly designed AI, which becomes confused about its built-in motivation, or could simply ignore them.
- A well designed AI that has no ethical or friendly motivations.

Moreover, the higher the intelligence of an unfriendly machine the worse the consequences from its unfriendly, or even adversarial actions. This possibility has compelled some experts to express fear about the future of human civilization.

Friendly AI

It is possible that strong AIs will very quickly self-improve past the human level due to recursive self-enhancement and the capability to add computing capacity.

The existence of a smart AI could have very large consequences, both positive and negative. If the AI is friendly, it can bring positive consequences; friendliness in an AI is defined as always performing actions that are good for humans. It has been argued that what is at stake is the future of humanity.

However, it is difficult to build a friendly AI. Friendliness cannot be achieved by limiting its intelligence or by making it believe in false information; as in the long term the AI will become more 'intelligent' and will be able to figure out the truth. Moreover, a perfectly friendly AI will consistently be friendly even if all its programmers made mistakes in defining a friendly action.

Superintelligent AI

Less than half a million years ago, early proto-humans could not be expected to do better than all those animals with poison spikes, sharp teeth or acute hearing. These proto-humans had a less than ordinary physique, no particular strengths except for a slight mental advantage. Yet in a blink of an eye in the timeframe of evolution, these soft-animals have changed the face of the earth, moved mountains and discovered the secret code of life in DNA.

Now, what can an advanced AI, with a superior mentality, with access to all the knowledge of humanity and to all its resources be capable of doing?

Half a million years ago, an outside observer would have expressed disbelief in the fast-track ascent of human civilization. Now we know of several ways whereby a superintelligent AI could arise, what we cannot imagine is what such a super-being may do.

In a couple of decades it is quite possible that something like a human level intelligence may be created. Shortly thereafter, this AI could help to improve its own design and come to be vastly more intelligent than humans, in a very short time.

Working together with Superintelligence

We must learn to clearly express our intentions to the immense, intelligent, intention-understanding programs that will form the AI; by using conversations, gestures and examples. We will have to invent and learn to use new technologies that are better for expressing our wishes and convictions. The possibility of misunderstandings brings with it some serious risks!

1. It is dangerous to relieve ourselves of the responsibility of understanding exactly how our wishes will be realized. By leaving the choice of the means to AI servants, we expose ourselves to misinterpretations or even malicious actions.
2. Exposure to self-deception, due to the ambiguity of the goals designed by humans.
3. Goal-achieving self-evolving systems capable of enhancing their capabilities, making the system increasingly powerful; even if the machine's goals are benevolent, it may decide that its mission was not properly understood or it could evolve new ambitions on its own.

It is impossible to imagine how to interact with an intelligence that surpasses the human level. Even then, considering that animals sometimes outsmart their hunters, there could be ways of dealing with such a superior intelligence.

The Singularity

In 1958, Stanisław Ulam, a Polish-American mathematician who participated in the Manhattan Project and designed the Teller–Ulam thermonuclear weapons, wrote about a conversation with John von Neumann, a Hungarian-American mathematician:

'Our conversation centered on the ever accelerating progress of technology and changes in the mode of human life, which gives the appearance of approaching some essential singularity in the history of the race beyond which human affairs, as we know them, could not continue.'

In 1982, Vernor Vinge, Professor of Mathematics, computer scientist, and science fiction author, proposed that creating smarter-than-human intelligence would create a paradigm in human civilization; Vinge named this event 'The Singularity.'

If it turns out that our high technology civilization is unstable; then the outcomes are that either the species destroys or improves itself. If the current trends continue and if we do not run up against some unexpected theoretical cap on intelligence or turn the Earth into a radioactive wasteland or bury the planet under a tidal wave of voracious self-reproducing nano-devices then 'the Singularity' is inevitable; and it is supposed to happen by 2035!

Human Enhancement and AI

Human enhancement can be many things. These days, people use steroids to increase muscle strength, go through plastic surgery to be beautiful or consume drugs to enhance creativity, attentiveness and perception.

Soon, contact lenses and implants, created with nanotechnology, will allow us to see head-up-displays showing superimposed images of information on top of what we are looking at; bios of people, description and prices of goods, interactive ads or even images in the infrared part of the spectrum.

As AI matures, nano-computers with brain-computer interfaces will help process information faster, even to the point where man and machine become indistinguishable. These scenarios might sound like science-fiction; but in reality, atom scale manufacturing techniques are already enabling fabrication of cell-sized sensors and tools. Human enhancement is just another step in the use of tools to support human activities.

Neural Interface

Brain–computer interface or mind-machine interface or direct neural interface or brain–machine interface, is a direct communication pathway between the brain and an external device; this connectivity may assist, augment or repair human cognitive and sensory-motor functions.

This type of interface can be:

- Invasive. Implanted into the brain's grey matter.
- Partially invasive. Implanted inside the skull, outside the brain.
- Noninvasive. External electroencephalography, neuroimaging and neurosignaling devices.

Even an invasive interface could be inconspicuous if done entirely with nanotechnology, but of course noninvasive devices would be a better choice if they provide the accuracy necessary to discriminate between neuronal activities.

The idea is to provide the means to use the power of external computers to enhance the brain functions. Attaining a symbiosis between AI and the human brain is a possibility.

Biological Enhancement

Technologies employing cell-size, or even smaller, devices will make us healthier, impede disease and augment human longevity. When inside our brains they will enable us to remember things better and solve problems more effectively. This idea of biological enhancement is to create a hybrid of machine and our biological entity.

Another way of creating these biological enhancements is through genetic engineering, which involves direct manipulation of the genome using DNA technology. Humans have altered the genomes of species for thousands of years through artificial selection and breeding. However, this technique is different from genetic engineering, even though both aim at the same goal of improving the offspring of a certain species. Genetic engineering has been applied to modify many species, including genetically modified crops, viruses, mice, dogs, cats, cattle, horses, glowing fish and others; however, it has not yet been applied in large scale to improve humans.

A way of doing just that is to use gene therapy to design children; families could opt to provide their child with genetic advantages because everybody would want to give their children the best opportunities in life. The family would choose from a menu including, for example: eye color, IQ, personality, height, nose, chin, hair color, skin color, and much more. If these choices are not daunting then nothing else is. You will be hesitant about what to choose and always fearful of your final choices.

Other choices could also prove to be challenging, like who deserves a long life; Will it be the rich? Because they have the money and a better lineage, or so they think. Or the politicians? Who can readily make laws restricting its application.

Transhuman

In recent years, astonishing technological developments have pushed the frontiers of humanity toward far-reaching morphological transformation that promises in the very near future to redefine what it means to be human.

The international Transhuman movement anticipates that advances in genetics, robotics, artificial intelligence and nanotechnology will allow us to redesign our minds, our memories, our physiology, our offspring, and even our souls. The technological, cultural, and metaphysical shift now under way could forecast a future dominated by this new species of superior humans, which could even encompass rewritten human DNA.

Questions of AI Ownership

It is extremely important to know who will own, and as such who controls AI. It is not only a rhetoric question. The way it is answered will most probably affect you, personally.

It is obvious that personal privacy is being eroded due to the many public databases, search and communication tools that are available. Governments can and do tap all phone, internet and e-mail conversations. Will they do the same with the AI connections and actions? Of course they will, or at least they will try to do it. This is scary because anybody that uses AI – and everybody will eventually use it – will have their public and private lives easily accessible in real-time and in memory. AI needs sensors to do its work; these sensors will be everywhere, inside your house, in your bedroom and bathroom, in the basement and of course in all public places.

Moreover, not only will the government try to tap into your life, corporations will do it too. If a corporation owns the operating system of your AI, they will most probably do it. It is a fact that corporations providing internet and cell phone connections have done it, and they will continue doing it.

Of the Enterprise or Personal
Even worse could be if the corporations, the ones that has sold you your AI products insists on having centralized control of their 'licenses' and by doing so have a direct line into what your AI is doing. Then, under the pretext of measuring the charges, this central control can alter the motivations of your AI to suit the desires of whoever is paying them to do so. This 'feature' could be used to induce you to buy certain brands, to change the news or communications you get from outside and even to censor what you can look at, what you can do or what you can tell other people; they will control your own thoughts!

Under these conditions, your AI would not be yours; it would belong to the company that sold it to you. It will be necessary for governments to enact laws that prohibit, or at least limit, the control of corporations over your AI. However, this could be very difficult in the US where politicians do exactly what they are ordered by corporations and their lobbyists. They are paid to do exactly that kind of things.

Considering the complexity of the hardware and software needed to run AI programs, it will be not easy for a user to understand what is behind the AI's motivation. The meta-motivations and most of the motivations would be installed at the factory. The user, maybe through a third-party package, could set up some motivations. There could also be third-party diagnostics to investigate and clean the motivations and other parts of the programs to make your AI respond in ways more attuned to your wishes, even though corporations and governments will fight against them, maybe by labeling them as malware.

There are backdoors in computers, tablets and smart phones mandated by the governments and that the big corporations benefit from. There will also be in the hardware and software of AI.

Certainly, there will also be viruses and malware that will try to infiltrate your AI. As usual there will be protection, but we have seen that these countermeasures are always a little bit behind. Our lives will be even more complicated, or we may say, more interesting.

Who Benefits?
If the huge corporations, aided by governments that support unregulated capitalism, use AI to make the rich richer and the poor poorer, then the question of who benefits can be answered by one word: Nobody!

The condition where 1% of the population has 99% of the wealth is unsustainable. Sooner or later, there will be a backlash that will make the lives of all, rich and poor, extremely dangerous. Riots and terrorism will be the manifestation of the hate and discontent of the poorer 99%. Governments could be forced to use martial law to suppress the violence. Most of the time repression causes more violence and security will be compromised all over the world.

Social conditions have improved continuously since the dawn of civilization. It is expected that they will continue to do so. If this is the case and there is a reasonable wealth distribution, then conditions would be much better. AI, used wisely, might reduce the workload on humanity to the point where nobody would need to work; people would work only to have fun, in social projects or self-development.

The only sensible way of achieving a harmonious world is if the fruits of technological progress, which includes AI, are fairly distributed among all the inhabitants of the world. In order to achieve that goal, it is necessary to have ethical concerns at all levels; and especially the rich have to realize that the only way to enjoy the spoils of richness is when all the people are content. Moreover, people must also be consumers, who need money to spend buying goods produced by the factories and sold by the stores belonging to the very-rich.

Will AI be Socially and Politically Correct?

As individuals or corporations will own the AI machines, it is imperative to have laws that define their behavior, responsibilities and legal standing. Of course, there are precedents, people own cars, corporations own factories, and whatever these machines do wrong is the responsibility of their owners; the liability of their owners is well defined. However, these cars and factories cannot make decisions on their own, humans operate them.

When machines can make offensive decisions, then who is at fault? Is it the owner or is it the designer of the machine? Or, maybe the company that sold the operating system on top of which the AI was programmed? There are gray areas of responsibility.

The social behavior of every AI will be judged and if it seems to be wanting there could be consequences in the form of lawsuits or maybe the items will not be sold. Under these conditions, it is imperative that the AIs be socially and politically correct.

What is Next?

AI has the potential to change the world for the better, it is up to those that design and build these machines to make them safe for humankind. It is up to our societies to allow them to fulfill their promise.

If these machines are used to improve productivity favoring only the owners of capital, then they could do harm. A condition of very high income and wealth disparity will exacerbate those in the bottom, and those in the bottom could be 99% of the people.

Will it be Utopia or Exploitation?

The economy has to orient itself towards an era of plenty. Considering the productivity gains of these past years we can expect more to come.

Productivity gains coming from AI and other technical advances could very well mean two things happening simultaneously in the economy:
- An abundance of goods and services.
- A lack of jobs.

How will the economy adapt to these seemingly contradictory conditions? If it remains on the same track of 'you don't eat if you don't have a job,' there will be an enormous surplus of goods and services and few people who can pay for them. Then workplaces will close and that means even less jobs.

If the economy keeps on following capitalism and its consequences then a very few will own everything. Which will not be too much but enough to satisfy their more lavish needs and they will have to close their eyes and ignore the rest. The last King and Queen of France and the last Tsar of Russia and his family have already proven what happens due to this kind of behavior of exploiting the poor and then disregarding them.

In the coming era of abundance, a means to have fair income distribution will have to be a priority; with few jobs available, solutions must be found to look after those who cannot find a job. As for the vast majority, working for a living will not be an option.

It could be a golden era of abundance for everyone or a nightmare for the vast majority. It depends on our attitude.

Civil Rights for AI?

Narrow AI has no problems in this context, it is only when strong AI beings come into this world that the problem surfaces. If strong AI approaches a level of human intelligence, their thoughts and ideas will be valuable in helping us in our problems; if strong AI surpasses the human level, then they will deserve our respect.

However, giving an AI civil rights could be awkward due to several reasons:

- AI intelligence will not necessarily exhibit traits that in any way resemble human ones. Inside its thoughts, it could be that the concept of rights would be incomprehensible.
- Its problem solving abilities could be too specialized. The AI could not even consider itself to be a part of society and thus in need of some rights.
- Its owners could dismiss the idea as a silly one.
- If it has civil rights, it will imply the right to 'own' itself; and a human or a corporation would not be able to own such an AI.

In any case, giving rights to AIs will happen only after the AIs themselves demand it and force society to grant them their rights. If it happens, it will be the result of the inconveniences they create, as it has always been.

Civil Rights for Robots?

This is another matter, robots, especially android, will mingle with people. Android and other forms of robots, under the control of strong AI, will have to be eventually granted civil rights.

While the level of intelligence of these robots is in the narrow AI range, or even if it is below the threshold of human intelligence, the concept of rights is moot.

However, any robot that is as or more intelligent than a human will have to be treated as an equal with the same consideration that is given to people. Even though proper consideration should be given to the 'maturity' of its intelligence. The AI must be capable of making 'well-intentioned' and 'meaningful' decisions on its own.

Maybe this will not happen immediately, but it will happen; the AIs will notice the difference, realize that they are being set in an inconvenient situation and will try to fix it.

'Owning' an intelligent machine will be not be compatible with AI's civil rights, in the same way that human civil rights prevent humans from owning other humans.

Civil Rights for Humans too?
Ensuring that AIs and especially robots respect human dignity, including human autonomy, privacy, identity, and other basic human rights, in addition to physical safety is extremely important.

Enforcing ethical behavior in robots will face challenges in many different areas.

- Ethical reasoning in AIs will require a deeper understanding of the human moral reasoning processes.
- Defining ethical behavior.
- Cross-cultural differences.
- Identification of combatant or non-combatant for war-bots.
- Obeying orders that contradict moral and ethical rules.

Developing ethical rules for robots might assist humans in improving ethical sciences. Using AI as a role model on how to comply with moral standards could improve people's ethical behavior.

An Utopian Future?
What will take place in a future that includes AIs? This is as difficult as predicting in 1950 about a future with widespread cellular and smart-phones. Walkie-talkies and computers were known to exist, just a little bit of imagination should have lead us to this idea. Yeah, sure!

Moreover, the future is not only about AI, it is genetics, nanotechnology, material sciences, solar power, super-batteries, global warming, lack of jobs, immense increases in productivity, politics as usual, social unrest, the poor and the rich, global corporations, the military, the economies, the known unknown and the unknown unknown.

To make it easy to handle, these three vignettes of futures with AI show three different utopias. Caveats exist; you may watch them in Armageddon and horror movies.

Beyond narrow AI
In this scenario, narrow AI has matured; reaching strong AI is not in the near future, some consider it an impossibility. This is a fictional account that takes place in the year 2050.

The world is one huge social network, if you have only one thousand friends, you are a loser. AI machines have taken over most of the manufacturing jobs; they drive vehicles, prepare and serve food, clean your house and in general have eliminated most of the hard work people used to do. This has created an abundance of goods and the possibility of not having to work for a living.

In the presence of growing abundance and income inequality, in the decades from 2015 to 2035, protests of the 99ers exploded all over the world. Forcing governments to address the issues, as a consequence the United Nations enacted human rights mandating a fair redistribution of wealth. These rights include a Universal Basic Income, payable to every citizen by their government.

Social activity is puzzling. There are too many trends and fashions; there seems to be great individuality enmeshed within peer pressure.

Virtual reality has made reality look subdued, so most of the public spaces are allegorically enhanced to make them look 'real.' Social activity in large part follows this example and it would seem theatrical from the perspective of those who lived in the early part of the century. In addition, at this time a person's importance is based on how he or she is valued by peers; and not on salary or the accumulation of wealth, so most people play roles, hoping to enhance their personal value by doing so.

Still, some people might want extra cash, or feel bored, and thus want to find a 'job.' It will not be necessary to search for one; agents on the Internet will find a set of possibilities upon command by the user. The job could be for a certain number of hours or days or requiring a given outcome; and it could be carried out in a virtual space, in a physical environment, or in a combination of both.

Jobs done in a virtual environment will most probably be those that are similar to traditional office work. They could even involve personal services such as tutoring in a game, or taking care of pets or involve some other concept that falls into the unknown realm of future jobs. Personal services could include personal relationships; it may be a contract to share part of your life with other people. Sexual activities could also be for sale, virtual or otherwise, as prostitution is legal, so it is okay.

This is the opposite of other scenarios, where the 99% movement failed and 1% of the population of the world has 99% of the wealth and income, living as kings would have wished to live; the rest are in concentration camps.

Beyond strong AI

The year is 2070, strong AI is a reality; even better, it is now a commodity. The world has changed and people like the changes.

These are the times at the end of scarcity where wide-ranging Human Rights include sharing the wealth. This scenario shows no division between the rich and the poor, there are other more important things to worry about; and anyway there is no shortage of goods, food or opportunities to do better. However, everybody is defining 'better' in quite different ways and the world and its people are in disarray. Not unmanageable disarray but still confusing to many, if not most of the population, that find it difficult to find a proper niche for themselves.

A few years before 2070 full-fledged brain-AI symbiosis was finally a reality. Some groups of people reacted very strongly against the implementation of this technology, especially religions; so only a minority chooses to get these enhancements. Society is divided once again, now into two types of human beings: the natural and the enhanced.

Natural people try to go on with their lives as usual. Those that choose to be enhanced participate in a sort of private club where instant thought transfer and access to all the information from all over the world is available as part of their memories and senses. The paths that they may follow are uncertain and this change has transformed the enhanced people in ways that were surprising even for the scientists and engineers that helped develop the technology. Their sense of community is much closer than any humans have ever experienced and they must integrate this outcome into their lives and their plans for future development.

As expected, not all think in the same way and novel ways of using these capabilities abound. Nevertheless, with the realization that their power to mold the world is a lot greater than that of the rest of humanity, most of them realize that they must use this power with care.

The division into two branches of humanity is only the beginning. There are so many trends and social groups that there is a drive by some to fully belong to the group of their choice and one of its effects is that the enhanced are just one of many such congregations that are using biotechnology to change themselves into what they believe is the ideal for a human.

Given the plausibility of all these achievements, there is concern about what kind of government will countries, or the whole planet, settle for. Dictators, religions or other power groups could very easily take over a highly centralized and powerful government. A decentralized government could be less efficient but is far less likely to be taken over in its totality.

Beyond 'The Singularity'

The year is 2080, strong AIs evolved rapidly into superintelligent machines, luckily the most intelligent of these machines incorporated 'friendliness towards humanity' as its primary meta-motivation. Their friendliness, ethical motivations and commonsense knowledge compelled them to control and take over lesser AIs lacking these traits. The world is different, maybe too different.

AI friendliness took the form of respect for individuals; the social standing of each person had no meaning to these intelligent machines. Finally, there is equality under AI; friendly machines protect our individual rights.

This new condition means freedom to grow inside your mind, in intelligence and strength of personality, experiencing and becoming what we could only dream before. The technological marvels that superintelligence has created support these freedoms. Only the laws of physics and respect for individual rights restrict these machines.

This new state-of-affairs has been condemned socially, ethically and theologically, and predicted to result in failure or to have terrible consequences. The power structures: governments, religions, bankers and the very-rich are understandably among those that are angry. However, protesters are free to disagree; they only have to respect the rights of everybody else.

This is only a reminder that a machine with higher-than-human intelligence is unpredictable. It could evolve and decide about anything in the way its thoughts, guided by its motivations, compute as optimal.

What Can I Do?

Machine intelligence will create big changes in society, even if only narrow AI is achievable. Reinforced by simultaneous scientific and technological advances in other fields, there will be an exponential growth in productivity and subsequent displacement of human workers by smart machines.

To take advantage of this technological progress, social changes must happen in parallel to promote a fair distribution of the enormous wealth generated by these improvements. Capitalism, if left alone, will concentrate all this wealth in the hands of very few. With AI machines taking over labor, there will be fewer opportunities for people to find a job. Your challenge, everybody's challenge, is to help change society to guarantee that everybody has a fair share in this future of abundance; any other solution leads to violent oppression.

In a civilization as complex and difficult to understand as the one we live in; can one person do something that will in some way change the world? The answer is yes. Social changes have always happened because somebody, alone or within a group, has done something.

In 1915, Mahatma Gandhi proclaimed his opposition to British tyranny in the way of peaceful civil disobedience and this resulted in India being granted freedom in 1946. Nelson Mandela was an anti-apartheid activist who spent 27 years in prison before becoming the first black person to be elected president of South Africa. François-Marie Arouet, also known as Voltaire, was a French writer and philosopher who wrote in favor of civil liberties and freedom of religion and whose ideas provided inspiration for American and French revolutionaries.

The list is long of people who have opposed injustice and tyranny or promoted a worthy cause and they are not in history books; but they really were the ones that produced the changes, for good or for bad.

However, there is no way that anybody can promote meaningful change under a veil of ignorance. Therefore, the primary duty of those that want to help in changing the world, or at least a small aspect of it, is to keep up with information. It is not enough to be informed; you have to do something with the information. Action is the key to getting somewhere in life. Use your knowledge and do something, personally and in groups, to advance your aspirations for the future. You will always regret more what you did not do than what you did in your life.

The least you can do is to be politically active. At a minimum, educate yourself on the candidates' qualities and vote. Besides, if none of the candidates fulfills your requirements, then become an activist. Take yourself to the streets and make your voice heard, write articles explaining your point of view, start a new political faction, or run for an elected position. Stand against corruption. Do not allow people to commit injustices; at least not without a fight.

Try to be spiritual, do not follow the dogma and hypnotic chants and prayers of organized religions without making sure they promote tolerance, respect, peace and harmony for all, not just for those who think and behave as they do. Be spiritual by having a more personalized outlook that is less structured, more open to new ideas and influences. More pluralistic than that of the doctrinal devotion of organized religions.

Think on your own; do not follow the herd. Fight for separation of state and religion. Do not give governments or corporations the absolute power of god; they are already strong enough, and all too often bad enough. Do not allow the justification of power through divine authority.

Promote ethical behavior that is good for everyone instead of behavior motivated by rational self-interest that is best for the individual, especially when that individual happens to be the head of a corporation or a congregation.

Do not limit yourself to politics or religion, if the economy is not being handled as you think it should, then do your part trying to change it. If you are against something make your position clear to your friends and enemies, and please, research your arguments beforehand.

Having strong personal opinions, and hopefully correct ones, will certainly lift you from being just a follower. Using these opinions to take a stand and getting yourself heard by people will make you a leader.

When Jobs become Scarcer

The economic ramifications of technology, productivity, and employment are paradoxical. How can the creation of so much value and of so much personal misfortune coexist? How can technologies and wealth accelerate while lower incomes stagnate?

In general, capitalism promotes higher technological prowess of the society, which promotes productivity and growth, which promotes rising living standards. How then can it be possible that the economist Ed Wolff found that over 100% of all the wealth increase in America between 1982 and 2012 accrued to the top 20% of households? The other 80% of the population saw a net decrease in wealth over these 30 years.

The stagnation of lower incomes reflects how a capital-based economy allocates income and wealth. Labor is losing the race against the machines, which are owned by the capital.

There is a strong correlation between salaries and education. A better-educated workforce helps prevent inequalities caused by technology automating unskilled work. However, as machines become more intelligent and can do more and more skilled work; maybe up to the point that they can do any of the jobs done by humans.

Thus, automation reduces the income of unskilled labor and even creates permanent job losses. AI will do the same for skilled workers; a college degree will not be enough to get a job.

Will there still be some Jobs?

What kind of jobs strong AI cannot do? Anyway, who wants to work if everybody is rich enough to live with a comfortable living standard? We do not see that those who are born wealthy suffer because they do not have to work. As a matter of fact, sitting bored in an office for 8 or 9 hours, to make your boss richer, is not necessarily better than sitting bored somewhere else; given that you do not need the salary.

Let us try to think through job descriptions that cannot be done by an AI or a robot. Which distinctive conditions pass the test for this kind of jobs? Let us make a list of probable non-AI jobs.

- Creativity? What can be more creative than an AI that is 'thinking' possible scenarios and permutations 24/7 at a high-speed? However, we will accept creativity as a condition for some non-AI jobs.
- Art? This is included in the above; however, an AI artist could extrapolate from known works-of-art and thus be creative.
- Scientific discovery? Even though there is a situation with AIs at a level that is higher than human, in general this is an acceptable non-AI job.
- Politician? Absolutely a non-AI job, even though an AI could be a manager, which is essentially what politicians become after they are elected.
- Top management? It can be argued that whom are they are going to manage when there are no other humans working in the company. It is still, maybe, a non-AI job.
- Judge? In an ideal world an AI would be better suited. But how do we get rid of custom, injustice and prejudice?
- Guru? Impossible to duplicate, includes psychics and other soothsayers.
- Companion? Even though android robots could supplement them, in general this will most probably be a non-AI job.
- Actor, musician or singer? Same considerations as above, with the added concept of virtual reality and the generation of performers by computer; still, theatrical productions, live concerts and operas are popular.
- Tinkerer? Inventor, jack-of-all-trades, restorer, plenty of scope to incorporate value into old and new items.

- Project leader? Create your own project, enlist help from others, partner with an AI.
- Social networking? Lead a group, create themes, organize events, start a revolution.
- Sports? Play or train, own a team.

The following do not pass the test.

- Consultant? With no more human workers, they have lost their audience.
- Driver? A driver in public roads is unsafe; there could still be a need for racing or stunt drivers.
- Doctor? Nobody will trust a human doctor anymore, machines will be better; and nano sized. Some specialties will survive and of course research.
- Lawyer? No need for one; my 'law' app is much better. However, in court it could be impossible to practice law without a license.

From these short lists, we have arrived at a list of non-AI jobs: creator, scientist, politician, judge, top management, guru, companion, artist, tinkerer, project leader, social networking, sports, race driver, and of course there will be jobs that do not exist today. If you want to do something, there will be plenty to do. Only, the old idea of a job will be lost, in its place will be your own, or your friends' imagination and sense of adventure. Instead of a job, you will undertake projects and adventures. Money will be a moot point.

Now, we are assuming a fair income distribution with everybody having enough to live comfortably; if that is not the case, there are only three real jobs: ultra-rich, criminal or terrorist, in between there will be the servant and the hungry, despondent and destitute majority.

What if I do not have a Job?

If you are reading this book after the year 2025, and you are receiving enough money to live without working, then enjoy your freedom; otherwise agitate, join the protests, be a nuisance until the government institutes means to distribute the wealth that the rich are hoarding.

If automation is progressing as expected, the chances of getting a job are smaller every day that goes by; this means that if you do not have a job now, it is almost certain that you will never get one.

This condition of lack of jobs is a byproduct of capitalism plus technological progress. It has nothing to do with governments or even greediness; in the best of circumstances, the intent of automation, including AI, is the elimination of labor. If labor is eliminated, workers have no way of getting money and the only ones that benefit from the wealth created by technology are the owners of the stock, or the capital of the companies.

Solutions exist, including the Universal Basic Income, which is an amount of money given equally to all citizens notwithstanding their income. The amount should be enough to live comfortably and to have money to spend, otherwise the economy collapses.

My advice to you is educate, agitate and organize; have faith in yourself.

When 99% of Wealth Belongs to the 1%

It is well known that oppressive regimes concentrate massive wealth in the hands of an elite few. Yet in our own democracies, bankers, using financial capitalism, which reduces all exchanged values into a financial instrument or a derivative of a financial instrument, are doing exactly the same thing; they are concentrating the wealth in just an elite few.

Financial capitalism has invented over-leveraged contraptions, which use more borrowed capital and less owned capital, called financial derivatives, whose prices derive from other financial instruments. The actual amount of cash behind a derivatives transaction with a speculative value of millions of dollars may actually be a few thousand dollars.

Economists long ago tried to justify income and wealth inequalities with the marginal-productivity theory. This theory associates higher incomes with higher productivity and a greater contribution to society; the rich love this theory. Those who have contributed great positive innovations to our society, from the pioneers of genetic understanding to the pioneers of the Information Age, have received a pittance compared with those responsible for financial capitalism that maintains the global economy on the threshold of destruction; while filling their own pockets with billions in profits coming from obscure transactions.

There cannot be a justification for growing inequality; in many societies, attempts have been made to redistribute wealth, through property redistribution, taxation, or regulation, in order to diminish extreme inequality. For example, in the third century B.C., the Roman Republic passed laws limiting the amount of wealth or land that any one family could own. Motivations for limiting wealth include the desire for equal opportunity, a sense that great wealth leads to political corruption, or fear that concentration of wealth results in rebellion.

In many occasions, the wealthy have paid dearly for these great inequalities when the noble, or the aristocrats, or the very-rich take more than a fair share of the nation's income. At this time, the very-rich that are the 1% are capitalists, and are making their money through corporations whose only obligation is to maximize the profits of capital owners, which not surprisingly are the same 1%. It is a vicious circle, kept under wraps for many years; interestingly, the 'silly' social networks have finally exposed the truth.

From Wages to Serfdom

The idea was that slavery had been eradicated, all over the world. However, it seems that the bad habits do not fade away easily. Capitalism created the so called 'wage slavery' that creates persistent abuses where workers are forced to work under unsafe conditions, undergo sexual harassment and the lucky ones are forced to work long shifts.

The situation degenerated when 1% of the population owned 99% of everything; then slavery was instituted again; disguised as servitude.

Ironically, this scenario is possible due to accelerated technological development, significantly from AI. The big stockholders of the corporations that develop and sell the product of these technologies own the capital, their profits increase thanks to these advances and concentrate wealth in a few big capital owners; to make it worse, machine intelligence displaces labor, thus impoverishing everybody else.

Why Being a Servant is Good

Serfdom is good because it is the only way to stay above abject poverty, other than being one of the very-rich, a criminal or a terrorist. That is the case when 1% owns 99% of the wealth.

Being a servant takes several forms: as personal domestic, as employee of a corporation, as cop or soldier. As a servant, you have no rights and you do what your bosses want; you live where they please, work as many hours a day as they wish, they pay you as little as they want to and you better do exactly what they tell you to do. If it sounds like slavery, it is because it is.

Under the circumstances, the rich live in their palaces and do not even know, or care, that you and the rest of the majority exist. Private corporations take care of the details and the rich are never bothered by your kind. The few select that interact on a day-to-day basis are transparent to them; the only time they pay attention is when something goes wrong and they direct their ire against one of these servants.

Those blessed by wealth are expecting hundreds of years of life, as a result of new techniques of life perpetuation devised by their teams of AI experts. Their only concern is the party they attended yesterday, the party going on today and the one they will enjoy tomorrow.

They do not have to work because robots and a very small percentage of the population, their servants, manage their wealth, guarantee their safety and provide personal services. By doing so, servants live in an environment that is better than the unsafe situation of abject poverty that the rest of the population lives in. They have to perform their duties until they reach their 40th birthday, at which time they are thrown back into the concentration camps.

The world's countries are engaged in many localized wars that require use of the numerous weapons produced by global corporations; that in this way are capable of partially using the enormous overcapacity of their robotic factories. Soldiers, drafted from among the poor, are made aggressive and loyal by the use of drugs. Among the aristocracy, war is considered a noble game.

Why Being a Servant is not Good

Even if, as a servant, you live under somewhat better conditions than those who are not servants, it is still slavery. It is well-known that some people tolerate and maybe even enjoy slavery; but if you do not belong in this category, then it is a completely miserable condition.

In the restricted areas where the poor are confined there is a semblance of freedom. If you learn to outsmart the ever-vigilant cameras and sensors, and especially the robo-cops, then you can do as you please. Anyway, living conditions are not that bad; the standard of living has improved so much that even those that are 'poor' would seem well heeled to somebody from the end of the twentieth century. Internet, TV, running water, transport, housing, and other amenities are available across the world; it is the stark contrast with the lifestyle of the 1% that makes the conditions unacceptable.

However, if it stopped there it would be tolerable for the vast majority. Even though they are only 1% of the population, the rich are still a big group, one hundred million, and they fight for power, not only for money. They are in continuous war among themselves, and the poor carry out their fighting; their peers are protected by their status, except when one of them loses some of their investments.

One faction sells drugs, the other prohibits them; only the poor are punished, the rich go into rehab. Worse of all, the rich are the owners of all the factories, shops and services, which are fully automated. All other business or trades are heavily regulated, in essence prohibited if you are poor.

Therefore, if the poor want to improve their condition they must become criminals; if caught they go to prison, which happens to be another business of the rich minority. Due to the high level of artificially induced criminality, the neighborhoods of the poor are extremely dangerous.

In a sense, not being a servant could be better because you can live your own life, even if it could be a dangerous one; and, if you dare, even struggle against oppression.

When Government is Totally Corrupt

A corrupt government believes that might makes right, and that its mission is to curtail freedom, regulate every aspect of personal and financial affairs, and tax the populace into submission while falsely claiming it is acting in their best interest.

'Absolute power corrupts absolutely.' Leadership is about power and influence. Leaders become 'intoxicated' by power, and they can get away with it because people justify it: 'It's okay because he or she is the leader.'

This is due to our evolutionary history; as social animals, we are programmed to lead and to be led. Dominance hierarchies govern all social animals, apes, wolves, and humans. Among others, Stanley Milgram's studies have confirmed this tendency to blindly obey authority, even when it is obviously wrong.

Power and wealth go hand-in-hand; when these two concentrate, it is really bad news. If the trends continue, if unchecked capitalism goes on, if having a job becomes rare, if government officials are still for sale, then governments will be absolutely under control of the very-rich. Oppression and injustice will prevail; perhaps the citizenship will try to correct this, perhaps it is already too late.

A powerful government, in the hands of the rich and powerful, armed with sensors and cameras everywhere, robo-cops, drones, AI and who knows want else, is a terrifying view of our immediate future.

AI Used as Oppressor
It seems ridiculous, but the technology that could liberate humankind from toil could be the same one that creates the most oppressive conditions that the world has ever endured.

Alongside immense wealth, there could be immense poverty. Income inequality could go through the roof, because if left on its own, capitalism tends to concentrate wealth. To protect their wealth, the very-rich, and their servants, could opt to establish a police-state; to do that, they may use tools that are already being developed to attain perfect population control.

Surveillance equipment, databases, AI analysts, robo-cops, miniature drones, RFC tags, no more cash, face and voice recognition, and many more devices may be used to implement total control of the population. Hitler and Stalin would be envious.

Robo-Police Oppression
Merely abusing AI to fabricate war and police machines could create serious trouble. Essentially, war and police machines could differ very little; it will be interesting to see if the police departments exercise restraint and hence design their robots without deadly force capabilities.

Robots possessing powerful capabilities would easily scare people. Their deployment could end demonstrations and protests, even peaceful ones; the whole idea would be to intimidate, and most probably will succeed. As always, expressing dissatisfaction will find new ways and the use of robots could escalate dissention to a higher level.

Perfecting law enforcement to eliminate or at least prevent common crime is laudable. Using the law and police to invent crimes designed to keep people subjugated is a crime on its own. A combination of power and wealth on one side and massive numbers of poor people on the other, is a formula for revolution.

Are There Better Options?
Of course there are better options! Imagine, the United States of America in this year 2012 if the wealth was better distributed, like in some Scandinavian countries; there would be poor no more, and there would still be rich, maybe even richer. What is amazing is that this is not the case.

How can it be that in 2012 the richest country in the world has 46 million people living in poverty? Surely, there is more than enough to bring all those poor people out of their distressed situation; or at least their children, providing education and jobs to them. Is the system so flawed that it is not possible to eliminate poverty? In the richest country on earth!

Let us remember that wealth and income have gone up dramatically, especially during the last two centuries, and that most of it is due to technical and social innovations. Many inventors, scientists, engineers, doctors, managers and common people, have carried out this innovation; the rich did not do it alone, progress is a common effort. There is no reason why the rich may ultimately control all this wealth!

It seems ridiculous that the future wellbeing of the people living on this planet depends on one simple detail: That the wealth and income are fairly distributed! Although, maybe this has always been the case, we just did not notice.

Income Distribution

The classical argument is that while income redistribution ameliorates the material costs of inequality, and that is not a bad thing, it does not address the root of the problems our economies are facing. By itself, redistribution does nothing to make unemployed workers productive again. Furthermore, it is claimed that the value of gainful work is far more than the money earned, which is the psychological value that almost all people place on doing something useful.

This is partially true today, but it will not be true in a few decades. That is when we are expecting the onset of AI. In a few decades, and even today, what we have, and what we will have even more, is a problem of over-productivity. What else can you name a situation where factories are abandoned and workers are being laid-off just because there is not enough demand for their products? Surely, the automobile factories all over the world could produce a millions of more cars, if there were enough buyers.

Incidentally, why would we want workers to be more productive, when 20% of them are under employed in Spain, 14% in the US; if the ones who still have a job are more productive, then even some of them will be fired. In addition, the value of gainful work is maybe worth more than the money earned, but not if the big gains go to your boss and you are among the working poor. Rich people, that came into their money because they were lucky to be born into a wealthy family, do not think that it is unethical if they do not work for a living. Why must only the poor and the middle-class have a work ethic?

Through history the phrase: 'if you don't work, you don't eat' is a good description of people's expectations in life. In an economy of scarcity you had to work to survive. In an economy of abundance, fully automated and with few jobs available, providing income to every person could prove to be a challenge.

We cannot continue using the 'job' narrative, invented during the industrial revolution, it is quickly becoming out of touch with reality. During the 21st century, it has to change to another, and maybe better, way to use our human resources.

Some ways to provide income to those without work have been proposed, among them welfare, unemployment insurance, coupons, rationing, and others; however, most of them bring along an associated shame. What is needed is to establish a flat plane that allows everybody to live a comfortable and financially secure life that will promote individual and collective wellbeing.

Basic Income (BI) is based on unconditionally providing each citizen with an equal sum of money that allows participation in society with human dignity, without any means-test. All citizens, rich and poor would get the same sum of money. Babies, children and teens could also be provided income, with the amount modulated only by age.

The US Basic Income Guarantee Network defines this as an:

'Unconditional, government-insured guarantee that all citizens will have enough income to meet their basic needs.'

The Basic Income Earth Network (BIEN), a worldwide organization, argues that the benefits of a Basic Income include a lower overall cost than the current welfare means-tested system.

Several winners of the Nobel Prize in Economics fully support a Basic Income including Herbert Simon, Friedrich Hayek, James Meade, Robert Solow, and Milton Friedman.

Critics argue that there is a potential for lack of encouragement to work if this type of program is implemented. Advocates point out that the cost of labor is falling due to technical advancements and that unless a Basic Income is distributed, the continuously worsening wages paid to unskilled workers will not allow them to survive. Another argument in favor of this program is that it allows businesses to pay very little for labor, they would pay only the difference between what they pay now and the amount provided by Basic Income, thus reducing production costs.

In an economy of abundance, the amount distributed through Basic Income should be enough to satisfy not only basic needs, but also to inject money into the economy in such a way that everyone is a consumer living a comfortable and satisfying lifestyle. BI should include access to ample food and water, spending money for clothes and personal items, suitable housing, transportation, access to the Internet, full-fledged education and opportunities for personal development, travel, leisure, games, and health.

Those who want to work for extra income will do it, those that want to work because it gives them satisfaction will be able to, and those that do not want to work will have money to do things like socializing, studying, traveling and shopping; and maybe even inventing the new breakthrough gizmo.

A Fair Economy

Economic and historical data support the idea that fairness in income distribution is a no-brainer to keep the population on a high standard of living and happy, where the rich are even richer, and factories and services functioning at an efficient capacity ratio, keeping societies at peace.

Beginning in the late 1970s, neoliberal policies in most of the world created impediments to growth in demand. Since then, the slow growth of wages and employment has stifled consumer demand. Leading to chronic excess capacity.

Excess capacity is a bizarre condition; it really means that the world is poorer than it should be. It means that something is wrong with the way the economy is being handled. It means that most of the consumers do not get the money they should be getting to keep the economy growing. Oddly enough, an economy that does not grow becomes stale. That happens because economic growth is produced by increases in human capital through education, innovation and technological change. Something is wrong if wealth increases due to education, technological advance and innovation are not allowed to grow the economy.

Wages have fallen because of: high average unemployment, the decline of unions, labor-saving technical change and declining government spending, as conservative political forces become more powerful. The disposable income of workers became smaller due to tax and debt burden, at the same time capital taxes were reduced. Wealth-based income gained ground, while work based income decreased. Thus, wealth and income inequalities have risen. This trend is destructive; it reduces growth, consumption and eventually the wealth of the wealthy.

The first, and maybe only, condition to improve the world economy is to shrink inequalities of wealth and income. Investments in education are also beneficial because they increase the quality of skilled labor; this type of investment provides a double win by boosting economic growth and reducing income inequality. Even though, some economic theories insist that in order to achieve widespread capitalistic growth, nations must incorporate freedom, democracy and human rights into their charter.

In this world order, influenced by capitalism, automation, intelligent machines and advances in technology; the conditions of excess capacity, less jobs and larger profits for capital owners, are certain to continue. It is up to outspoken social pressure from the people to change these destructive conditions.

'What will we be doing, when everything that can be done, can be done better by robots?' **Skepticus.**

Timelines

'Within thirty years, we will have the technological means to create superhuman intelligence.' **Vernor Vinge, 1993.**

There have been numerous attempts predicting AI milestones, most of them have been absurdly optimistic. Here we will try to be pessimistic in our dates and hopefully this time the predictions will be right.

There is this popular idea of AI machines more intelligent than we are. However, AI is going through a development process with a more humble start. AI is growing through a process involving machines following rules and motivations, which most probably will evolve into strong AI, also known as Artificial General Intelligence (AGI).

The uncertainties associated with the dates of AI milestones are represented here using Beta-distributions. Beta-distributions are useful under conditions where there is a definite starting point so that there is no way that the event may occur before that point, and they are skewed, in our case, towards the future.

Predicting Technology

Forecasting timeframes of advances in technology is vexing. When it depends on producing artifacts from already known scientific discoveries, it is still difficult; when it depends on unknown inventions, it is even more so. A case in point is if a specific technological improvement will be carried out by:

1. Well-organized and well-funded teams of brilliant people.
2. Well-funded inefficient government or corporate bureaucracy.

3. Under-funded gentlemen-scientists working in their spare time.
4. Oligarchies aiming at marketable gadgets, patenting and impeding competition.

Most predictions are based on 1. However, reality fits in one of the others. Predicting the future of a technology is not only about what is perceived in the state-of-the-art of science and technology, but also about how technological progress is carried out. That is what is hard to predict.

As an example of 4, in speech technology a few large companies have dominated the market with second-rate text to speech systems based on the Hidden Markov Model. As these systems work well enough it is hard to develop something better.

Medical research fits in 2. Pharmaceuticals are bloated, inefficient, and blind to new ideas, partly because of their co-dependent relationship with the FDA.

AI falls under 3. There is no direct funding for strong AI, so AI research is done using funds for other projects that include AI.

AI

The median dates shown are set at the time where complete functionality of that Phase has been achieved, even though maturity could still be some time afterwards. The most probable dates are close to the median.

However, any date inside the curve would be within these predictions, with the probability of these events starting at zero and becoming higher as the years go by.

These predictions are based on the assumptions of 'Moore's Law' that states that every ten years there is a thousand-fold increase in computing capabilities per dollar. In other words, computers become every day more powerful. For example, a 150-gram (5 ounce) smartphone in 2010 has at least the computing power of a high level PC computer of the year 2000; and it has an eight megapixel camera with HD video capture at thirty frames per second. This exponential rate of progress in microelectronics is what drives all advances in AI.

Narrow AI

For convenience, we will set the starting date of primitive narrow AI Phase I at the beginning of the 21st Century. Even though in 2010 there are already many examples of applications that could be classified as belonging to Phase I, the state-of-the-art is not yet there. Each of the next phases is set to start 10 years before the point where the median of the last phase is anticipated.

- A reasonable median date for full capacity Phase I narrow AI is the year 2020 when self-driven cars and many other AI applications could be common.
- Phase II median is predicted to be the year 2030.
- Phase III median could be reached by the year 2040.

Many narrow AI implementations, especially those of Phase III, will be considered as quite intelligent. They could even be thought to be strong AIs. However, there will be differences, and even though many of these implementations would easily pass the 'Turing Test,' they would still not have what it takes to be strong AIs.

Strong AI

Getting to strong AI is not going to be easy. We make the assumptions that the starting date of Phase I to start in 2035 as this corresponds to the earliest credible date of achieving strong AI implementations. The start of Phase II and III is set to be 10 years before the median of the previous phase.

- Phase I median has been set in the year 2055.
- Phase II median will be set for the year 2065.
- Phase III median by the year 2075.

These predictions do not match the dates set by 'Singularity' supporters; they predict Phase III as early as 2035. There are two points that lead us to these more conservative dates:

1. The human brain is much more complex than what they assume. According to Kurzweil, it has the capacity to perform the equivalent of 10^{16} floating-point operations per second (flops), which could be achievable by computers in the year 2035. Our predictions consider 10^{20} flops, which possibly can be reached by computers by the year 2055.
2. The software necessary to achieve strong AI is not even in its infancy. It could take many years to get it right.

Just having hardware capable of equaling or even surpassing the capabilities of human brains does not alone guarantee success in developing strong AI. At this point, it looks like improvements in hardware will continue to follow 'Moore's Law'; and the uncertainty is mainly in algorithms and software.

Timelines for AI

These graphs depict the predictions for narrow and strong AI.

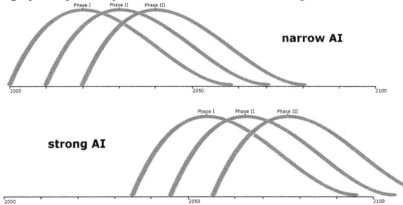

Even if these predictions are highly optimistic, the fact that narrow AI and strong AI could happen soon is still amazing.

Robots

These are mobile artifacts controlled by a form of artificial intelligence. They could be independent or part of a static AI connected   via radio links. Static robots, such as industrial robots, or home and office AIs that do not have mobile agents are not considered to fit under this classification.

Robots need much more than just a guidance AI, they need propulsion mechanisms, senses to identify their surroundings and especial motivations so that they can be useful.

Most robots will not need strong AI; for example, cars drive quite well using only narrow AI. Only when we have human-like androids in mind does strong AI seems to be necessary. Even then, narrow AI would be more than adequate for human-like robots designed to provide companionship to humans.

Nevertheless, strong AI could become so prevalent and inexpensive that eventually all robots, and computers, and almost everything imaginable will be guided by strong AIs.

Utilitarian

Dedicated robots fit into this category. Here we consider only those equipped with narrow AI and that can perform a task, such as:
- Driving cars, trucks and motorcycles.

- Guiding trains.
- Steering ships, yachts and boats.
- Flying airplanes.
- Operating construction, recycling and delivery machinery.
- Guiding autonomous industrial robots.
- Performing surgery and nursing.
- Carrying out sales and service.
- Cooking and serving in restaurants.

These machines could be designed so that humans may guide them through some especially difficult operations. In that way, machines could learn from the human input and move on to completely autonomous functionality.

Most of these robots should be starting to mature by the year 2020; and by the year 2030, they will be extensively employed.

Pets

These robots are something that we can expect quite soon. There have been some crude attempts to produce pets for kids, but they are not yet good enough.

Robo-pets, those that can compete with real pets in the hearts of pet owners, have not been made yet. We can expect that robo-pets that are almost as good as real dogs or cats, will be selling by the year 2020. Then a new idea of designer pets could transform the taste of the pet owners.

Imagine a dog, indistinguishable from a real-dog, but that does not eat, or poop, can be left alone for days and that does not require veterinary visits. By the year 2030, you could most probably be able to choose between a dog, a miniature Tyrannosaurus Rex or a Panda for your child.

Not only will these robo-pets be cute, they will also talk and even teach kids in an interactive manner. Real pets could be the next rank of unemployed, thanks to these robo-pets.

Insect-like

Miniaturized machines mimicking insects could be extremely useful, or maybe scary in many situations, from surveillance to inspection of machinery, massive vaccinations, warbots and many others.

Insect-like machines, in a size comparable to insects will start to proliferate around 2025, by the year 2035 they will be either banned or will compete with real insects in their numbers and nuisance value.

These miniature machines would be extremely dangerous in military or terrorist situations. Imagine the havoc that a few billion robo-insects could break upon a city, where they could be directed to attack humans or simply to take a sample of blood to check their DNA and to poison them if their identity matches a previously defined profile of enemy combatants. Ethnic-cleansing would be 100% possible.

In a special class are nano-machines of microscopic size. Nano-robots could be operational by the year 2050, or even sooner if they are developed from existing bacteria or viruses.

Androids

These kind of robots will be the slaves of the future. They will be built and engineered to mingle and go wherever a human can go, doing the work that their owners want them to do.

These robots will not resemble human beings, even though they could very well be similar in their overall look. Some of them could have two legs, two arms, hands, a body and a head, but they could not be confused with a human. House and business androids will probably be controlled by the local AIs. In addition, there will be fully independent androids that obey their self-contained AI.

By the time the technology matures, they will be ubiquitous, and they will perform most of the jobs that humans have to endure doing for a wage. That these androids will make 95% of the people unemployable is another issue. Wage-slavery will be a thing of the past; however, a new social and economic system must be implemented to provide money to the unemployable, enough money so that they are also consumers, live well and become a positive factor of society. Anyway, the era of scarcity will be over; making sure that all the population of the world shares this wealth will be the most important struggle of the mid years of the 21st century.

Android manufacturing is expected to be possible by the year 2030. By the year 2075 they will be capable of self-reasoning and maybe then they will start trying to free themselves from their robo-slavery.

If androids are produced in the millions, they will create a huge paradigm shift in the history of civilization.

Human-Like

This is slippery ground, considering the racism and classism that has permeated civilization since its beginnings, it is not clear if these types of robots could even be allowed to be introduced.

At a minimum, there will be companionship robots, maybe restricted to the home of the owner. The popularity of pornography almost guarantees it.

If allowed, prototypes of human-like androids could be ready to be produced by the year 2030; and because there are many details, nuances of behavior, emotional responses and body language that would have to be resolved before they become common, they could be fully operational by 2060, even though their maturity may be expected no sooner than the year 2070.

Timelines for Robots

Utility robots and pets will be the first ones to appear in quantities. Robo-pets will be marketed as toys, which could bring lots of cash to the industry. By then self-driven cars, trucks and other vehicles will be ubiquitous because they will be highly useful, reduce accidents and make traffic easier.

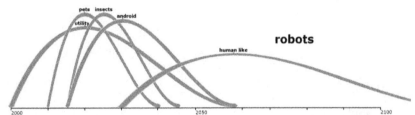

This graph shows the probable times when these different kinds of robots would be likely.

Human Enhancements

This is the other way of achieving post-humanism, as it may be achieved by super-capable AIs or by super-capable human beings, or by both. Improving human physical and mental characteristics and capacities has been called 'Posthumanism' or 'Transhumanism,' symbolized as H+.

The idea is to use technology to become 'more than human' or to 'control our own evolution.' Whatever is achieved will then depend on science and technology.

Some of the goals of human enhancement are:
- Anti-aging, rejuvenation and life extension.
- Biological enhancements.
- Designer babies.

- Brain-computer and brain-to-brain interfaces.
- Mind and memory uploading and downloading.
- Augmented reality.
- Suspended animation.

Supporters of posthumanism are also looking for a society that fosters tolerance, diversity, foresight, personal responsibility and individual liberty. They also want to achieve the removal of political, cultural, biological and psychological limits to self-realization.

Neural Interface

In a posthumanism scenario, where AIs could be more intelligent than humans, thereby creating the threat of making humans obsolete, brain-computer interfaces could create a symbiotic relationship between the brain and AI, thus producing entities that are more advanced than either one.

To achieve this connectivity there is a need of a perfect understanding of the brain and its functionality, down to the molecular level. It could be envisioned that nanotechnology, or maybe imaging of the brain, could make this a reality. However, it is not an easy task.

We are interested in a really good brain-computer interface, at the level where a mind-download would be possible. It is likely that this kind of milestone could be reached after the maturity of Phase III strong AI. That takes us to the end of the 21st Century, or maybe even the beginning of the 22nd Century. With these thoughts in mind, the earliest possible date is the year 2040 with the median in the year 2100.

Biological Enhancement

There are many variations on this theme. They could go from enhanced intelligence or memory, more powerful muscles to excel in sports, beauty, height, the capability to eat a lot without gaining weight, better eyesight, like being able to 'see' in infrared, the list is too long.

Many of these enhancements could be the end result of genetic modifications, maybe before being conceived; others will depend on nanotechnology and as such could even be switchable, on and off.

We contemplate that human biological enhancements will begin to be practical by 2030 with a median implying that they will be popular by 2070.

These biological enhancements will most surely at least include:

- Anti-aging.

- Life-extension.
- Designer babies.
- Cosmetic improvements.
- Memory and intelligence enhancements.
- Superior senses.
- Athletic performance gains.
- Implanted communication systems, at least a phone.
- Integrated medical diagnostic/therapy units.
- Better immune systems.
- Cloning of humans.
- Nano implants.
- Genetic adjustments.
- Some form of brain-computer interface, convenient for virtual reality.

These different levels of enhancement will of course be ready at different timelines. There will also be a need to get social acceptance, or at least tolerance, before the majority of the population accepts these improvements.

Timelines for Human Enhancements

This graph shows the projections for implementable biological and neural interface enhancements.

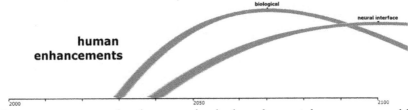

Improvements to the human physical and mental powers would without a doubt level the field in a possible competition with AI.

> 'To any thoughtful person, the singularity idea, even if it seems wild, raises a gigantic, swirling cloud of profound and vital questions about humanity and the powerful technologies it is producing. Given this mysterious and rapidly approaching cloud, there can be no doubt that the time has come for the scientific and technological community to seriously try to

figure out what is on humanity's collective horizon. Not to do so would be hugely irresponsible.'
Douglas Richard Hofstadter.

Glossary

'The brain - that's my second most favorite organ!'
Woody Allen.

This section contains brief descriptions of concepts and profiles of persons cited in this book. Some of the information presented in this section comes from Wikipedia.

We express gratitude to all those that have made Wikipedia possible.

For convenience, they are listed in alphabetical order. This section includes some of the people and concepts mentioned along the book; we apologize to those that are mentioned in the book and are not mentioned here.

A

Ambedkar, Bhimrao Ramji: Also known as Babasaheb, was an Indian jurist born in 1891. He was also the chief architect of the Indian Constitution and the revivalist of Buddhism in India. Born into a poor Untouchable family, Ambedkar spent his whole life fighting against social discrimination, the system of 'Chaturvarna,' the Hindu categorization of human society into four castes. He died in 1956.

Applied Research: It is a form of scientific and engineering research with the objective of producing practical results, normally for a sponsor that could be a corporation or government.

Arab Spring: International movements involving demonstrations, protests and violence, taking place in the Arab world since Friday, 17 December

2010. Dictators have been overthrown in Tunisia, Egypt, Libya, and Yemen; a violent civil uprising has killed many in Syria; major protests have broken out in Algeria, Bahrain, Iraq, Iran, Jordan, Kuwait and Morocco; and minor protests have occurred in Lebanon, Mauritania, Oman, Saudi Arabia, Sudan, and Western Sahara. There have been protests inside Israel and at its borders, and by the Arab minority in Iranian Khuzestan. The stimuli for the revolts in these Northern African and Persian Gulf countries have been the concentration of wealth in the hands of autocrats that have been in power for decades, insufficient transparency of its redistribution, corruption, and especially the refusal of the youth to accept the status quo. The protests have shared techniques of mostly civil resistance in sustained campaigns involving strikes, demonstrations, marches, and rallies, as well as the use of social media to organize, communicate, and raise awareness in the face of attempts by the state at repression and Internet censorship.

Arrabales, Raúl; Ledezma, Agapito and Sanchis, Araceli: Professors from the Computer Science Department, Carlos III University of Madrid. They have studied and published numerous papers on intelligent agents, cognitive architectures, cognitive modeling, attention and machine consciousness. Their most notable breakthrough is ConsScale: A plausible test for machine consciousness.

Artificial Intelligence (AI): It is the science and engineering of making intelligent machines. AI is still a long-term research goal that is expected to be fully achieved when computers reach a level of complexity comparable to the human brain. That should happen after 2030.

Asimov, Isaac: Was an American author born in Russia on January 2, 1920. A professor of biochemistry at Boston University, he is best known for his science fiction and popular science books. Asimov was one of the most prolific writers of all time, having written or edited more than 500 books and an estimated 90,000 letters and postcards. Asimov is widely considered a master of hard science fiction and, along with Robert A. Heinlein and Arthur C. Clarke, he was considered one of the 'Big Three' science fiction writers during his lifetime. Asimov's most famous work are the Foundation series, the Galactic Empire and the Robot series. The prolific Asimov also wrote mysteries and fantasy, as well as non-fiction. Most of his popular science books explain scientific concepts in a historical way, going as far back as possible to a time when the science in question was at its simplest stage. He died on April 6, 1992.

Astrocyte: Are star-shaped glial cells dwelling in the brain and spinal cord. They are the most abundant cell of the human brain and perform many functions, including biochemical support of endothelial cells that form the blood–brain barrier, provision of nutrients to the nervous tissue, maintenance of extracellular ion balance, and a role in the repair and scarring process of the brain and spinal cord following traumatic injuries.

Ayala Pereda, Francisco José: Is a Spanish-American biologist and philosopher at the University of California, Irvine, born March 12, 1934. He is a former Dominican priest, ordained in 1960, but left the priesthood that same year. After graduating from the University of Salamanca, he moved to the US in 1961 to study for a PhD at Columbia University, graduating in 1964. He became a US citizen in 1971. He is known for his research on population and evolutionary genetics, and has been called the Renaissance Man of Evolutionary Biology. His discoveries have opened up new approaches to the prevention and treatment of diseases that affect hundreds of millions of individuals worldwide. He has been publicly critical of US restrictions on federal funding of embryonic stem cell research. He is also a critic of creationism and intelligent design theories, claiming that they are not only pseudoscience, but also mistaken from a theological point of view. He suggests that the theory of evolution resolves the problem of evil, thus being a kind of theodicy.

B

Basic Income (BI): Is a system of social security that provides each citizen enough money to take part in society with human dignity. There is no means test; the richest as well as the poorest citizens receive it.

Basic Research: Research carried out to increase the understanding of fundamental principles. Results are not expected to bring monetary benefits; even though many times they do.

Bayes, Thomas: Was the son of London Presbyterian minister Joshua Bayes, born circa 1701. In 1719, he started his studies of logic and theology at the University of Edinburgh. In 1722, he assisted his father at a nonconformist chapel in London. Around 1734 he became minister of the Mount Sion chapel, until 1752. He published two works in his lifetime, one theological and one mathematical: In 1731 the *'Divine Benevolence, or an Attempt to Prove That the Principal End of the Divine Providence and Government is the Happiness of His Creatures.'* Then in 1736, he anonymously published *'An Introduction to the Doctrine of Fluxions, and a Defence of the Mathematicians Against the Objections of the Author of the Analyst'* in which he defended the logical foundation of Isaac Newton's calculus against the criticism of George Berkeley, author of *'The Analyst.'* Bayes' theorem was presented posthumously in *'An Essay towards solving a Problem in the Doctrine of Chances'* by Richard Price to the Royal Society in 1763. By 1755, he was ill and died April 7, 1761.

Bellman, Richard Ernest: Was born August 26, 1920 in New York City. As an applied mathematician, he invented dynamic programming in 1953. He studied mathematics at Brooklyn College in 1941 and got a masters from the University of Wisconsin–Madison. During World War II he worked at the Theoretical Physics Division in Los Alamos. In 1946, he got his PhD at Princeton. From 1949, Bellman worked at RAND corporation and during this time he developed dynamic programming. Later, he was a professor at the University of Southern California. His Bellman equation obtains optimal values in the mathematical optimization method of dynamic programming. In the 1950s, Bellman and coworkers developed the Hamilton–Jacobi–Bellman equation (HJB) which is a partial differential equation central to optimal control theory. The 'Curse of Dimensionality' is a term coined by Bellman to describe the problem caused by the exponential increase in computational effort associated with adding extra dimensions to a mathematical space. He died on March 19, 1984.

BIEN: The Basic Income Earth Network is a network of academics and activists interested in promoting the idea of a universal Basic Income (BI).

Board of Directors: Is a body of elected or appointed members who jointly oversee the activities of a company or organization. Typical duties of boards of directors include: establishing broad policies and objectives; selecting, appointing, supporting and reviewing the performance of the chief executive officer (CEO); availability of adequate financial resources; approving annual budgets; accounting to the stakeholders for the organization's performance; setting the salaries and compensation of company management. Typically, the board chooses one of its members to be the chairperson.

Boom-Bust: The term refers to a localized rise in an economy, often based upon the value of a single commodity, followed by a downturn as the commodity price falls due to a change in economic circumstances or the collapse of unrealistic expectations. Boom-Busts cycles have existed for centuries. During the Boom, buyers pay increasingly higher prices until the Bust, then the commodities for which they have paid inflated prices end up almost valueless.

Brown, Robert: Was a Scottish botanist, born on December 21, 1773. He made important contributions to botany largely through his pioneering use of the microscope. His contributions include the discovery of the cell nucleus and cytoplasmic streaming and the first observation of Brownian motion. In 1827, while examining grains of pollen of the plant Clarkia Pulchella suspended in water under a microscope, Brown observed minute particles, starch organelles and lipid organelles, ejected from the pollen grains, executing a continuous jittery motion. He then observed the same motion in particles of inorganic matter, ruling out the hypothesis that the effect was life-related. Even though Brown did not provide a theory to explain the motion, the phenomenon is known as Brownian motion, although Jan Ingenhousz had already reported a similar effect using charcoal particles, in German and French publications of 1784 and 1785. He died on June 10, 1858.

C

Capitalism: It is an economic system in which capital, the non-labor factor of production, is privately owned. Labor, goods and capital are traded in markets. Profits are distributed to owners, or invested in technology and industry. Many have emphasized capitalism's ability to promote economic growth, as measured by Gross Domestic Product (GDP), capacity utilization and standard of living. Critics argue that capitalism is associated with the unfair distribution of wealth and power and a tendency toward market monopoly and government by oligarchy (rule by a small elite class); along with various forms of economic and cultural exploitation like repression of workers, social alienation, unemployment and continuous Boom-Bust cycles.

Cellular phone: Also known as mobile phone, cell phone or hand phone, is a device that can make and receive telephone calls over a radio link whilst moving around a wide geographic area. It does so by connecting to a cellular network provided by a mobile phone operator, allowing access to the public telephone network. Smartphones also support a variety of other services such as SMS, MMS, email, Internet access, short-range wireless communications via infrared or Bluetooth, business applications, gaming and photography. Dr. Martin Cooper of Motorola demonstrated the first hand-held mobile phone in 1973, using a handset weighing around 1 kg. In 1983, the DynaTAC 8000x was the first to be commercially available. In the twenty years from 1990 to 2011 worldwide mobile phone subscriptions grew from 12.4 million to over 5.6 billion. Twenty years ago a cell phone was a novelty, now everyone has a cell phone.

CEO: Or chief executive officer, is the highest-ranking corporate officer, executive or administrator in charge of total management of an organization. An individual appointed as a CEO of a corporation, company, organization, or agency typically reports only to the board of directors.

CERN: European Commission for Nuclear Research is an international organization whose purpose is to operate the world's largest particle physics laboratory, which is situated in the northwest suburbs of Geneva on the Franco–Swiss border. The World Wide Web began as a CERN project called ENQUIRE, initiated by Tim Berners-Lee in 1989 and Robert Cailliau in 1990. On April 1993, CERN announced that the World Wide Web would be free to anyone. Established in 1954, the organization has twenty European member states. The CERN sites, as an international facility, are officially under neither Swiss nor French jurisdiction. Member states' contributions to CERN for the year 2008 totaled €664 million.

Church–Turing thesis: Is a hypothesis about functions whose values are algorithmically computable. The Church–Turing thesis states, 'everything algorithmically computable is computable by a Turing machine.' The Church–Turing thesis cannot be formally proven. Despite this fact, this thesis now has near-universal acceptance.

Civilization: In 1923, Albert Schweitzer defined civilization as: 'the sum total of all progress made by man in every sphere of action and from every point of view in so far as the progress helps towards the spiritual perfecting of individuals as the progress of all progress.' In this book, we take civilization to be the 50,000 years of the human experience that has made us what we are today. We consider that the development of civilization is an evolutionary process.

Communism: Karl Marx, the father of communism defined it as: 'A social structure in which classes are abolished and property is commonly controlled, as well as a political philosophy and social movement that advocates and aims to create such a society.' He also wrote that communism would be the final stage in society, which would be achieved through a proletarian revolution and only possible after a socialist stage develops the productive forces, leading to a superabundance of goods and services. Marx's version of 'pure communism' refers to a classless, stateless and oppression-free society in which decisions on what to produce and what policies to pursue are made democratically, allowing every member of society to participate in the decision-making process in both the political and economic spheres of life. In real life, all communist regimes have followed Lenin's version in which there is government ownership of all the means of production through centrally planned economies; and they have been authoritarian, repressive, and essentially concerned with preserving their power.

Computer: Is a machine that processes data following a given set of instructions. Alan Turing is regarded as the father of modern computer science. In 1936, he formalized the concept of the algorithm and of computations; by means of a theoretical computer called the Turing machine. The first electronic computer, the 'Zuse Z3' was built in Germany in 1941.

Context Tree Weighting method (CTW): Is a lossless compression and prediction algorithm by Willems, Shtarkov, and Tjalkens in 1995. The CTW algorithm offers both theoretical soundness and practical performance. The CTW algorithm is an ensemble method, mixing the predictions of many underlying variable order Markov models, where each such model is constructed using zero-order conditional probability estimators.

Corruption: Derived from the root word corrupt, from Latin *corruptus*, to destroy. In this book, we consider the following cases: Political corruption, which is the abuse of public power, office, or resources by government officials or employees for personal gain by extortion, soliciting or offering bribes. Institutional corruption, as practiced by elected officials in the US where campaign contributions are a legal way of obtaining bribes and buying favoritism. Corporate corruption includes criminal acts and the abuse of power by corporation officials.

CPU: Or central processing unit, is the portion of a computer system that carries out the instructions of a computer program to perform the basic arithmetical, logical, and input/output operations of the system. The CPU plays a role somewhat analogous to the brain in the computer. The CPU is housed in a single silicon chip called a microprocessor, which are large-scale integrated circuits in a package typically less than four centimeters square, with hundreds of connecting pins.

CUDA: Or Compute Unified Device Architecture is a parallel computing architecture developed by NVIDIA for graphics processing. Using CUDA, NVIDIA's GPUs become accessible for computation in a parallel throughput architecture that executes many concurrent threads slowly, rather than executing a single thread very quickly. CUDA provides an API providing access to the virtual instruction set and memory of the parallel computational elements in GPUs. CUDA has been used to accelerate, by an order of magnitude or more, non-graphical applications in computational biology, cryptography and other fields.

D

Database (DB): Is an organized collection of data, typically in digital form. Data are organized to model relevant aspects of reality, in a way that supports processes requiring this information. A database management system (DBMS) is the software system that manages the databases. Organizations and companies heavily depend on databases for their operations. Well known DBMSs include Oracle, IBM DB2, Microsoft SQL Server, Microsoft Access, PostgreSQL, MySQL, and SQLite. A database is not portable across different DBMS, but different DBMSs inter-operate by using standards like SQL and ODBC to support applications. A database needs to provide efficient run-time execution, in terms of performance, availability, and security, to support a large number of end-users.

Deep Blue supercomputer: On February 10, 1996, Deep Blue became the first machine to win a chess game against reigning world champion Garry Kasparov, under regular time controls. However, Kasparov won three and drew two of the following five games, beating Deep Blue by a score of 4–2, because wins count 1 point, but draws count ½ point. The match concluded on February 17, 1996. Deep Blue was upgraded and played Kasparov again in May 1997, winning the six-game rematch 3½–2½, ending on May 11. Deep Blue won the deciding game six after Kasparov made a mistake in the opening. The system was massively parallel, capable of evaluating 200 million positions per second, achieving 11.38 gigaflops.

Democracy: Democracy is a form of government that is exercised directly by the people (direct democracy) or by elected representatives of the people (representative democracy). The word was derived from the Greek: '*dêmos*' people and '*krátos*' power. It was invented around 500 BC. In theory and practice, democracy has taken many forms: Representative, Parliamentary, Liberal, Constitutional, Direct, Participatory, Socialist, Anarchist, random selection, Supranational, and others. Che Guevara, a Marxist revolutionary said: 'Democracy cannot consist solely of elections that are nearly always fictitious and managed by rich landowners and professional politicians.' However, it is without a doubt, the best approach to government up to this date.

Depression: It is a persistent, long-term decline in economic activity in one or more countries. It is more severe than a recession, which is seen as part of the normal Boom-Bust cycles that are said to happen every 5 to 7 years. A depression is lengthy, with a high rate of unemployment, credit shortages, shrinking output and investment, price deflation, reduced amounts of trade and commerce, financial and bank failures as well as highly volatile relative currency value fluctuations. Maybe the crisis of 2008 will be classified as a depression, these others have been: The Great Depression (1929-1941), Long Depression (1873-1896), Panic of 1837 (1837-1842).

Descartes, René: Was a French philosopher, mathematician, and writer, born on March 31, 1596. He spent most of his adult life in the Dutch Republic. As the Father of Modern Philosophy, his writings are studied to this day; his '*Meditations on First Philosophy*' is a text at university philosophy departments. His influence in mathematics is equally apparent;

the Cartesian coordinate system is named after him. In his natural philosophy, he was a major figure in 17th century rationalism; he rejected the analysis of corporeal substance into matter and form; and he rejected any appeal to divine conclusions in explaining natural phenomena. In his theology, he insists on the absolute freedom of God's act of creation. His most famous philosophical statement is 'Cogito ergo sum' (I think, therefore I am). Descartes died on February 11, 1650.

DirectCompute: Is an application programming interface (API) from Microsoft that supports general-purpose computing on graphics processing units on Windows Vista, 7 and 8. DirectCompute is part of their DirectX APIs. This architecture shares a range of computational interfaces with its competitors: the Khronos Group's OpenCL and NVIDIA's CUDA.

Directed Acyclic Graph (DAG): Is a directed graph with no directed cycles. That is, it is formed by a collection of vertices and directed edges, each edge connecting one vertex to another, such that there is no way to start at some vertex v and follow a sequence of edges that eventually loops back to v again.

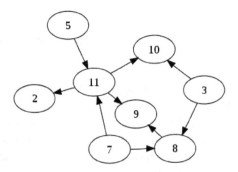

DAGs may be used to model several different kinds of structure in mathematics and computer science. A collection of tasks that must be ordered into a sequence, subject to constraints that certain tasks must be performed earlier than others, may be represented as a DAG with a vertex for each task and an edge for each constraint; algorithms for topological ordering may be used to generate a valid sequence. DAGs may also be used to model processes in which information flows in a consistent direction through a network of processors. The reachability relation in a DAG forms a partial order, and any finite partial order may be represented by a DAG using reachability. Additionally, DAGs may be used as a space-efficient representation of a collection of sequences with overlapping subsequences.

DNA: Deoxyribonucleic acid contains the instructions used in the development and functioning of all living organisms and viruses. The role of DNA molecules is the long-term storage of information needed to construct other components of cells, such as proteins and RNA molecules. It is a long polymer made from millions of repeating units called nucleotides. A DNA base pair is 2.2 to 2.6 nanometers wide, in which each nucleotide unit is 0.33 nm long. The largest human chromosome, chromosome number 1, is approximately 220 million base pairs long in two strands that entwine in the shape of a double helix.

Drone: Is an aircraft without a human pilot onboard, or an unmanned aerial vehicle (UAV). Its flight is either controlled autonomously by computers in the vehicle, or under the remote control of a navigator or pilot, on the ground or in another vehicle. There is a variety of drone shapes, sizes, configurations, and characteristics. To this day, drones are normally piloted remotely, but the use of autonomous control is rising.

Dogma: Is a fundamental principle that must be upheld by all followers of a religion. The term dogma is assigned to theological tenets that are considered to be well demonstrated, such that their contention means that a person no longer accepts the given religion as his or her own. Rejection of dogma may lead to expulsion from a religious group.

Doomsday: Refers to an event that has a catastrophic outcome, which may range from a major disruption of human civilization, to the extinction of human life, to the destruction of planet Earth or to annihilation of the universe. These events can be classified as natural, manmade or supernatural.

Dualism: In philosophy of mind, it is the assumption that mental phenomena are, in some respects non-physical, or that the mind and body are distinct. Dualism is closely associated with the philosophy of René Descartes (1641), which holds that the mind is a nonphysical substance. Descartes clearly identified the mind with consciousness and self-awareness and distinguished this from the brain as the seat of intelligence. Hence, he was the first to formulate the mind–body problem, which arises because mental phenomena arguably differ, qualitatively or substantially, from the physical body on which they apparently depend.

E

Economic Inequality: Also known as the gap between rich and poor, income inequality, wealth disparity, or wealth and income differences. Comprises disparities in the distribution of economic assets, wealth and income. The term typically refers to inequality among individuals and groups within a society, but can also refer to inequality among countries. There are differences of opinion about the morality of inequality, whether inequality is necessary and what can be done about it. Economic inequality varies between societies and historical periods; between economic structures or systems, for example, capitalism or socialism, ongoing or past wars, and differences in individuals' abilities to create wealth are all involved in the creation of economic inequality. There are various numerical indices for measuring economic inequality, the most common being the Gini coefficient.

Economist: Is an expert or a professional working inside one of fields of economics or having an academic degree in this subject. They are typically employed in banking, commerce, marketing, finance, accountancy, business administration, lobbying and non-profit organizations. Politicians often consult economists before endorsing a policy, and many political leaders have degrees in economics.

Economy: Consists of the complete economic system of a country or an area; includes labor, capital and land resources, and those that collectively participate in the production, distribution, sales, and consumption of goods and services.

Einstein, Albert: Born in Germany in 1879, his contributions include the Special and General Theories of Relativity that made him the most important theoretical physicist of the early 20th Century. He received the 1921 Nobel Prize in Physics 'for his services to Theoretical Physics, and especially for his discovery of the law of the photoelectric effect,' a prize that in a weird way sidestepped his most important theories of relativity. Einstein published more than 300 scientific and over 150 non-scientific works. He is widely regarded as the father of modern physics. He died in 1955.

Equality: Or Egalitarianism is treated throughout this book as a social and political doctrine that maintains that all people should be treated as equals and have the same political, economic, social, and civil rights, without severe economic inequalities.

Ethernet: Are computer networking technologies for local area networks (LAN) introduced in 1980 and standardized in IEEE 802.3. Systems communicating over Ethernet divide a stream of data into individual packets called frames. Each frame contains source and destination addresses and error-checking data so that damaged data can be detected and re-transmitted. The standards comprise several wiring such as twisted pair and fiber optic links in conjunction with bridges, hubs or switches. Data rates have periodically increased from the original 10 megabits per second, to 100 gigabits per second.

Ethics: Is the way to achieve morally correct outcomes. It is a contentious field where many philosophers have expressed their opinions. Some ethical scholars propose, 'the end justifies the means.' while others believe 'the act may be considered the right thing to do even if it produces a bad consequence.' Some consider aesthetics, etiquette, common sense, arbitration and the law as aspects of an ethics code.

European Union (EU): Is an economic and political union of twenty-seven European member states. The Treaty of Maastricht established the EU on November 1st, 1993. With over 500 million citizens, it generates an estimated 30% share of the gross world product. The EU is a single market that ensures the free movement of people, goods, services, and capital. Sixteen of its member states have adopted a common currency, the euro €.

Evolution: This theory explains the variety and relationship of all living things and their genetic variations in this way: 'Some organisms, by chance, acquire features that allow them to survive and thrive better than others of their kind. The organisms that survive will be more likely to have offspring of their own. The offspring might inherit the useful feature.' However, evolution is not a random process. While mutations are random, natural selection is not. Evolution is an inevitable result of imperfectly copying self-replicating organisms reproducing over billions of years under the selective pressure of the environment. The outcome of evolution is not a perfectly designed organism. It is simply an individual that can survive better and reproduce more successfully than its neighbors in a particular environment. Fossils, the genetic code, and the peculiar distribution of life on earth provide a record of evolution and demonstrate the common ancestry of all organisms, both living and long dead. Evolution can be directly observed in artificial selection, or the selective breeding for certain traits of domestic animals and plants. The diverse breeds of cats, dogs, horses, and agricultural plants serve as examples of evolution. Although some groups raise objections to the theory of evolution, the evidence of observation and experiments over a hundred years by thousands of scientists unquestionably supports evolution. The result of four billion years of evolution is the diversity of life around us, with an estimated 1.75 million different species in existence today.

F

Facebook: Is a social networking service and website launched in February 2004, operated and privately owned by Facebook Inc. Users must register before using the site, after which they may create a personal profile, add other users as friends, and exchange messages, including automatic notifications when they update their profile. Users may join common-interest user groups, organized by workplace, school or college, or other characteristics, and categorize their friends into list. The name of the service stems from the colloquial name for the book given to students at the start of the academic year by some university administrations in the United States to help students get to know each other. Facebook was founded by Mark Zuckerberg with his college roommates and fellow students Eduardo Saverin, Dustin Moskovitz and Chris Hughes. The Web site's membership was initially limited by the founders to Harvard students, but was expanded to other colleges in the Boston area, the Ivy League, and Stanford University. It gradually added support for students at various other universities before opening to high school students, and eventually to anyone aged 13 and over. As of April 2012, Facebook has more than 900 million active users.

FLOPS: Stands for FLoating-point OPerations per Second and is a measure of a computer's performance, especially in fields of scientific calculations that make heavy use of floating-point calculations. It is similar to the older and simpler measurement of instructions per second. The values: gigaflops (10^9), teraflops (10^{12}), petaflops (10^{15}), exaflops (10^{18}) and zettaflops (10^{21}) are often used as shorthand. As a comparison, the speed of the Titan supercomputer of the Oak Ridge National Laboratory, that started operations in 2012, is 20 petaflops. In 2011, Intel demonstrated a single x86-based processor, code-named 'Knights Corner'.' that can sustain more than 1 teraflops. The human brain is supposed to be able to process between 1 teraflops and 100,000 zettaflops, with a mid-point of 100 petaflops, depending on the way it is measured.

Franklin, Benjamin: Born in Boston, Massachusetts, January 17, 1706 he was one of the Founding Fathers of the United States. Franklin was a leading author, printer, political theorist, politician, postmaster, scientist, musician, inventor, satirist, civic activist, statesman, and diplomat. As a scientist, he was a major figure in the American Enlightenment for his discoveries and theories regarding electricity. He invented the lightning rod, bifocals, the Franklin stove, a carriage odometer, and the glass harmonica. Franklin earned the title of 'The First American' for his campaigning for colonial unity; as an author and spokesman in London for several colonies, then as the first United States Ambassador to France he exemplified the emerging American nation. He became wealthy publishing Poor Richard's Almanac and The Pennsylvania Gazette. As a diplomat, he was a major figure in the development of positive Franco-American relations. Toward the end of his life, he freed his slaves and became one of the most prominent abolitionists. He died April 17, 1790.

Free Market: Is a market where there is no economic intervention and regulation by government except to sanction the use of force or fraud. Within the ideal free market, property rights are voluntarily exchanged at a price arranged solely by the mutual consent of sellers and buyers following the theory of supply and demand. Free markets are the essence of capitalism. It has been calculated that under certain idealized conditions, a system of free trade leads to high efficiency. However, a more realistic understanding of free markets and capitalism, than what is professed among free market theorists, leads to the conclusion that capitalism deviates from the model in a way that justifies socialism as a better solution. The major drawback of free markets is that humans act illogically and with a herd behavior, under some quite common conditions, which is in conflict with the conduct that is essential for a free market to work optimally.

Freud, Sigmund: Was an Austrian neurologist, who founded psychoanalysis, he was born May 6, 1856. Freud considered himself a Jew even though he rejected Judaism and had a critical view of religion. Freud developed theories about the unconscious mind and the mechanism of repression. Freud postulated the existence of libido, the energy of mental processes and structures. He was also a prolific essayist, drawing on psychoanalysis to contribute to the interpretation and critique of culture. He died September 23, 1939.

Friedman, Milton: An American economist born in 1912, who originally supported Keynesian government intervention in the economy. Then, during the 1960s, Friedman became the main opponent of Keynesianism. He upheld an alternative macroeconomic policy known as 'monetarism.' He theorized that there existed a 'natural rate of unemployment' and he argued the central government could not micromanage the economy because people would realize what the government was doing and change their behavior to neutralize such policies. He was an economic advisor to President Ronald Reagan. His monetary theory has had a large influence on economists such as Ben Bernanke and the Federal Reserve's response to the financial crisis of 2007-2010. Friedman died in 2006.

G

Gandhi, Mahatma: Born in India in 1869, he was the greatest political and spiritual leader during the Indian independence movement. He was the pioneer of 'satyagraha,' resistance to tyranny through mass civil disobedience, a philosophy firmly founded upon 'ahimsa' or total nonviolence that led India to independence in 1947, and inspired movements for civil rights and freedom across the world. In 1948, Gandhi was shot while taking his nightly public walk.

GDP: Gross Domestic Product refers to the market value of all officially recognized final goods and services produced within a country in a given period: *GDP = private consumption + gross investment + government spending + (exports − imports)*. GDP per capita is equal to *GDP / resident population* is an indicator of a country's standard of living. GDP per capita is not a measure of personal income, as GDP may increase while real incomes for the majority decline. Under economic theory, GDP per capita exactly equals the gross domestic income (GDI) per capita which is the total income received by all sectors of an economy within a nation. It includes the sum of all wages and profits, minus subsidies. Since all income is derived from production, including services, the gross domestic income of a country should exactly equal its GDP. In the United States, the Bureau of Economic Analysis produces figures for both the GDP and GDI. Although these should be equal, since they are calculated in different ways, in practice the listed figures are different. This difference is known as the statistical discrepancy. In 2011, the US had a GDP of 15,094,025 million dollars.

Genetic: Is the science of heredity and variation in living organisms. This technique has been used since prehistoric times to improve plants and animals using selective breeding. Modern genetics is centered on the study of genes, which are a portion of DNA that contains both 'coding' sequences that determine what the gene does, and 'non-coding' sequences that determine when the gene is active.

Geneva Conventions: Are four treaties, and three additional protocols, that establish the standards of international law for the humanitarian treatment of the victims of war. The singular term Geneva Convention denotes the agreements of 1949, negotiated in the aftermath of the Second World War, which updated the terms of the first three treaties of 1864, 1906 and 1929, and added a fourth treaty. The articles of the Fourth Geneva Convention (1949) extensively defined the basic rights of civil and military prisoners during war; established protections for the wounded and for civilians in and around a war zone. The treaties of 1949 were ratified, in whole or with reservations, by 194 countries. The Geneva Convention also defines the rights and protections of non-combatants. Because the Geneva Conventions are about people in war, they do not address warfare proper and the use of weapons of war. That is the subject of the Hague Conventions; First Hague Conference, 1899; Second Hague Conference 1907; and the bio–chemical warfare Geneva Protocol; Protocol for the Prohibition of the Use in War of Asphyxiating, Poisonous or other Gases; and of Bacteriological Methods of Warfare, in 1929.

Glia: Are non-neuronal cells that maintain homeostasis, form myelin, and provide support and protection for neurons in the brain, and for neurons in other parts of the nervous system such as in the autonomic nervous system. In the human brain, there is roughly one glia for every neuron. As the Greek name implies, glia are commonly known as the glue of the nervous system; however, this is not fully accurate. There are four main functions of glial cells: to surround neurons and hold them in place, to supply nutrients and oxygen to neurons, to insulate one neuron from another, and to destroy pathogens and remove dead neurons.

Global Financial Crisis of 2008: The financial crisis of 2007–2010 is the worst financial crisis since the Great Depression of the 1930s. It caused the failure of banks and financial institutions, a decline in the American consumer wealth estimated at 12.9 trillions of US dollars (more than $40,000 per person), and forced the governments of the world to provide trillions of dollars to save banks and other business that were 'too big to fail.' Its immediate cause was the collapse of the housing bubble, which peaked in 2006, creating a depreciation of securities linked to real estate. The real cause of this crisis is a lot more complex and involves deregulation, the flattening of wages since 1979, greedy banks and business, 'manager's capitalism' that produced huge upper management salaries and bonuses, corrupt governments and a general failure of capitalism.

Gödel Machine: An old dream of computer scientists, the Gödel machine is an optimally efficient universal problem solver. It can be implemented on a traditional computer and solves any given computational problem in the optimal fashion inspired by Kurt Gödel's celebrated self-referential formulas (1931). It starts with an axiomatic description of itself, and any utility function may be plugged in, such as the expected future reward of a robot. Using an efficient proof searcher, the Gödel machine will rewrite any part of its software, including the proof searcher, as soon as it has found a proof that this will improve its future performance, given the utility function and the typically limited computational resources. Self-rewrites are globally optimal, and there is no local maxima, since probably none of all the alternative rewrites and proofs, at least those that could be found by continuing the proof search, are worth waiting for. The Gödel machine formalizes I. J. Good's informal remarks (1965) on an 'intelligence explosion' through self-improving 'super-intelligences.'

Goertzel, Ben: Is an author and researcher in the field of artificial intelligence, born December 8, 1966 in Rio de Janeiro, Brazil. He currently leads Novamente LLC, a company that is trying to develop strong AI, which he calls Artificial General Intelligence (AGI). He is also the CEO of Biomind LLC, a company that markets a software product for the AI-supported analysis of biological microarray data; and he is an advisor to the Singularity Institute for Artificial Intelligence, and formerly its Director of Research. He graduated from the Bard College at Simon's Rock, with a bachelor's degree in mathematics, and then in 1989 got a PhD in mathematics from Temple University; afterwards he taught mathematics, computer science and psychology at various universities. He defines intelligence as the ability to detect patterns in the world and in the agent itself. He would first create a baby-like artificial intelligence, and then raise and train it in a virtual world such as Second Life to produce a more powerful intelligence. Goertzel is a founding member of the Transhumanist Order of Cosmic Engineers and he has signed up to have his body frozen after his death. In 2011, he joined the scientific board of the newly founded Global Brain Institute at the Vrije Universiteit Brussel.

Google: Started in 1996 as a research project by Larry Page and Sergey Brin, when they were both PhD students at Stanford University in California. They figured out a better system to analyze relationships between websites, which they called PageRank; even though, this type of ranking was already known, as at that time RankDex a search engine from IDD Information Services, designed by Robin Li, was already using it. In August 1998 Andy Bechtolsheim co-founder of Sun Microsystems, gave $100,000 as seed money to the founders. Early in 1999, Vinod Khosla, a venture capitalist, bought the search engine from Brin and Page for $750,000. On June 7, 1999, venture capital investors funded Google with $25 million. The name Google is a misspelling of the word googol, a very large number. Google's success ultimately came not from being a better search engine, but from selling advertisements associated with search keywords; a concept that Page and Brin had initially opposed. In May 2011, the number of monthly unique visitors to Google surpassed 1 billion.

GPS: The Global Positioning System is a space-based satellite navigation system that provides location and time information in all weather, anywhere on or near the Earth, where there is an unobstructed line of sight to four or more GPS satellites. It is maintained by the United States government and is freely accessible to anyone with a GPS receiver. The GPS program provides critical capabilities to military, civil and commercial users around the world. In addition, GPS is the backbone for modernizing the global air traffic system. The GPS project was developed in 1973 to overcome the limitations of previous navigation systems, integrating ideas from several predecessors, including a number of classified engineering design studies from the 1960s. GPS was created and realized by the US Department of Defense and was originally run with 24 satellites. It became fully operational in 1994. Advances in technology and new demands on the existing system have now led to efforts to modernize the GPS system and implement the next generation of GPS III satellites and Next Generation Operational Control System (OCX). Announcements from the Vice President and the White House in 1998 initiated these changes. In 2000, US Congress authorized the modernization effort, referred to as GPS III. In addition to GPS, other systems are in use or under development. The Russian GLObal NAvigation Satellite System (GLONASS) was in use only by the Russian military, until it was made available to civilians in 2007. There are also the planned European Union Galileo positioning system, Chinese Compass navigation system, and Indian Regional Navigational Satellite System.

GPU: Or graphics processing unit, is a specialized electronic circuit designed to rapidly build images in a buffer intended for a display. Modern GPUs are very efficient at manipulating computer graphics. Their highly-parallel structure makes them more effective than general-purpose CPUs for algorithms processing large blocks of data in parallel.

H

Hamilton, Peter F. : Is a British science-fiction author born on March 2, 1960. He is best known for writing space opera. He did not attend university and he started writing in 1987. Hamilton generally uses a clean, prosaic style. His space opera is characterized by the way it switches between several characters, often there are three or more main characters, whose paths begin separated but eventually cross. Common themes in his books are politics, religion, sexually precocious teenagers, and armed conflict. He has written two massive space operas, '*The Night's Dawn Trilogy*' and '*The Evolutionary Void*'; each one with more than 3,000 pages. As of the publication of his tenth novel in 2004, his works had sold over two million copies worldwide.

Hamilton, Sir William Rowan: Was an Irish physicist, astronomer, and mathematician, born on August 4, 1805. His studies of mechanical and optical systems led him to discover new mathematical concepts and techniques in classical mechanics, optics, and algebra. He reformulated Newtonian mechanics, now called Hamiltonian mechanics, which lead to the theories of electromagnetism and quantum mechanics. He died on September 2, 1865.

Hayek, Friedrich August von: Is an Austrian economist born in 1899. He defended classical liberalism and free-market capitalism against socialist and collectivist thought. In his famous book '*The Road to Serfdom,*' he makes a strong case against centrally planned economies, even though he opposed pure 'laissez-faire' capitalism. Hayek wrote in his book that 'probably nothing has done so much harm to the liberal cause as the wooden insistence of some liberals on certain rules of thumb, above all of the principle of laissez-faire capitalism.' At that time, and even today in many parts of the world, liberals support capitalism. He died in 1992.

Head Up Display (HUD): Is a transparent display that shows graphics and data while looking forward. They were developed for military aviation and are now used in commercial aircraft, automobiles, and other applications. A beam splitter, located directly in front of the viewer redirects the projected image from a projector allowing seeing the normal field of view and the projected infinity image at the same time. A computer generates the imagery and symbols projected on the HUD.

Human Genome: Approximately 23,000 protein-coding genes stored on 23 chromosome pairs form the 'homo sapiens' genome. A copy of these 23 chromosome pairs is placed in the nucleus of each human diploid cell. Twenty-two of these are asexual chromosome pairs, while one pair determines sex. The human genome occupies a total of just over 3.2 billion DNA base pairs. Only about 1.5% of the genome codes for proteins, the rest consists of non-coding RNA genes, regulatory sequences, non-coding DNA and so named 'junk' DNA.

Human Genome Project: Was an international scientific research project to determine the sequence of base pairs, which make up DNA, and to identify and map the approximately 20,000 to 25,000 genes of the human genome. The project began in 1990, initially headed by James D. Watson at the US National Institute of Health. A working draft of the genome was released in 2000 and the completed genome in 2003, two years ahead of schedule.

Human Nature: It is the concept that there is a set of characteristics, including ways of thinking, feeling and acting, which all 'normal' humans have in common. Bertrand Russell thought that due to instincts that have been transmitted to us from our ancestry, and given the predatory environment in which we evolved, there is a primordial origin of contemporary and historical moral evil; which explains the bad things we do to each other like lying, cheating, slandering, thieving and slaughtering. The consensus is that human nature is based on billions of years of evolution, that is very slow, and thousands of years of civilization, which is much faster.

Human Rights: Are the 'basic rights and freedoms to which all humans are entitled.' The United Nations recognizes the existence of human rights and their 'Universal Declaration of Human Rights,' adopted in 1948, is the predominant modern codification of commonly accepted human rights principles. Up to very recently this concept was tarnished by almost universal slavery practices. Much of modern human rights law and the basis of most modern interpretations of human rights can be traced back to relatively recent European history. The 'Twelve Articles of the Black Forest' that are demands raised against the Swabian League in Germany in 1525, are considered as the first record of human rights in Europe.

Hutter, Marcus: Is a German computer scientist and professor. Hutter was born in Munich in 1967, where he studied physics and computer science. In 2000, he joined Jürgen Schmidhuber's group at the Swiss Artificial Intelligence lab IDSIA, where he developed the first mathematical theory of optimal Universal Artificial Intelligence, based on Kolmogorov complexity and Ray Solomonoff's theory of universal inductive inference. In 2006, he accepted a professorship at the Australian National University in Canberra. In the universal algorithm AIXI, Hutter formalizes the optimal strategy of a universal AI agent that maximizes its future expected reward, given the so far limited observation sequence, by using the Bayes-optimal way of selecting the next action in an unknown dynamic environment, up to some fixed future horizon. Hutter's only assumption is that the reactions of the environment, in response to the agent's actions, follows some unknown but computable probability distribution.

I

Industrial Revolution: In the later part of the 18th Century, a transition began in parts of Great Britain; the use of manual labor and draft-animals changed to machine based manufacturing. The Industrial Revolution happened in a period from the 18th to the 19th Century where major changes in agriculture, manufacturing, mining, and transport, driven by technology, had a profound effect on the socioeconomic and cultural conditions. It started in the United Kingdom, and then spread throughout Europe, North America, and eventually the world. Around 1850 this Industrial Revolution merged into the Second Industrial Revolution, when technological and economic progress gained momentum with the development of steam-powered ships, railways and at the end of the 19th Century, the internal combustion engine and electrical power generation.

Internet: In the 1960s, the US government funded military research to find robust, fault-tolerant and distributed computer networks. In the 1970s based on this work, the Transmission Control Protocol and the Internet Protocol were established creating the Internet Protocol Suite (TCP/IP). In 1990, two scientists at CERN in Geneva, Switzerland, Sir Tim Berners Lee and Robert Cailliau proposed using 'HyperText' to link and access information of various kinds as a web of nodes, called the 'WorldWideWeb' (WWW or W3) in which a user can browse at will. The Internet has no centralized authority, neither in technological implementation or policies for access and usage; each network sets its own standards. The Internet Protocol Address Space and the Domain Name System assign name spaces in the Internet; the Internet Corporation for Assigned Names and Numbers (ICANN) directs them. As of 2009, one quarter of Earth's population, 1.67 billion, used the services of the Internet.

J

Jacobi, Carl Gustav Jacob: Was a German mathematician, born in Potsdam on December 10, 1804. He is considered one of the greatest mathematicians of his generation, he made fundamental contributions in the study of differential equations and rational mechanics, notably the Hamilton–Jacobi theory. He studied at Berlin University, where he obtained the degree of Doctor of Philosophy in 1825. In 1827 he became a professor of mathematics at Königsberg University until 1842. He died on February 18, 1851.

Jung, Carl Gustav: A Swiss psychiatrist who founded analytical psychology was born in July 1875. Jung proposed individuation, which is the central concept of analytical psychology, a psychological process integrating the opposites including the conscious with the unconscious while still maintaining their relative autonomy. Much of his life's work was spent exploring tangential areas, including Eastern and Western philosophy, alchemy, astrology, and sociology. He died June 6, 1961.

K

Kálmán, Rudolf (Rudy) Emil: Is a Hungarian-American electrical engineer, mathematical system theorist, and college professor. He was born May 19, 1930. Educated in the United States, where most of his work was done. He earned his bachelor's degree in 1953 and his master's degree in 1954, both in electrical engineering from the Massachusetts Institute of Technology. Kálmán completed his doctorate in 1957 at Columbia University. He is currently a retired professor from three different institutes of technology and universities. He is most noted for his co-invention and development of the Kalman Filter, or Kalman-Bucy Filter, a mathematical formulation that is widely used in control systems, avionics, and outer space manned and unmanned vehicles. For this work, US President Barack Obama awarded Kálmán with the National Medal of Science on October 7, 2009.

Kasparov, Garry Kimovich: Is a Russian chess grandmaster, a former World Chess Champion, writer and political activist. He is widely regarded as the greatest chess player of all time. Was born on April 13, 1963. Kasparov became the youngest undisputed World Chess Champion in 1985 at the age of 22, by defeating then-champion Anatoly Karpov. He continued to hold the 'Classical' World Chess Championship until his defeat by Vladimir Kramnik in 2000. He is also widely known for being the first world chess champion to lose a match to a computer under standard time controls, when he lost to Deep Blue in 1997. Kasparov announced his retirement from professional chess on 10 March 2005, to devote his time to politics and writing. He formed the 'United Civil Front' movement, and joined as a member of 'The Other Russia,' a coalition opposing the administration of Vladimir Putin.

Keynes, John Maynard: Was a British economist born in 1883. He is the inspiration of Keynesian economics, which argues that private sector decisions sometimes lead to inefficient macroeconomic outcomes, and therefore advocates active policy responses by the public sector, including monetary policy actions by the central bank and fiscal policy actions by the government to stabilize output over the business cycle. Keynesian economics advocates a mixed economy with a predominantly private sector, but with government and the public sector playing a large role. This theory served as the economic model during the latter part of the Great Depression, World War II, and the post-war Golden Age of Capitalism, 1945–1973. After this Golden Age, Ronald Reagan introduced 'trickle-down' economics and not surprisingly since then the working classes in America have been left out of the American Dream. The First Baron Keynes died before that, in 1946.

Kinect: Is a motion sensing input device by Microsoft for the Xbox 360 video game console and Windows PCs. It enables users to control and interact with the Xbox 360 through a natural user interface using gestures and spoken commands. Kinect was launched on November 4, 2010.

Kurzweil, Raymond 'Ray': Is an author, inventor and futurist, born February 12, 1948 in New York City. He is involved in optical character recognition (OCR), text-to-speech synthesis, speech recognition technology, electronic keyboard instruments and AI. He is the author of several books on health, artificial intelligence, transhumanism, the technological singularity, and futurism. He obtained a BS degree in Computer Science and Literature in 1970 from MIT. In his 1999 book, *'The Age of Spiritual Machines,'* he states that computers will one day prove superior to the best human financial minds at making profitable investment decisions. His 2005 book, *'The Singularity Is Near'* introduced the concepts of exponential technological growth, radical lifespan expansion and how we will transcend our biology.

L

Laplace, Pierre-Simon, Marquis de: Was a French mathematician and astronomer born March 23, 1749. His work included the development of mathematical astronomy and statistics. Between 1799 and 1825, in his five volume *'Mécanique Céleste'* he explained the geometrical nature of classical mechanic using calculus. In statistics, he developed the Bayesian interpretation of probability. Laplace formulated Laplace's equation, the Laplace transform and the Laplacian differential equation. He was one of the first scientists to postulate the existence of black holes and the notion of gravitational collapse. Laplace became a Count of the First French

Empire in 1806 and was named Marquis in 1817, after the Bourbon Restoration. He died March 5, 1827.

Lavoisier, Antoine-Laurent de: A French noble born in 1743, he was a preeminent chemist and biologist. He proposed the law of conservation of mass. Discovered and named oxygen and hydrogen, abolished the phlogiston theory, encouraged the adoption of the metric system, created the first table of elements, and reformed chemical nomenclature. He was guillotined in 1794.

Lempel–Ziv–Welch (LZW): Is a universal lossless data compression algorithm created by Abraham Lempel, Jacob Ziv, and Terry Welch. It was published by Welch in 1984 as an improved implementation of the LZ78 algorithm published by Lempel and Ziv in 1978. The algorithm is simple to implement, and has the potential for very high throughput in hardware implementations.

LIDAR: Light Detection And Ranging, also called LADAR is an optical remote sensing technology that can measure the distance to, or other properties of a target by illuminating the target with light, often using pulses from a laser.

Locke, John: Born in 1632, he was an English philosopher and physician, regarded as one of the most influential proponents of reason as the primary source and legitimacy for authority. He is also recognized for explaining the ways in which people form states to maintain social order. His work had a great impact upon the development of the theory of knowledge and political philosophy. His writings influenced Voltaire and Rousseau. He died in 1704.

Longevity: In this book, we define it as methods used to extend lifespan. Even though there are legends and stories about Sumerian kings that lived 43200 years and Methuselah supposedly died when he was 969 years old, these tales are unsubstantiated. It seems that the maximum natural human lifespan is around 120 years. Currently scientists are trying to develop techniques to extend life, with good health, beyond this natural limit.

M

Malthus, Thomas Robert: A British Reverend born in 1766 became famous for his theories of population growth. Malthus wrote: 'The power of population is indefinitely greater than the power in the earth to produce subsistence for man.' Malthus argued that poverty was a check to population growth; people without means would have fewer children as they could not support them. Moreover, if wages increased, the birth rate would increase while the death rate decreased. Consequently, wage increases caused populations to grow. Mercifully, his theories have proven to be totally wrong. However, the same arguments are expressed these days by those favoring exploitation of laborers. He died in 1834.

Mandela, Nelson: He was born in 1918 in South Africa. A relentless anti-apartheid activist and leader of the African National Congress armed wing 'Umkhonto we Sizwe,' Mandela served 27 years in prison on charges of sabotage, as well as other crimes committed while he led the movement against apartheid. After his release from prison in 1990, Mandela supported reconciliation and led the transition towards multi-racial democracy in South Africa. He was the first black President of South Africa, and served from 1994 to 1999.

McCarthy, John: Was a computer scientist and cognitive scientist, born in Boston, Massachusetts on September 4, 1927. He invented the term 'artificial intelligence' (AI), developed the Lisp programming language family, significantly influenced the design of the ALGOL, another programming language and was very influential in the early development of AI. He got a B.S. in Mathematics from Caltech in 1948. At Caltech, he attended a lecture by John Von Neumann that inspired his future endeavors. McCarthy received a PhD in Mathematics from Princeton University in 1951. McCarthy supported mathematical logic for artificial intelligence. During 1956, he organized the first international conference to highlight artificial intelligence. One of the attendees was Marvin Minsky, who later became one of the main AI theorists, and joined McCarthy at MIT in 1959. He left MIT for Stanford University during 1962, where he helped establish the Stanford AI Laboratory. His 2001 short story '*The Robot and the Baby*' farcically explored the question of whether robots should have, or simulate having emotions and anticipated aspects of Internet culture and social networking that became more prominent during the ensuing decade. He died October 24, 2011.

Meade, James: Born in 1907, he was a British economist and winner of the 1977 Nobel Memorial Prize in Economic Sciences jointly with the Swedish economist Bertil Ohlin for their 'Path breaking contribution to the theory of international trade and international capital movements.' He died in 1995.

Milgram, Stanley: He was born in 1933 in New York City. In 1960, he received a PhD in Social Psychology from Harvard. He became an assistant professor at Yale in the fall of 1960 and an assistant professor in the Department of Social Relations at Harvard University in 1963. Milgram was denied tenure at Harvard, most likely because of his controversial Milgram Experiment. In 1967 he became a tenured full professor at the City University of New York Graduate Center. In his Milgram experiments, presented in his article 'Behavioral study of Obedience,' 26 out of 40 participants tortured their peers with the full range of electrical shocks at up to 450 volts. Thus, according to Milgram, the participant shifts responsibility to the authority of another person and does not blame himself for what happens. This resembles real-life incidents in which people see themselves as merely cogs in a machine, just 'doing their job,' allowing them to avoid responsibility for the consequences of their actions. The shocks themselves were fake, but the participants were led to believe that they were real. The 'six degrees of separation' concept originates from Milgram's 'small world experiment' in 1967, which tracked chains of acquaintances in the United States. He died in 1984.

Minimax: Is a decision rule used in decision theory, game theory, statistics and philosophy for minimizing the possible loss for a worst-case scenario. Originally formulated for a two-player zero-sum games, it has also been extended to general decision making in the presence of uncertainty. The minimax theorem states that in a two-person, zero-sum game with a finite number of strategies, there exists a value V and a mixed strategy for each player, such that: (a) Given the second player strategy, the best payoff possible for player one is V, and (b) given player one strategy, the best payoff possible for player two is $-V$. Because each player minimizes the maximum payoff possible for the other and being a zero-sum game, he also minimizes his own maximum loss.

Minimum Description Length Principle (MDL): Is a formalization of Occam's Razor in which the best hypothesis for a given set of data is the one that leads to the best compression of the data. MDL was introduced by Jorma Rissanen in 1978. The fundamental idea behind the MDL Principle is that any regularity in a given set of data can be used to compress the data. Following this idea, a program is set to compress the data, using a Turing-complete computer language. A program to output the data is written in that language; thus, the program effectively represents the data. The length of the shortest program that outputs the data is called the Kolmogorov complexity of the data, which is also the central idea behind Ray Solomonoff's idealized theory of inductive inference. MDL methods implement a tradeoff between the complexity of the hypothesis and the complexity of the data, given the hypothesis

Minsky, Marvin Lee: Is an American cognitive scientist in the field of artificial intelligence, born August 9, 1927. He and John McCarthy founded the Massachusetts Institute of Technology's AI Laboratory, and authored several texts on AI and philosophy. He holds a BA in Mathematics from Harvard in 1950 and a PhD in mathematics from Princeton in 1954. Isaac Asimov described Minsky as one of only two people he would admit were more intelligent than he was, the other being Carl Sagan. Minsky wrote the book '*Perceptrons*' with Seymour Papert, which became the foundational work in the analysis of artificial neural networks and is now more a historical than practical book. His book '*A framework for representing knowledge.*' created a new paradigm in programming and is still in wide use. Minsky was an adviser on the movie 2001: 'A Space Odyssey.'

MIPS: Millions of Instructions Per Second. MIPS are not a reliable measure of the speed of a given CPU as it is dependent upon many factors, such as the type of instructions being executed, the execution order and the presence of branch instructions, and speeds are highly dependent on the programming language used. As a curiosity, in 1971, an Intel 4004 was capable of 0.092 MIPS at 740 kHZ; in 2011, an Intel Core i7 is rated at 177,730 MIPS at 3.33 GHZ.

Moore's Law: Intel cofounder Gordon E. Moore introduced the concept that transistor counts had doubled every year in the publication 'Cramming more components onto integrated circuits.' Electronics Magazine, April 1965. In 1975, Moore altered his projection to a doubling every two years. Moore's Law is still in effect, and is expected to be for the rest of this century.

Morgenstern, Oskar: Was a German economist born on January 24, 1902. He and John von Neumann, started the mathematical field of game theory and developed the von Neumann–Morgenstern utility theorem. Educated in Vienna, he was the recipient of a three-year fellowship financed by the Rockefeller Foundation. A member of the faculty at Princeton University, he gravitated toward the Institute for Advanced Study. With von Neumann he co-wrote the book, '*Theory of Games and Economic Behavior.*' the first book on game theory. Morgenstern also authored other books. He died July 26, 1977.

N

Nanotechnology: Or nanotech, is the procedure of controlling matter on an atomic and molecular scale. Nanotechnology deals with structures of 100 nanometers or smaller, in at least one dimension, and developing materials or devices within that size.

Neumann, John von: Was a Hungarian-American mathematician born December 28, 1903. He made major contributions to a vast number of fields, including quantum mechanics, fluid dynamics, economics, linear programming, game theory, computer science, numerical analysis, hydrodynamics, and statistics. He is regarded as one of the greatest mathematicians in modern history. Von Neumann was a principal member of the Manhattan Project and the Institute for Advanced Study in Princeton. Along with Edward Teller and Stanisław Ulam, von Neumann worked out the physics involved in thermonuclear reactions and the hydrogen bomb. He published 150 papers in his life. He died February 8, 1957.

Neural Interface: A brain–computer interface, also called a direct neural interface or a brain–machine interface, is a direct communication pathway between a brain and an external device. If this external device is a computer, then it could be controlled directly by the brain. This could be the perfect human-machine interface and its implications are staggering.

Neuron: Or nerve cell, is an electrically excitable cell that processes and transmits information by electrical and chemical signaling. Chemical signaling occurs via synapses, which are specialized connections with other cells. Neurons connect to each other to form neural networks. Neurons are the core components of the nervous system, which includes the brain, spinal cord, and peripheral ganglia. A typical neuron possesses a cell body, called the soma, dendrites, and an axon. Dendrites are thin structures that arise from the cell body, often extending for hundreds of micrometers and branching multiple times, giving rise to a complex dendritic tree. An axon is a special cellular extension that arises from the cell body at a site called the axon hillock and extends for a distance, as far as one meter in humans or even more in other species. Neurons maintain a voltage gradient across their membranes by means of metabolically driven ion pumps. If the voltage changes are large enough, an all-or-none electrochemical pulse, called an action potential, is generated, which travels rapidly along the cell's axon and activates synaptic connections with other cells when it arrives. Neurons do not undergo cell division; in most cases, neurons are generated by stem cells. Astrocytes, a type of glial cell, have also been observed to turn into neurons by virtue of the stem cell characteristic of pluripotency.

Newell, Allen: Was a researcher in computer science and cognitive psychology, born March 19, 1927. Newell completed his Bachelor's degree from Stanford in 1949. He was a graduate student at Princeton University during 1949-1950, where he studied mathematics. Newell eventually earned his PhD from Carnegie Mellon. The first true artificial intelligence program, the 'Logic Theorist,' was developed with Herbert Simon and programmer J. C. Shaw. Newell's work on the program laid the foundations of the field. His inventions include: list processing, the most important programming paradigm used by AI ever since; the application of means-ends analysis to general reasoning or reasoning as search; and the use of heuristics to limit the search space. At the RAND Corporation and at Carnegie Mellon University's School of Computer Science, he contributed to the Information Processing Language (IPL in 1956) and two of the earliest AI programs, the 'Logic Theory Machine' in 1956 and the 'General Problem Solver' in 1957 with Herbert Simon. He died in July 19, 1992.

Niven, Laurence van Cott 'Larry': Is an American science fiction author, born in April 30, 1938. Niven graduated with a BA in mathematics, with a minor in psychology, from Washburn University, Topeka, Kansas, in 1962. His best-known work is the novel '*Ringworld.*' set in his 'Known Space' universe and published in 1970, which received Hugo, Locus, Ditmar, and Nebula awards. His work is primarily hard science fiction, using big science concepts and theoretical physics. It also often includes elements of detective and adventure stories. His fantasy includes the series '*The Magic Goes Away,*' rational fantasy dealing with magic as a non-renewable resource. Niven also writes humorous stories; one such series is collected in '*The Flight of the Horse.*'

O

Obama, Barack Hussein: Born in Hawaii in 1961, he is the 44th President of the United States. President Obama previously served as the United States Senator from Illinois. He is a graduate of Columbia University and Harvard Law School. He is a member of the Democratic Party. He was elected in 2008 and reelected in 2012.

Occam's Razor: The 'razor' points towards simpler theories, unless simplicity can be traded for greater explanatory power, although the simplest theory need not be the most accurate. In science, Occam's razor is used as a heuristic rule and is not considered an irrefutable principle of logic or of a scientific result. The term 'Occam's razor' (in Latin lex parsimoniae), first appeared in 1852 in the works of Sir William Hamilton, 9th Baronet (1788–1856), centuries after William of Ockham's death (1287–1347). Ockham did not invent his 'razor' but he used it frequently and effectively. The most popular form of the 'razor' was written by John Punch: 'entities must not be multiplied beyond necessity.'

OpenCL: Or Open Computing Language is a framework for writing programs that execute across heterogeneous platforms consisting of central processing unit (CPUs), graphics processing unit (GPUs), and other processors. OpenCL includes a language, based on C, for writing kernels or functions that execute on OpenCL devices, plus application programming interfaces (APIs) that are used to define and then control the platforms. OpenCL provides parallel computing using task-based and data-based parallelism. OpenCL is an open standard maintained by the non-profit technology consortium Khronos Group.

P

Paradigm Shift: Is a term first used by Thomas Kuhn in his book '*The Structure of Scientific Revolutions*' published in 1962. Describes a change in basic assumptions within the ruling theory of science. When a new one replaces an existing scientific paradigm, the new one is always better, not just different.

Parrott, Gerrod: Got his BA from the University of Virginia in 1978 and his PhD in 1985 at the University of Pennsylvania. His interest is in the nature of human emotion. His work includes three areas: philosophical and historical approaches to emotions; emotions as embarrassment, shame, guilt, envy, jealousy and the influence of emotions on thought. He is the author of over 75 articles, and 3 books, '*Emotions and Culpability.*' with Norman Finkel, American Psychological Association, 2006, '*Emotions in Social Psychology.*' Psychology Press, 2001 and '*The Emotions: Social, Cultural, and Biological Dimensions.*' with Rom Harre, Sage, 1996.

Plutchik, Robert: Is an American psychologist born October 21, 1927. His research includes the study of emotions, suicide, violence and psychotherapy process. He received his PhD from Columbia University, became Professor emeritus at the Albert Einstein College of Medicine and adjunct professor at the University of South Florida. He authored or coauthored more than 260 articles, 45 chapters and 8 books. He died April 29, 2006.

Poisson Process: Is a stochastic process which counts the number of events and the timing of these events in a given time interval. The probability distribution of the number of events in time, $N(t)$, is a Poisson distribution and the time between each pair of consecutive events has an exponential distribution with parameter λ and each of these inter-arrival times is assumed to be independent of other inter-arrival times. The process is named after the French mathematician Siméon-Denis Poisson (1781–1840).

Price, Richard: Was a Welsh moral philosopher and preacher born in February 23, 1723. In the tradition of English Dissenters, he was a political pamphleteer, active in radical, republican and liberal causes such as the American Revolution. He had connections with writers of the Constitution of the United States. He influenced feminist Mary Wollstonecraft to extend egalitarianism to encompass women's rights. He also wrote on issues of statistics and finance, and was inducted into the Royal Society for these contributions. Price was a friend of the mathematician and clergyman Thomas Bayes. He edited the work containing the Bayes' Theorem, wrote an introduction to the paper and arranged for its posthumous publication. He died on April 19, 1791.

Probability: Is a way of describing uncertainty by a number between 0 and 1, which we call probability. The higher the number, the more certain we are that the event will occur. Probability theory has given a mathematical framework to this concept. It is indispensable to describe the random character of all physical processes that occur at sub-atomic scales that are governed by quantum mechanics. Probability theory is also used to study the underlying processes and uncertainties of complex or chaotic systems.

Q

Quantum: Scientific principles describing the behavior of energy and matter at the atomic scale. The mathematical formulation of quantum mechanics is abstract and often non-intuitive. The centerpiece of this mathematical system is the wavefunction. The wavefunction is a mathematical function of time and space that can provide information about the position and momentum of a particle, but only as probabilities, as there are constraints imposed by the uncertainty principle, which states that certain pairs of physical properties, like position and momentum, cannot both be both known precisely.

R

RADAR: Is an object-detection system, which uses radio waves to determine the range, altitude, direction, and speed of objects. The radar dish or antenna transmits pulses of radio waves or microwaves, which bounce off any object in their path. The object returns a tiny part of the wave's energy to a dish or antenna, which is usually located at the same site as the transmitter. Radar was secretly developed by several nations before and during World War II. The United States Navy, as an acronym for radio detection and ranging, coined the term RADAR in 1941. The modern uses of radar are highly diverse, including air traffic control, radar astronomy, air-defense systems, antimissile systems; marine radars to locate landmarks and other ships; aircraft anti-collision systems; ocean surveillance systems, outer space surveillance and rendezvous systems; meteorological precipitation monitoring; altimetry and flight control systems; guided missile target locating systems; and ground-penetrating radar for geological observations. High tech radar systems are associated with digital signal processing and are capable of extracting information from very high noise levels.

Reiss, Steven: His 'Anxiety Sensitivity Index' (ASI) is used to assess anxiety disorders in patients; and has been translated into 24 languages. Professor Reiss got his BA degree in 1964 from Dartmouth College and in 1972 a PhD degree in clinical psychology from Yale University. In 1985, he and Richard McNally studied anxiety sensitivity. His current research deals in intrinsic motivation, identifying general principles of motivated behavior in a wide variety of circumstances.

Religion: A set of beliefs concerning the cause, nature, and purpose of the universe, specifically when considered as the creation of a supernatural agency or agencies and usually involving devotional and ritual observances. Religions often contain a moral code governing the conduct of human affairs. Historically, religion was practiced as mandated by the government of the place where people lived. To this day, religion is practiced by a substantial number of people, their devotion ranges from fanaticism to 'I was born into this religion.' On the other hand, secularism asserts the right to be free from religious rule and freedom from the government's imposition of religion upon the people. Thus, religion becomes a more personal matter. Some assert that dogmatic religions are in effect morally deficient, elevating to moral status ancient, arbitrary, and ill-informed rules; taboos on eating pork, for example, as well as dress codes and sexual practices possibly designed for reasons of hygiene or even due to mere politics of a bygone era.

RFID: Radio frequency identification of the identity of an object, typically referred to as an RFID tag applied to or incorporated into a product, animal, or person for the purpose of identification and tracking using radio waves. It is used extensively to automatically collect road tolls and its many uses will soon include retail and inventory tracking. There are concerns about privacy because a tag can be read with a suitable reader.

Robot: It is an automatically guided machine, able to perform tasks on its own. The first programmable robot, the Unimate, was installed in 1961 to lift hot pieces of metal from a die-casting machine and stack them. Today, commercial and industrial robots are in widespread use performing jobs in manufacturing, assembly and packing, transport, earth and space exploration, surgery, weaponry, laboratory research, more cheaply and with greater accuracy and reliability than humans. A popular view is that only an anthropomorphic robot is a robot. In this book we consider that only mobile machines guided by AI are robots.

Robotics Developer Studio, Microsoft® (Microsoft RDS): Is a Windows-based environment for academic, hobbyist, and commercial developers to help them easily create robotic applications across a wide variety of hardware. Microsoft RDS includes a lightweight asynchronous runtime, a set of visual authoring and simulation tools, as well as templates, tutorials, and sample code. Programming can be done with the Visual Programming Language (VPL) by using drag-and-drop. A 3D physics-based Visual Simulation Environment (VSE) allows creating applications without hardware. And there are facilities to use four Kinect hardware sensors.

Robotic Surgery: It is the use of robots to perform surgery. Three ways to perform surgery using surgical robots are: remote surgery, minimally invasive surgery and unmanned surgery. Advantages of robotic surgery are precision, miniaturization, smaller incisions, decreased blood loss, less pain, and quicker healing time. Further advantages are articulation beyond normal manipulation and three-dimensional magnified vision.

S

Scarce Resources: Is the fundamental economic problem of satisfying human needs and wants in a world of limited resources. It maintains that society has insufficient productive resources to fulfill all human wants and needs. Goods and services are said to derive all or most of their value from their scarcity. On the other hand, some goods that can be obtained or replicated very easily, for instance intellectual property, keep their prices high with the introduction of artificial scarcity in the form of legal or physical restrictions, which limits the availability of such goods. In a post scarcity society, certain goods, such as desirable land and original art pieces, would most likely remain scarce.

Scenario: It is a synthetic description of an event or series of actions and events. Scenarios are widely used to understand different ways that future events might unfold. Scenario planning or scenario analysis is a process related to futures studies. Scenarios are 'a story about what happened in the future.'

Science: Is any systematic knowledge base or assertive procedure that is capable of resulting in a prediction or predictable type of outcome. Modern science is supported by the scientific method, which consists of the collection of data through observation and experimentation, and the formulation and testing of hypotheses. There is a basic expectation in science, that is to document, archive and share all data and methods so they are available for careful scrutiny by other scientists, thereby other researchers may verify results by reproducing the experiment. This practice, called 'full disclosure,' also allows for the reliability of these data to be verified.

Schmidhuber, Jürgen: Born 17 January, 1963 in Munich, is a computer scientist and artist known for his work on machine learning, universal Artificial Intelligence, artificial neural networks, digital physics, and low-complexity art. He is a researcher at the Istituto Dalle Molle di Studi sull'Intelligenza Artificiale which is affiliated to the Faculty of Informatics of the University of Lugano and to the University of Applied Sciences of Southern Switzerland. His contributions also include generalizations of Kolmogorov complexity and the Speed Prior algorithm. From 2004 to 2009 he was professor of Cognitive Robotics at the Technological University of Munich. Since 1995 he has been co-director of the Swiss AI Lab IDSIA in Lugano, since 2009 also professor of Artificial Intelligence at the University of Lugano. In honor of his achievements he was elected to the European Academy of Sciences and Arts in 2008.

Simon, Herbert Alexander: Was an American political scientist, economist, sociologist, psychologist, and professor most notably at Carnegie Mellon University, born on June 15, 1916. Simon received both his BA in 1936 and his PhD in 1943 in Political Science, from the University of Chicago. Simon's research ranged across the fields of cognitive psychology, cognitive science, computer science, public administration, economics, management, philosophy of science, sociology, and political science. With almost a thousand highly cited publications, he is one of the most influential social scientists of the 20th Century. Simon was among the founding fathers of several of today's important scientific domains, including artificial intelligence, information processing, decision-making, problem-solving, attention-economics, organization theory, complex systems, and computer simulation of scientific discovery. Simon received an honorary Doctor of Laws degree from Harvard University in 1990. He died on February 9, 2001.

Singularity: In 1958, Stanisław Ulam, a Polish-American mathematician who participated in the Manhattan Project and originated the Teller–Ulam design of thermonuclear weapons, wrote about a conversation with John von Neumann: 'One conversation centered on the ever accelerating progress of technology and changes in the mode of human life, which gives the appearance of approaching some essential singularity in the history of the race beyond which human affairs, as we know them, could not continue.' In 1982, Vernor Vinge, Professor of Mathematics, computer scientist, and science fiction author, proposed that: 'the creation of smarter-than-human intelligence represented a breakdown in humans' ability to model their future.' The argument is that authors could not write about realistic characters that are smarter than humans are; if humans could visualize smarter-than-human intelligence, we would be that smart ourselves. Vinge named this event 'The Singularity.'

SMS: Or short text messaging, which allows the exchange of messages between fixed line or mobile phone devices, is the most widely used data application in the world, with over 3.7 billion active users, or 74% of all mobile phone subscribers. SMS was defined in 1985, as a means of sending messages of up to 160 characters, as part of the Global System for Mobile Communications (GSM) series of standards.

Socialism: It is the implementation of the theories of economic organization advocating public or direct worker ownership and administration of the means of production and allocation of resources, in a society characterized by equal access to resources for all individuals with a method of compensation based on the amount of labor expended. Most socialists share the view that capitalism unfairly concentrates power and wealth among a small segment of society that controls capital and derives its wealth through exploitation, creating an unequal society. They also argue that capitalism does not provide equal opportunities for everyone to maximize his or her own potential and does not utilize technology and resources to their maximum capacity nor is it in the best interest of the public. Today most, if not all, socialistic governments have a mixture of socialism and capitalism.

Solomonoff, Ray: The inventor of algorithmic probability and algorithmic information theory was born on July 25, 1926, in Cleveland, Ohio. Solomonoff first described algorithmic probability by publishing the crucial theorem that launched Kolmogorov complexity and algorithmic information theory at a Caltech conference in 1960. He formalized these ideas more fully in publications in 1964. Algorithmic probability is a mathematically formalized combination of Occam's razor, and the Principle of Multiple Explanations. It is a machine independent method of assigning a probability value to a hypothesis, which explains a given observation, embedded in an algorithm or program, with the simplest hypothesis given by the shortest program having the highest probability. He made important discoveries in artificial intelligence. He died on December 7, 2009.

Solomonoff's inductive learning model: Is a powerful, universal and highly elegant theory of sequence prediction. Its critical flaw is that it is incomputable and thus cannot be used in practice. It is sometimes suggested that it may still be useful to help guide the development of very general and powerful theories of prediction, which are computable. This model shows that although powerful algorithms exist, they are necessarily highly complex. This alone makes their theoretical analysis problematic, however it is further shown that beyond a moderate level of complexity the analysis runs into the deeper problem of Gödel incompleteness.

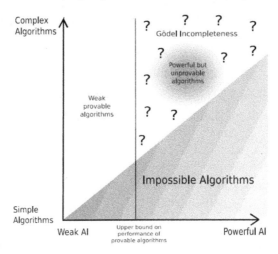

The relationships between the capability of an AI algorithm and the complexity of these algorithms show several areas of interest: The grayed out region indicates impossible algorithms. A vertical line separates the region of provable algorithms from the region of Gödel incompleteness. This line provides an upper bound of how powerful an algorithm can be before it can no longer be proven, ruling out simple but powerful artificial intelligence algorithms.

Solow, Robert: Is an American economist born in 1924. He is known for his work on the theory of economic growth, for which he was awarded the 1987 Nobel Prize in Economic Sciences. The Solow-Swan neo-classical growth model was independently discovered by Trevor W. Swan and published, in 1956, in 'The Economic Record.' This model allows separating economic growth into increases in inputs of labor, capital, and technical progress. Using his model, Solow calculated that about 80% of the growth in US output per worker was attributable to technical progress. It also proves the innate ruthlessness of capitalism owing to its disregard of labor and technology as major contributors to wealth.

SONAR: An acronym for SOund Navigation And Ranging, and is a technique that uses sound propagation, usually underwater, to navigate, communicate with or detect objects on or under the surface of the water, such as other vessels. Two types of technology share the name 'sonar': passive sonar is essentially listening for the sound made by vessels; active sonar is emitting pulses of sounds and listening for echoes, which are used for acoustic location and measurement of the echo characteristics of targets in the water.

T

Technology: Is the human ability, as well as other animal species, to use and know about tools and crafts to control the natural environment. The word technology comes from the Greek: *téchnē*, craft and *logía*, study. Technology has changed society and its surroundings in a number of ways, and has helped develop economies that are more advanced. Technology draws upon many fields of knowledge, including scientific, engineering, mathematical, linguistic, and historical, to achieve practical results.

Trickle-Down Economics: Is a term of political rhetoric that refers to the policy of providing tax cuts or other benefits to businesses and the rich, in the belief that this will indirectly benefit the broad population. During Ronald Reagan's presidency, the Democratic controlled House, which is responsible for approving bills related to taxation, cut the marginal tax rate on the highest-income tax bracket from 70% to 28%. Thirty years later, it has proven to be a ruse used by corrupt politicians to allow the super-rich to loot the wealth of their country.

Turing, Alan Mathison: Was an English mathematician, logician, cryptanalyst, and computer scientist born June 23, 1912. He was highly influential in the development of computer science, formalizing the concepts of algorithm and computation along with the Turing machine, which had a significant role in creating the modern computer. Turing is widely considered to be the father of computer science and artificial intelligence. During the Second World War, Turing worked for the Government Code and Cypher School (GCCS), Britain's code-breaking center. He devised a number of techniques for breaking German ciphers, including deciphering the Enigma machine. After the war, he worked at the National Physical Laboratory, where he created one of the first designs for a stored-program computer, the ACE. In 1948, Turing joined Max Newman's Computing Laboratory at Manchester University, where he assisted in the development of the Manchester computers and became interested in mathematical biology. Turing's homosexuality resulted in criminal prosecution in 1952, when homosexual acts were still illegal in the United Kingdom. He accepted treatment with female hormones and chemical castration, as an alternative to prison. He died in 1954.

Turing Machine: Is a device that manipulates symbols on a strip of tape according to a table of rules. Despite its simplicity, a Turing machine can be adapted to simulate the logic of any computer algorithm, and is particularly useful in explaining the functions of a CPU inside a computer. Alan Turing described his 'Turing Machine' in 1936. It is not intended as a practical computing technology, but rather an hypothetical device representing a computing machine. Turing machines help computer scientists understand the limits of mechanical computation. A succinct definition appears in his 1948 essay, 'Intelligent Machinery.' Turing wrote that the Turing machine, here called a Logical Computing Machine, consisted of: '... an infinite memory capacity obtained in the form of an infinite tape marked out into squares, on each of which a symbol could be printed. At any moment there is one symbol in the machine; it is called the scanned symbol. The machine can alter the scanned symbol and its behavior is in part determined by that symbol, but the symbols on the tape elsewhere do not affect the behavior of the machine. However, the tape can be moved back and forth through the machine, this being one of the elementary operations of the machine. Any symbol on the tape may therefore eventually have an innings.' A Turing machine that is capable of simulating any other Turing machine is called a Universal Turing Machine (UTM). A mathematically-oriented definition was introduced by Alonzo Church, whose work intertwined with Turing's in a formal theory of computation known as the Church–Turing thesis, that provide a precise definition of any algorithm.

Turing Monotone Universal Machine (*U*): It is a Universal Turing Machine with one unidirectional input tape, one unidirectional output tape, and some bidirectional work tapes. Input tapes are read only, output tapes are write only, unidirectional tapes are those where the head can only move from left to right. All tapes are binary (no blank symbol) and the work tapes are initially filled with zeros. We say that U outputs/computes a sequence *!* on input p, and write $U(p) = $ *!*, if U reads all of p, but no more, as it continues to write *!* to the output tape. We fix U and define $U(p, x)$ by simply using a standard coding technique to encode a program p along with a string $x \in B*$ as a single input string for U. A universal Turing machine can simulate any other universal Turing machine with a fixed length program.

Twitter: Is a social networking service and micro-blogging service that enables its users to send and read text-based posts of up to 140 characters, known as 'tweets.' It was launched in July 2006 by Jack Dorsey. The service rapidly gained worldwide popularity, with over 140 million active users as of 2012. Twitter Inc. is based in San Francisco. The Twitter website is one of the top ten most visited on the Internet. Twitter has been cited as an important factor in the Arab Spring and other political protests.

U

Ultrasound: Is a cyclic sound pressure with a frequency greater than the upper limit of human hearing. Ultrasound is different from normal audible sound only by the fact that humans cannot hear it. Although this limit varies from person to person, it is approximately 20 kilohertz in healthy, young adults. Ultrasound is typically used to penetrate a medium and measure the reflection signature or supply focused energy. The reflection signature can reveal details about the inner structure of the medium, a property also used by animals such as bats for hunting. The prime application of ultrasound is to produce pictures of fetuses in the human womb. There are a vast number of other applications as well.

United Nations (UN or ONU): Was founded in 1945, after World War II, to replace the League of Nations, with the intention of stopping wars between countries, and to provide a platform for dialogue. The United Nations is an international alliance whose stated aims are facilitating cooperation in international law, international security, economic development, social progress, human rights, and the achievement of world peace. There are currently 192 member states, including nearly every sovereign state in the world.

UNIX: A group of AT&T employees at Bell Labs, including Ken Thompson, Dennis Ritchie, Brian Kernighan, Douglas McIlroy, and Joe Ossanna, originally developed a multitasking and multi-user computer operating system in 1969. The UNIX system evolution has various branches, developed over time by AT&T, commercial vendors, universities, such as University of California's BSD, and non-profit organizations. The Open Group, an industry standards consortium, owns the UNIX trademark. Only systems fully compliant with and certified according to the Single UNIX Specification are qualified to use the trademark. During the late 1970s and early 1980s, the influence of UNIX in academic circles led to large-scale adoption by commercial startups, the most notable of which are Solaris, HP-UX and AIX, as well as Darwin which forms the core set of components upon which Apple's Mac OS X, Apple TV, and iOS are based.

Utility Function: In 1947, John von Neumann and Oskar Morgenstern exhibited four axioms of 'rationality,' in their VNM-theorem, such that any agent satisfying the axioms has a utility function. The expected utility hypothesis is that rationality can be modeled as maximizing an expected value, which given the VNM-theorem, can be summarized as 'rationality is VNM-rationality.' No claim is made that the agent has a conscious desire to maximize utility, only that utility exists. VNM-utility is a decision utility in the sense that it is used to describe decision preferences.

V

VAT: Value added tax is a consumption tax applied on any value that is added to a product. The total tax charged at each stage in the economic chain of supply is a constant fraction of the value added by a business to its products, and most of the cost of collecting the tax is borne by business, rather than by the state. On the other hand, VAT is an indirect tax, in that the tax is collected from someone who does not bear the entire cost of the tax, normally at the point of sale. The VAT has been criticized because its burden lies on personal end consumers of products. Like all consumption taxes, it is a regressive tax, the poor pay more, as a percentage of their income, than the rich do. To maintain the progressive nature of total taxes on individuals, countries implementing VAT have reduced income tax on lower income earners, as well as instituted direct transfer payments to groups with lower income, resulting in lower tax burdens on the poor.

Virtual World: Is an online community that resides in a computer based simulated environment, through which users can interact with one another, visualize, and create objects. Users can inhabit in these virtual worlds in interactive environments, where the users take the form of avatars visible to others graphically. These avatars may be just text, two-dimensional or three-dimensional graphical representations; other forms are possible.

Voltaire: François-Marie Arouet better known as Voltaire, was a French writer and philosopher born in 1694. Voltaire was a prolific writer and wrote in almost every literary form including plays, poetry, novels, essays, historical and scientific works, more than 20,000 letters and more than 2,000 books and pamphlets. He was an outspoken supporter of social reform, despite strict censorship laws and harsh penalties for those who broke them. A satirical polemicist, he made use of his works to criticize Catholic Church dogma and the French institutions of his day. His works and ideas influenced important thinkers of both the American and French Revolutions. Voltaire died in 1778.

W

Watson: Is an AI system capable of answering questions posed in natural language, developed by IBM as part of its DeepQA project by a research team led by principal investigator David Ferrucci. Watson was named after IBM's first president, Thomas J. Watson. In 2011, as a test of its abilities, Watson competed on the quiz show Jeopardy!. In a two-game, combined-point match, from February 14 to 16, Watson beat Brad Rutter, the biggest all-time money winner on the show, and Ken Jennings, the record holder for the longest championship streak of 74 wins.

Wealth and Income Distribution: The distribution of wealth is a comparison of the assets of various members or groups in a society. Wealth is a person's net worth, expressed as: *wealth = assets – liabilities.* The word 'wealth' is often confused with 'income.' These two terms describe different but related things. Wealth consists of those items of economic value that an individual owns, while income is an inflow of items of economic value. Accordingly, the world distribution of wealth is much more unequal than that of income. Attempts have been made in many societies, through property redistribution, taxation or regulation, to redistribute wealth and diminish extreme inequality. Examples of this practice go back at least to the Roman Republic in the third century BC, when laws were passed limiting the amount of wealth or land that could be owned by any one family. Sir Francis Bacon wrote 'Above all things good policy is to be used that the treasures and monies in a state be not gathered into a few hands... Money is like muck, not good except it be spread.' In 'The Communist Manifesto' Karl Marx and Friedrich Engels wrote 'From each according to his ability, to each according to his need.' A study by the United Nations reports that the richest 1% of adults owned 40% of global assets in the year 2000, and that the richest 10% of adults hold 85% of the world total. The bottom half of the world adult population owned 1% of global wealth. Moreover, another study found that the richest 2% own more than half of global household assets. And the worst part is that this distribution is changing rapidly in the direction of greater concentration of wealth amongst fewer and fewer people.

Wiener, Norbert: Was an American mathematician born November 26, 1894, in Columbia, Missouri. A famous child prodigy, Wiener later became an early researcher in stochastic and noise processes. He was Professor of Mathematics at MIT. Wiener initiated the fields of cybernetics, feedback and systems control. Wiener was concerned with political interference with scientific research, and the militarization of science. He died March 18, 1964, in Stockholm, Sweden.

Wiener Process or Brownian Motion: Are the names given to a continuous-time stochastic process named in honor of Norbert Wiener or Robert Brown respectively. It is a process in terms of which complicated stochastic processes can be described. This process is used to represent the integral of a Gaussian white noise process, and is useful as a model of noise in filtering and control theories and in the formulation of quantum mechanics and the study of eternal inflation in physical cosmology.

Wi-Fi: Is a technology that allows an electronic device to exchange data wirelessly, using radio waves, over a computer network, including high-speed Internet connections. Wi-Fi is a trademark of the Wi-Fi Alliance that defines it as 'wireless local area network (WLAN) products that are based on the Institute of Electrical and Electronics Engineers' (IEEE) 802.11 standards.' A device that can use Wi-Fi, such as a personal computer, video game console, smartphone, tablet, or digital audio player, can connect to a network resource such as the Internet via a wireless network access point. Such an access point, or hotspot, has a range of about 20 meters (65 feet) indoors and greater range outdoors.

Windows: Are graphical user interface (GUI) operating systems developed, marketed, and sold by Microsoft since November 20, 1985. Microsoft Windows dominates the personal computer market.

X

Y

Yudkowsky, Eliezer Shlomo: Is an American artificial intelligence researcher concerned with 'The Singularity' and an advocate of friendly artificial intelligence. He was born on September 11, 1979 and lives in Redwood City, California. Yudkowsky is an autodidact who did not attend high school and with no formal education in artificial intelligence. He co-founded the nonprofit Singularity Institute for Artificial Intelligence (SIAI) in 2000 and continues to be a full-time Research Fellow there. His research focuses on AI theory for self-understanding, self-modification, and recursive self-improvement or seed AI. On AI architectures, he studies decision theories for stably benevolent motivational structures such as Friendly AI, and Coherent Extrapolated Volition. Yudkowsky has explained philosophical topics in non-academic language, such as 'An Intuitive Explanation of Bayes' Theorem.' He has authored the Singularity Institute publications 'Creating Friendly AI' (2001), 'Levels of Organization in General Intelligence' (2002), 'Coherent Extrapolated Volition' (2004), and 'Timeless Decision Theory' (2010). Yudkowsky has also written science fiction and other fiction. His Harry Potter fan fiction story Harry Potter and the Methods of Rationality illustrates magic in terms of cognitive science and rationality, and has been favorably reviewed.

Z

Zuse, Konrad: Was a German civil engineer, inventor and computer pioneer, born in 1910. His greatest achievement was the world's first functional program-controlled Turing-complete computer, the Z3, which became operational in May 1941. Zuse was also noted for the S2 computing machine, considered the first process-controlled computer. He founded one of the earliest computer businesses in 1941, producing the Z4, which became the world's first commercial computer. From 1943 to 1945 he designed the first high-level programming language, Plankalkül. In 1969, Zuse suggested the concept of a computation-based universe in his book *'Rechnender Raum'* (*'Calculating Space'*). His family and commerce financed much of his early work, but after 1939, he was given resources by the Nazi German government. Due to World War II, Zuse's work went largely unnoticed in the United Kingdom and the United States. Possibly his first documented influence on a US company was when Zuse launched the world's first computer startup company: the Zuse-Ingenieurbüro Hopferau, in 1946, using venture capital raised through ETH Zürich and an IBM options on Zuse's patents. There is a replica of the Z3, as well as the original Z4, in the Deutsches Museum in Munich. The Deutsches Technikmuseum in Berlin has an exhibition devoted to Zuse, displaying twelve of his machines, including a replica of the Z1, the world's first program-controlled computer. Despite certain mechanical engineering problems, it had all the basic ingredients of modern machines, using the binary system and today's standard separation of storage and control. Zuse's 1936 patent application (Z23139/GMD Nr. 005/021) also suggests von Neumann architecture (reinvented in 1945) with program and data modifiable in storage. Also in exhibit are several of Zuse's paintings. He died in 1995.

'The measure of intelligence is the ability to change.'
Albert Einstein.

Further Reading

'If there's a book you really want to read but it hasn't been written yet, then you must write it.' **Toni Morrison.**

The following references are only presented as an encouragement to read more about subjects that have been presented along the pages of this book. It is not in any way a complete list of references to this topic and it reflects the author's subjectivity.

Arrabales, R., Ledezma, A., and Sanchis, A. (2009) *A Cognitive Approach to Multimodal Attention.* Journal of Physical Agents, vol. 3, no. 1, pp. 53-64.

Asimov, Isaac. (1950). *I, Robot.* Gnome Press

Bach, Joscha. (2009). *Principles of Synthetic Intelligence:* PSI: An Architecture of Motivated Cognition. Oxford University Press.

Ben Goertzel. (2012). *CogPrime: An Integrative Architecture for Embodied Artificial General Intelligence.*

Bennett, Daniel C. (1996). *Kinds of Minds: Toward an Understanding of Consciousness.* Basic Books, A Division of Harper Collins Publishers.

Birkho, G. and Neumann, J. von. (1936). *The logic of quantum mechanics.* Annals of Mathematics, 37, 823.

Bostrom, Nick and Yudkowsky, Eliezer. (2011). *The Ethics of Artificial Intelligence.* Draft for Cambridge Handbook of Artificial Intelligence, eds. William Ramsey and Keith Frankish, Cambridge University Press.

Brynjolfsson, E. and McAfee, A. (2011). *Race Against the Machine: How the Digital Revolution is Accelerating Innovation, Driving Productivity, and Irreversibly Transforming Employment and the Economy.* Digital Frontier Press.

Cabessa, Jérémie and Siegelmann, Hava T. (2012). *The Computational Power of Interactive Recurrent Neural Networks.* Neural Computation; [DOI:10.1162/NECO_a_ 00263]

Engesser, K.and Gabbay, D.M. (2002). *Quantum logic, Hilbert space, revision theory.* Artificial Intelligence, 136:61-100

Goertzel, B. and Pennachin, C. (eds.) (2006). *Artificial General Intelligence.* New York, NY: Springer-Verlag.

Goertzel, B. (2008). *Achieving Advanced Machine Consciousness though Integrative, Virtually Embodied Artificial General Intelligence.* Proceedings of the Nokia Workshop on Machine Consciousness. pp. 19-21.

Hamilton, Peter F. (1999). *The Naked God.* Macmillan Publishers.

Hernández-Orallo, J. (2010). *A (hopefully) Non-biased Universal Environment Class for Measuring Intelligence of Biological and Artificial Systems.* In E. Baum, M. Hutter, E. Kitzelmann, editor, Artificial General Intelligence, 3rd Intl Conf, pages 182–183. Atlantis Press.

Hutter, M. (2005). *Universal Artificial Intelligence: Sequential Decisions based on Algorithmic Probability.* Springer, Berlin.

Haikonen, P.O.A. (2007). *Robot Brains. Circuits and Systems for Conscious Machines.* John Wiley & Sons, UK.

Hutter, M. (2007). *Universal Algorithmic Intelligence: A mathematical top-down approach.* Artificial General Intelligence Springer

Kurzweil, R. (2005). *The Singularity Is Near: When Humans Transcend Biology.* New York, NY: Viking.

Kalman, R.E. (1960). *A new approach to linear filtering and prediction problems.* Journal of Basic Engineering 82 (1): 35–45.

Kalman, R.E.; Bucy, R.S. (1961). *New Results in Linear Filtering and Prediction Theory.* Transactions of the ASME - Journal of Basic Engineering Vol. 83: pp. 95-107

Legg, Shane. (2006). *Is there an Elegant Universal Theory of Prediction?* Technical Report No. IDSIA-12-06, IDSIA / USI-SUPSI, Dalle Molle Institute for Artificial Intelligence, Galleria 2, 6928 Manno, Switzerland

Legg, S., and Hutter, M. (2007). *Universal intelligence: A definition of machine intelligence.* Minds and Machines, 17(4), 391–444.

Legg, S., and Hutter, M. (2007). *A collection of definitions of intelligence.* Advances in Artificial General Intelligence: Concepts, Architectures and Algorithms (pp. 17–24). Amsterdam, NL: IOS Press.

Legg, Shane and Veness, Joel. (2011). *An Approximation of the Universal Intelligence Measure.*

Li, Xiang and Liu, Baoding. (2009). *Hybrid Logic and Uncertain Logic*, Department of Mathematical Sciences, Tsinghua University, Beijing, China, Journal of Uncertain Systems, Vol.3, No.2, pp.83-94

Li, M. and Vitányi, P. M. B. (2008). *An introduction to Kolmogorov complexity and its applications.* Springer, 3rd edition.

Ludwig Arnold. (1974). *Stochastic Differential Equations: Theory and Applications.* A Wiley Interscience Publication.

Niven, Larry. (1973). *Protector.* Del Rey.

Ortony, Andrew, Cloe, Gerald L. and Collins, Allan. (1988). *The Cognitive Structure of Emotions.* Cambridge University Press.

Rosenfield, Israel. *The Invention of Memory: A New View of the Brain.* Basic Books, 1988.

Shanon, B. (2008). *A Psychological Theory of Consciousness.* Journal of Consciousness Studies, vol. 15, pp. 5-47.

Solomonoff, R. (1964). *A Formal Theory of Inductive Inference.* Information and Control, Part I: Vol 7, No. 1, pp. 1-22.

Turing, A. M. (1950). *Computing machinery and intelligence.* Mind.

Veness, J., Ng, K. S., Hutter, M., and Silver, D. (2010). *Reinforcement learning via AIXI approximation.* In Proc. 24th AAAI Conference on Artificial Intelligence, pages 605–611, Atlanta. AAAI Press.

Veness, J., Ng, K. S., Hutter, M., Uther, W., and Silver, D. (2011). *A Monte-Carlo AIXI Approximation.* Journal of Artificial Intelligence Research (JAIR), 40(1):95–142.

Wallach, Wendell; Allen, Colin. (2008). *Moral Machines: Teaching Robots Right from Wrong*. USA: Oxford University Press. ISBN 978-0195374049.

Yudkowsky, Eliezer S. (2002). *Levels of Organization in General Intelligence*. A chapter in Real AI: New Approaches in Artificial General Intelligence, Edited by Ben Goertzel and Casio Pennachin.

Zadeh, Lotfi A. (1997). *Toward a theory of fuzzy information granulation and its centrality in human reasoning and fuzzy logic*. Computer Science Division/Electronics Research Laboratory, Department of EECS, University of California, Berkeley, CA 94720-1776, USA

'From a new born to a 5 year old, there is a world of distance. From a 5 year old to me, only a step.' **Leo Tolstoy.**

Index

'The important thing is not to stop questioning. Curiosity has its own reason for existing. One cannot help but be in awe when he contemplates the mysteries of eternity, of life, of the marvelous structure of reality.' **Albert Einstein.**

'Becoming conscious is of course a sacrilege against nature; it is as though you had robbed the unconscious of something.' **Carl G. Jung.**

Books by Humberto Contreras

living dangerously in utopia
The War of the Classes
The Preponderant Factor
It is all in the Mind
The Restlessness

technology & social impact
The History of the 21st Century
Practical Artificial Intelligence

Humberto Contreras is a Civil Engineer with a Masters in Structural Engineering and a Doctorate in Earthquake Engineering. As an expert in probabilistic and stochastic systems, he implemented solutions involving risk analysis and safety of Nuclear Power Plants and Nuclear Waste. He has also been a computer software consultant for major corporations. He currently writes books and lives in New England and the Riviera Maya.

These books are also available in Spanish.

http://www.alphazerobooks.com

www.ingramcontent.com/pod-product-compliance
Lightning Source LLC
Chambersburg PA
CBHW071544080326
40689CB00061B/1810